Foundations in Accountancy/ ACCA

MANAGEMENT ACCOUNTING (FMA/MA)

Welcome to BPP Learning Media's Practice & Revision Kit for MA. In this **Practice & Revision Kit**, which has been reviewed by the **ACCA examining team**, we:

- Include **Do you know?** Checklists to test your knowledge and understanding of topics

- Provide you with **two** mock exams including the Specimen Exam

Note
Foundations in Accountancy FMA and ACCA MA are examined under the same syllabus and study guide.

FOR EXAMS FROM 1 SEPTEMBER 2019 TO 31 AUGUST 2020

First edition May 2011
Eight edition February 2019

ISBN 9781 5097 2413 0
(Previous ISBN 9781 5097 1754 5)

e-ISBN 9781 5097 2440 6

British Library Cataloguing-in-Publication Data
A catalogue record for this book
is available from the British Library

Published by

BPP Learning Media Ltd
BPP House, Aldine Place
London W12 8AA

www.bpp.com/learningmedia

Printed in the United Kingdom

Your learning materials, published by BPP Learning
Media Ltd, are printed on paper obtained from traceable
sustainable sources.

Contents

Question index

Helping you with your revision

BPP Learning Media – ACCA Approved Content Provider

As an ACCA **Approved Content Provider**, BPP Learning Media gives you the **opportunity** to use revision materials reviewed by the ACCA examining team. By incorporating the ACCA examining team's comments and suggestions regarding the depth and breadth of syllabus coverage, the BPP Learning Media Practice & Revision Kit provides excellent, **ACCA-approved** support for your revision.

These materials are reviewed by the ACCA examining team. The objective of the review is to ensure that the material properly covers the syllabus and study guide outcomes, used by the examining team in setting the exams, in the appropriate breadth and depth. The review does not ensure that every eventuality, combination or application of examinable topics is addressed by the ACCA Approved Content. Nor does the review comprise a detailed technical check of the content as the Approved Content Provider has its own quality assurance processes in place in this respect.

Selecting questions

We provide signposts to help you plan your revision.

- A full **question index** listing questions that cover each part of the syllabus, so that you can locate the questions that provide practice on key topics, and see the different ways in which they might be tested

Attempting mock exams

There are two mock exams that provide practice at coping with the pressures of the exam day. We strongly recommend that you attempt them under exam conditions. **Mock Exam 1** is the Specimen Exam. **Mock Exam 2** reflects the syllabus coverage of the exam.

Using your BPP Practice & Revision Kit

Aim of this Practice & Revision Kit

To provide the practice to help you succeed in computer based examinations for FMA/MA *Management Accounting*.

To pass the examination you need a thorough understanding in all areas covered by the syllabus and teaching guide.

Recommended approach

- Make sure you are able to answer questions on **everything** specified by the syllabus and teaching guide. You cannot make any assumptions about what questions may come up in your exam. The examining team aim to discourage 'question spotting'.

- Learning is an **active** process. Use the **DO YOU KNOW?** Checklists to test your knowledge and understanding of the topics covered in FMA/MA *Management Accounting* by filling in the blank spaces. Then check your answers against the **DID YOU KNOW?** Checklists. Do not attempt any questions if you are unable to fill in any of the blanks – go back to your **BPP Interactive Text** and revise first.

- When you are revising a topic, think about the mistakes that you know that you should avoid by writing down **POSSIBLE PITFALLS** at the end of each **DO YOU KNOW?** Checklist.

- Once you have completed the checklists successfully, you should attempt the questions on that topic. Each section has a selection of **MULTIPLE CHOICE QUESTIONS**.

- Each mark carries with it a time allocation of 1.2 minutes (including time for selecting and reading questions). A 10 mark multi task question should therefore be completed in 12 minutes.

- You should attempt each bank of questions to ensure you are familiar with their styles and to practise your technique. Ensure you read **Tackling Multiple Choice Questions** on page xi to get advice on how best to approach them.

- Once you have completed all of the questions in the body of this Practice & Revision Kit, you should attempt the **MOCK EXAMS** under examination conditions. Check your answers against our answers to find out how well you did.

Passing the FMA/MA exam

To access Foundations in Accounting syllabuses, visit the ACCA website
www2.accaglobal.com/students/fia

The exam

This is a computer-based exam. All questions in the exam are compulsory. This means you cannot avoid any topic, but also means that you do not need to waste time in the exam deciding which questions to attempt.

There are 35 MCQs and other types of objective test question (OTQ) in Section A (for example, number entry, multiple response and multiple response matching) and three multi-task questions in Section B.

The multi-task questions will come from each of syllabus areas D Budgeting, E Standard Costing and F Performance Measurement. Note: Budgeting MTQs in Section B can also include tasks from B2 Forecasting techniques. B4 Spreadsheets could be included in any of the MTQs, as either the basis for presenting information in the question or as a task within the MTQ.

This means that the examining team is able to test most of the syllabus at each sitting, and that is what they aim to do. So you need to have revised right across the syllabus for this exam.

Revision

This kit has been reviewed by the FMA/MA examining team and contains the Specimen Exam. Working through the questions in the Kit provides excellent preparation for the exam. It is important to tackle questions under exam conditions. Allow yourself just the number of minutes shown next to the questions in the index and don't look at the answers until you have finished. For questions you answer incorrectly, think about your answer and the correct answer. If you require further clarification, refer to the explanation of the topic provided in your Interactive Text. Question practice is an essential part of your revision, so don't neglect it.

Passing the exam

The following points will help you pass the exam:

- Read the question carefully.

- Don't spend more than the allotted time on each question. Don't become bogged down. If you are having trouble with a question, stop, think, decide on your best option and answer the question. Move on!

Approach to examining the syllabus

FMA/MA is a two-hour exam.

The exam is structured as follows.

	No of marks
Section A	
35 compulsory objective test questions of 2 marks each	70
Section B	
3 compulsory multi-task questions of 10 marks each	30
	100

The computer-based examination

Computer-based examinations (CBEs) are available for most of the Foundations In Accountancy exams. The CBE exams for the first seven modules can be taken at any time, these are referred to as 'exams on demand'. The Option exams can be sat in June and December of each year, these are referred to as 'exams on sitting'. FAU and FFM are moving from paper-based exams (PBE) to CBE format from the December 2019 exam sitting, and FTX will follow from the June 2020 exam sitting. There will be no parallel running of PBE and CBE exams.

Computer-based examinations must be taken at an ACCA CBE Licensed Centre.

How do CBEs work?

- Questions are displayed on a monitor

- Candidates enter their answer directly onto the computer

- Candidates have two hours to complete the examination

- Candidates sitting exams on demand are provided with a Provisional Result Notification showing their results before leaving the examination room.

- The CBE Licensed Centre uploads the results to the ACCA (as proof of the candidate's performance) within 72 hours.

- Candidates sitting the Option exams will receive their results approximately five weeks after the exam sitting once they have been expert marked

- Candidates can check their exam status on the ACCA website by logging into myACCA

Benefits

- Flexibility – the first seven modules, exams on demand, can be sat at any time

- Resits for the first seven modules can also be taken at any time and there is no restriction on the number of times a candidate can sit a CBE

- Instant feedback for the exams on demand as the computer displays the results at the end of the CBE

For more information on computer-based exams, visit the ACCA website.

www.accaglobal.com/gb/en/student/exam-entry-and-administration/computer-based-exams.html

Tackling Multiple Choice Questions

This exam includes MCQs. You have to **choose the option that best answers the question**. The incorrect options are called distracters. There is a skill in answering MCQs quickly and correctly. By practising MCQs you can develop this skill, giving you a better chance of passing the exam.

You may wish to follow the approach outlined below, or you may prefer to adapt it.

Step 1	Skim read all the MCQs and identify what appear to be the easier questions.
Step 2	Attempt each question – **starting with the easier questions** identified in Step 1. Read the question **thoroughly**. You may prefer to work out the answer before looking at the options, or you may prefer to look at the options at the beginning. Adopt the method that works best for you.
Step 3	Read the four options and see if one matches your own answer. Be careful with numerical questions as the distracters are designed to match answers that incorporate common errors. Check that your calculation is correct. Have you followed the requirement exactly? Have you included every stage of the calculation?
Step 4	You may find that none of the options matches your answer.
	• Re-read the question to ensure that you understand it and are answering the requirement
	• Eliminate any obviously wrong answers
	• Consider which of the remaining answers is the most likely to be correct and select the option
Step 5	If you are still unsure make a note and continue to the next question.
Step 6	Revisit unanswered questions. When you come back to a question after a break you often find you are able to answer it correctly straight away. If you are still unsure have a guess. You are not penalised for incorrect answers, so **never leave a question unanswered!**

After extensive practice and revision of MCQs, you may find that you recognise a question when you sit the exam. Be aware that the detail and/or requirement may be different. If the question seems familiar read the requirement and options carefully – do not assume that it is identical.

Using your BPP products

This Kit gives you the question practice and guidance you need in the exam. Our other products can also help you pass:

- **Interactive Text** introduces and explains the knowledge required for your exam
- **Passcards** provide you with clear topic summaries and exam tips.

You can purchase these products by visiting www.bpp.com/learningmedia.

Questions

Do you know? – Accounting for management

Check that you can fill in the blanks in the statements below before you attempt any questions. If in doubt, you should go back to your BPP Interactive Text and revise first.

- Good information should be ...., ..., ..., and .... It should inspire confidence, it should be appropriately communicated, its volume should be manageable, it should be timely and its cost should be less than the benefits it provides.

- Information for management is likely to be used for

  - ....
  - ....
  - ....

- The main objective of profit making organisations is to .... A secondary objective of profit making organisations might be to increase .... of its goods/services.

- The main objective of non-profit making organisations is usually to .... and services. A secondary objective of non-profit making organisations might be to minimise the .... involved in providing the goods/services.

- Long-term .... planning, also known as corporate planning, involves selecting appropriate .... so as to prepare a long-term plan to attain the objectives.

- Anthony divides management activities into .... planning, ... control and .... control.

- Tactical (or management) control: 'the process by which managers assure that .... are obtained and used effectively and efficiently in the accomplishment of the organisation's objectives'.

- Operational control: 'the process of assuring that specific .... are carried out .... and ....

- .... accounts are prepared for individuals external to an organisation: shareholders, customers, suppliers, tax authorities, employees.

- .... accounts are prepared for internal managers of an organisation.

- There is no legal requirement to prepare .... accounts.

- .... accounts are both an historical record and a future planning tool.

- .... accounts concentrate on the business as a whole, aggregating revenues and costs from different operations, and are an end in themselves.

- Cost accounting information is, in general, unsuitable for ....

- *Possible pitfalls*

  Write down the mistakes you know you should avoid.

Did you know? – Accounting for management

Could you fill in the blanks? The answers are in bold. Use this page for revision purposes as you approach the exam.

- Good information should be **relevant**, **complete**, **accurate**, and **clear**. It should inspire confidence, it should be appropriately communicated, its volume should be manageable, it should be timely and its cost should be less than the benefits it provides.

- Information for management is likely to be used for

    - **Planning**
    - **Control**
    - **Decision making**

- The main objective of profit making organisations is to **maximise profits**. A secondary objective of profit making organisations might be to increase **output** of its goods/services.

- The main objective of non-profit making organisations is usually to **provide goods** and **services**. A secondary objective of non-profit making organisations might be to minimise the **costs** involved in providing the goods/services.

- Long-term **strategic** planning, also known as corporate planning, involves selecting appropriate **strategies** so as to prepare a long-term plan to attain the objectives.

- Anthony divides management activities into **strategic** planning, **management** control and **operational** control.

- Tactical (or management) control: 'the process by which managers assure that **resources** are obtained and used effectively and efficiently in the accomplishment of the organisation's objectives'.

    Operational control: 'the process of assuring that specific **tasks** are carried out **effectively** and **efficiently**'.

- **Financial** accounts are prepared for individuals external to an organisation: shareholders, customers, suppliers, tax authorities, employees.

    Management accounts are prepared for internal managers of an organisation.

- There is no legal requirement to prepare **management** accounts.

- **Management** accounts are both an historical record and a future planning tool.

- **Financial** accounts concentrate on the business as a whole, aggregating revenues and costs from different operations, and are an end in themselves.

- Cost accounting information is, in general, unsuitable for **decision making**.

- *Possible pitfalls*

    - Forgetting the differences between financial and management accounting

1 Accounting for management · 24 mins

1.1 Which TWO of the following statements about qualities of good information are true?

☑ It should be relevant for its purposes

☐ It should be communicated to the right person

☑ It should be completely accurate — *accurate but not completely*

☐ It should be provided whatever the cost **(2 marks)**

1.2 The sales manager has prepared a manpower plan to ensure that sales quotas for the forthcoming year are achieved. This is an example of what type of planning?

○ Strategic planning
○ Tactical planning
○ Operational planning
○ Corporate planning **(2 marks)**

1.3 Which TWO of the following statements about management accounting information are true?

☑ They may include non-financial information

☐ They are required by law to be produced

☑ They are used to aid planning

☐ They are for use by parties external to the organisation **(2 marks)**

1.4 Which of the following statements is/are correct?

(i) A management control system is a term used to describe the hardware and software used to drive a database system which produces information outputs that are easily assimilated by management.

(ii) An objective is a course of action that an organisation might pursue in order to achieve its strategy.

(iii) Information is data that has been processed into a form meaningful to the recipient.

● (i), (ii) and (iii)
○ (i) and (iii)
○ (ii) and (iii)
○ (iii) only **(2 marks)**

1.5 Good information should have certain qualities.

Which TWO of the following are required as qualities of good management information?

☑ Complete

☐ Extensive

☐ True and fair

☑ Accurate **(2 marks)**

1.6   Monthly variance reports are an example of which one of the following types of management information?

    ○   Tactical
    ○   Strategic
    ○   Non-financial
    ○   Operational   **(2 marks)**

1.7   Which of the following statements is/are correct?

    (i)   Information for decision-making should incorporate uncertainty in some way.
    (ii)   The data used to prepare financial accounts and management accounts are the same.

    ○   (i) is true and (ii) is false
    ○   (ii) is true and (i) is false
    ○   Both are true
    ○   Both are false   **(2 marks)**

1.8   Use the drop down list to select which of the following processes occurs at the business planning stage.

Select...   ▼
Obtaining data about actual results
Taking corrective action
Comparing actual performance with budget
Establishing objectives

                                                                  (2 marks)

1.9   Which of the following statements is correct?

    ○   Management accounting systems provide information for use in fulfilling legal requirements.
    ●   Management accounting systems provide information for the use of decision-makers within an organisation.
    ○   Management accounting systems provide information for use by shareholders.
    ○   Management accounting systems provide information for use by tax authorities.   **(2 marks)**

1.10   Which TWO of the following would be data rather than information?

    ☐   Sales increase/decrease per product in last quarter
    ☐   Total sales value per product
    ☐   Total material usage
    ☐   Sales staff commission as a percentage of total sales   **(2 marks)**

                                                            (Total = 20 marks)

Do you know? – Sources of data

Check that you can fill in the blanks in the statements below before you attempt any questions. If in doubt, you should go back to your BPP Interactive Text and revise first.

- Data may be .... (collected specifically for the purpose of a survey) or .... (collected for some other purpose).

  You will remember that primary data are data collected especially for a specific purpose. The advantage of such data is that the investigator knows where the data .... and is aware of any inadequacies or limitations in the data. Its disadvantage is that it can be very .... to collect primary data.

- Secondary data sources may be satisfactory in certain situations, or they may be the only convenient means of obtaining an item of data. It is essential that there is good reason to believe that the secondary data used is .... and ....

- The main sources of secondary data are:

–	– ....
–	– ....
–	– ....
–	– ....

- The main characteristics of big data are .... and .... and ....

  The key role of Big Data is to analyse all relevant .... and to generate a .... model of what the outcome of the decision will be. Only data that has been ...., or in a digital form, can be analysed (for example from social media, audio/video content, financial data, GPS data, banking transactions and web server logs).

- *Possible pitfalls*

  Write down the mistakes you know you should avoid.

Could you fill in the blanks? The answers are in bold. Use this page for revision purposes as you approach the exam.

- Data may be **primary** (collected specifically for the purpose of a survey) or **secondary** (collected for some other purpose).

  You will remember that primary data are data collected especially for a specific purpose. The advantage of such data is that the investigator knows where the data **came from** and is aware of any inadequacies or limitations in the data. Its disadvantage is that it can be very **expensive** to collect primary data.

- Secondary data sources may be satisfactory in certain situations, or they may be the only convenient means of obtaining an item of data. It is essential that there is good reason to believe that the secondary data used is **accurate** and **reliable**.

- The main sources of secondary data are: **Governments; banks; newspapers; trade journals; information bureaux; consultancies; libraries and information services**.

- The main characteristics of big data are **volume** and **velocity** and **variety.**

  The key role of Big Data is to analyse all relevant **information** and to generate a **predictive** model of what the outcome of the decision will be. Only data that has been **digitised**, or in a digital form, can be analysed (for example from social media, audio/video content, financial data, GPS data, banking transactions and web server logs).

- *Possible pitfalls*

  - Mixing up the different types of sampling.
  - Not knowing the advantages and disadvantages of the sampling methods.

2a Sources of data   14 mins

2a.1 Which TWO of the following are primary sources of data?

☑ Historical records of transport costs to be used to prepare forecasts for budgetary planning

☐ The *Annual Abstract of Statistics*, published by the Office for National Statistics in the United Kingdom

☐ Data collected by a bank in a telephone survey to monitor the effectiveness of the bank's customer services

☑ Focus group feedback about potential flavours of a new biscuit   **(2 marks)**

2a.2 Which TWO of the following statements regarding different types of data are true?

☐ Secondary data are data collected especially for a specific purpose.

☐ Discrete data can take on any value.

☐ Qualitative data are data that cannot be measured.

☐ Population data are data arising as a result of investigating a group of people or objects.

(2 marks)

2a.3 Government statistics can be a useful source of data and information.

Which of the following types of data in the drop down list is most likely to be obtained from government statistics?

Select... ▼
Foreign exchange rates
Population data
Details of industry costs
Interest rates

(2 marks)

2a.4 Which of the following statements concerning Big Data analytics is correct?

● Big Data analytics relies on digital information
○ Big Data analytics relies on written information
○ Big Data analytics relies on verbal information
○ Big Data analytics relies on confidential information

(2 marks)

2a.5 Which of the following statements are true?

1 Big data analytics allows businesses to analyse and reveal insights in data which they have previously been unable to analyse.

2 In order for organisations to analyse big data and to gain insights from it, the source data needs to be structured within a software package.

3 One of the key features of big data is the speed with which data flows into an organisation, and with which it is processed.

○ 1 and 2 only
● 1 and 3 only
○ 2 and 3 only
○ 1, 2 and 3   **(2 marks)**

2a.6 Which of the following statements are true?

1 One of the uses of exploiting big data analytics for profit making organisations is to lead to increased profit margins.

2 One of the uses of exploiting big data analytics in non profit-seeking organisations is to lead to reduced costs.

3 Big data analytics show correlation and causation between variables.

- O 1 and 2 only
- O 1 and 3 only
- O 2 and 3 only
- O 1, 2 and 3 **(2 marks)**

(Total = 12 marks)

2b Presenting information   12 mins

2b.1 The cost of materials for product A are as follows.

Material W: $2,250
Material X: $3,000
Material Y: $3,600
Material Z: $150

If the material proportions were displayed on a pie chart, how many degrees would material Y represent?

☐ degrees

(2 marks)

The following information relates to questions 2b.2 to 2b.3.

	Number of ice-creams sold			
	April	May	June	July
Mint choc chip	600	760	725	900
Chocolate	300	335	360	525
Strawberry	175	260	310	475
Blueberry	75	90	100	90

2b.2 The data may be illustrated by the following chart.

What type of chart is it?

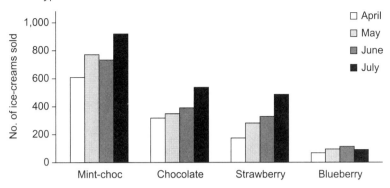

O   Simple bar chart
●   Multiple bar chart
O   Component bar chart
O   Ogive   (2 marks)

2b.3 Which of the following statements is true?

X   Sales of mint choc chip rose steadily over the four months
O   Total sales fell in the month of July
●   In June, the gap between sales of strawberry and sales of chocolate reduced
X   Sales of blueberry rose in May and July   (2 marks)

2b.4 The table below shows a company's sales figures for the first six months of the year.

	Jan	Feb	Mar	Apr	May	June	Total
Product	$'000	$'000	$'000	$'000	$'000	$'000	$'000
A	800	725	725	400	415	405	3,470
B	210	210	180	150	175	160	1,085
C	25	50	60	95	125	140	495
Total	1,035	985	965	645	715	705	5,050

What kind of graph or chart would you use to show the fluctuations of total monthly sales figures across the six months?

O   Percentage component bar chart
O   Scatter diagram
O   Line graph
O   Pie chart   (2 marks)

2b.5 **The following question is taken from the July to December 2017 exam period**

Which of the following would be best suited to represent the relationship between a company's advertising expenditure and its sales revenue?

1   A pie chart
2   A bar chart
3   A scatter graph

O   1 only
O   2 only
O   3 only
●   2 and 3   (2 marks)

(Total = 10 marks)

Check that you can fill in the blanks in the statements below before you attempt any questions. If in doubt, you should go back to your BPP Interactive Text and revise first.

- A .... cost is a cost that can be traced in full to the product, service or department that is being costed. An .... cost is a cost that is incurred in the course of making a product, providing a service or running a department but which cannot be traced directly and in full to the product, service or department.

- In classification by function, costs are classified as follows

  - .... These are associated with the factory.

  - .... These are costs associated with general office departments.

  - .... These are costs associated with sales, marketing, warehousing and transport departments.

- A .... cost is a cost which is incurred for a particular period of time and which, within certain activity levels, is unaffected by changes in the level of activity. A .... cost is a cost which tends to vary with the level of activity. Many items of expenditure are part .... and part .... and are called .... costs.

- The distinction between production and non-production costs is the basis of valuing ....

- A .... centre is a department or organisational function whose performance is the direct responsibility of a specific manager.

  .... centres are similar to cost centres but are accountable for costs and revenues.

  An .... centre is a profit centre with additional responsibilities for capital investment and possibly for financing, and whose performance is measured by its return on investment.

- The basic principle of cost behaviour is that as the level of activity rises, costs will usually ....

- The effect of increasing activity levels on unit costs is as follows. (Tick as appropriate)

	Rises	Falls	Remains constant
Variable cost per unit	☐	☐	☐
Fixed cost per unit	☐	☐	☐
Total cost per unit	☐	☐	☐

- The fixed and variable elements of semi-variable costs can be determined by the .... method.

- *Possible pitfalls*

  Write down the mistakes you know you should avoid.

Did you know? – Cost classification and cost behaviour

Could you fill in the blanks? The answers are in bold. Use this page for revision purposes as you approach the exam.

- A **direct** cost is a cost that can be traced in full to the product, service or department that is being costed. An **indirect** cost is a cost that is incurred in the course of making a product, providing a service or running a department but which cannot be traced directly and in full to the product, service or department.

- In classification by function, costs are classified as follows

    - **Production or manufacturing costs**. These are associated with the factory.

    - **Administration costs**. These are costs associated with general office departments.

    - **Marketing or selling and distribution costs**. These are costs associated with sales, marketing, warehousing and transport departments.

- A **fixed** cost is a cost which is incurred for a particular period of time and which, within certain activity levels, is unaffected by changes in the level of activity. A **variable** cost is a cost which tends to vary with the level of activity. Many items of expenditure are part **fixed** and part **variable** and are called **semi-variable** costs.

- The distinction between production and non-production costs is the basis of valuing **inventory**.

- A **responsibility** centre is a department or organisational function whose performance is the direct responsibility of a specific manager.

    Profit centres are similar to cost centres but are accountable for costs and revenues.

    An **investment** centre is a profit centre with additional responsibilities for capital investment and possibly for financing, and whose performance is measured by its return on investment.

- The basic principle of cost behaviour is that as the level of activity rises, costs will usually **rise**.

- The effect of changing activity levels on unit costs is as follows. (Tick as appropriate)

	Rises	Falls	Remains constant
Variable cost per unit			✓
Fixed cost per unit		✓	
Total cost per unit		✓	

- The fixed and variable elements of semi-variable costs can be determined by the **high-low** method.

- *Possible pitfalls*

    - Getting confused between fixed and variable costs – particularly if they are expressed per unit.
    - Not grasping the difference between direct and indirect costs.

3a Cost classification   29 mins

3a.1 A firm has to pay a 20c per unit royalty to the inventor of a device which it manufactures and sells.

How would the royalty charge be classified in the firm's accounts?

Select... ▼
~~Selling expense~~
(Direct expense)
~~Production overhead~~
~~Administrative overhead~~

(2 marks)

3a.2 Which TWO of the following would be classed as indirect labour?

☒ Assembly workers in a company manufacturing televisions

☑ A stores assistant in a factory store

☑ Factory cleaning staff

☒ Plasterers in a construction company

☒ A consultant in a firm of management consultants   **(2 marks)**

3a.3 A manufacturing firm is very busy and overtime is being worked.

How would the amount of overtime premium contained in direct wages normally be classed?

○ Part of prime cost
○ Factory overheads
○ Direct labour costs
○ Administrative overheads   **(2 marks)**

3a.4 A company makes chairs and tables.

Which TWO of the following items would be treated as an indirect cost?

☐ Wood used to make a chair

☐ Metal used for the legs of a chair

☑ Staple to attach fire retardant labels to chairs

☐ Fabric to cover the seat of a chair

☑ The salary of the sales director of the company   **(2 marks)**

3a.5 Which TWO of the following is the manager of a profit centre likely to have control?

☐ Selling prices

☐ Controllable costs

☐ Apportioned head office costs

☐ Capital investment in the centre   **(2 marks)**

3a.6 Which of the following best describes a controllable cost?

    ○   A cost which arises from a decision already taken, which cannot, in the short run, be changed.

    ○   A cost for which the behaviour pattern can be easily analysed to facilitate valid budgetary control comparisons.

    ○   A cost which can be influenced by its budget holder.

    ○   A specific cost of an activity or business which would be avoided if the activity or business did not exist.   **(2 marks)**

3a.7 Which TWO of the following items might be a suitable cost unit within the credit control department of a company?

    ☐   Stationery cost

    ☐   Telephone bill

    ☐   Customer account

    ☐   Cheque received and processed   **(2 marks)**

3a.8 Which of the following best describes a period cost?

    ○   A cost that relates to a time period which is deducted as expenses for the period and is not included in the inventory valuation.

    ○   A cost that can be easily allocated to a particular period, without the need for arbitrary apportionment between periods.

    ○   A cost that is identified with a unit produced during the period, and is included in the value of inventory. The cost is treated as an expense for the period when the inventory is actually sold.

    ○   A cost that is incurred regularly every period, eg every month or quarter.   **(2 marks)**

3a.9 A company employs four supervisors to oversee the factory production of all its products. How would the salaries paid to these supervisors be classified?

    ○   As a direct labour cost
    ○   As a direct production expense
    ○   As a production overhead
    ○   As an administration overhead   **(2 marks)**

3a.10 A company manufactures and sells toys.

Which TWO of these costs are classified as distribution costs?

    ☐   Rental of the finished goods warehouse

    ☐   Depreciation of its own fleet of delivery vehicles

    ☐   Costs associated with a marketing campaign

    ☐   Commission paid to sales staff   **(2 marks)**

3a.11 Which of the following describes a cost centre?

    ○   A unit of output or service for which costs are ascertained
    ○   A function or location for which costs are ascertained
    ○   A segment of the organisation for which budgets are prepared
    ○   An amount of expenditure attributable to a particular activity   **(2 marks)**

3a.12 The overhead expenses of a company are coded using a five digit coding system, an extract from which is as follows:

Cost centre	Code no	Types of expense	Code no
Machining	10	Indirect materials	410
Finishing	11	Depreciation of production machinery	420
Packing	12	Indirect wages	430
Stores	13	Maintenance materials	440
Maintenance	14	Machine hire costs	450
		Depreciation of non-production equipment	460

The coding for the hire costs of a packing machine is 12450.

Which is the coding for the issue of indirect materials issued from stores to the machining department?

- O 10410
- O 10440
- ● 13410
- O 13440

(2 marks)

(Total = 24 marks)

3b Cost behaviour   48 mins

3b.1 Fixed costs are conventionally deemed to be which of the following?

- O Constant per unit of output
- O Constant in total when production volume changes
- O Outside the control of management
- O Easily controlled

(2 marks)

3b.2 The following data relate to the overhead expenditure of a contract cleaners at two activity levels.

| Square metres cleaned | 13,500 | 15,950 |
| Overheads | $84,865 | $97,850 |

What is the estimate of the overheads if 18,300 square metres are to be cleaned?

$ [110,308]

(2 marks)

handwritten working:
diff 2,450
$12,985
$T = fc + 5.3(q)$
$vc = 5.3$
$T = 13,318 + 5.39$
$97,850$
$- 84,865$
$12,985$
$15,950$
$- 13,500$
$2,450$
$84,865 = fc + 5.3 (13,500)$

The following information relates to questions 3b.3 to 3b.7.

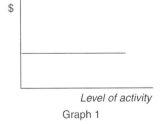

Level of activity
Graph 1

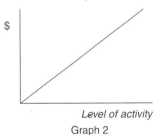

Level of activity
Graph 2

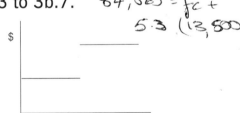

Level of activity
Graph 3

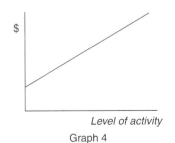

Level of activity
Graph 4

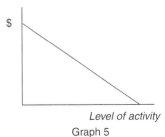

Level of activity
Graph 5

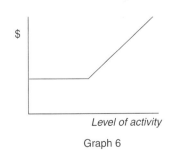

Level of activity
Graph 6

Which one of the above graphs illustrates the costs described in questions 3b.3 to 3b.7?

3b.3   A linear variable cost – when the vertical axis represents cost incurred.

○   Graph 1
○   Graph 2
○   Graph 4
○   Graph 5

(2 marks)

3b.4   A fixed cost – when the vertical axis represents cost incurred.

○   Graph 1
○   Graph 2
○   Graph 3
○   Graph 6

(2 marks)

3b.5   A linear variable cost – when the vertical axis represents cost per unit.

○   Graph 1
○   Graph 2
○   Graph 3
○   Graph 6

(2 marks)

3b.6   A semi-variable cost – when the vertical axis represents cost incurred.

○   Graph 1
○   Graph 2
○   Graph 4
○   Graph 5

(2 marks)

3b.7   A step fixed cost – when the vertical axis represents cost incurred.

○   Graph 3
○   Graph 4
○   Graph 5
○   Graph 6

(2 marks)

3b.8   A company has recorded the following data in the two most recent periods.

Total costs of production $	Volume of production Units
13,500	700
18,300	1,100

(handwritten)
$T = fc + 12(Q)$
$13500 (fc + 12(700))$
$13500 = fc + 8400$

$23\ 500$
$-\ 8\ 400$
$5100 = fc$

$ \boxed{5,100}

(handwritten right side)
Diff
Total = 18,300 - 13,800 = 4,800
Volume = 1,100 - 700 = 400

18,300
13,500
4,800

$\frac{4,800}{400} = 12 = VC$

What is the best estimate of the company's fixed costs per period?

(2 marks)

3b.9   A production worker is paid a salary of $650 per month, plus an extra 5 cents for each unit produced during the month. How is this type of labour cost best described?

✗   A variable cost
✗   A fixed cost
✗   A step cost
●   A semi-variable cost

(2 marks)

3b.10 What type of cost is supervisor salary costs, where one supervisor is needed for every ten employees added to the staff?

Select... ▼

A fixed cost

A variable cost

A mixed cost

A step cost

(2 marks)

3b.11 The following information for advertising and sales has been established over the past six months:

Month	Sales revenue $'000	Advertising expenditure $'000
1	155	3
2	125	2.5
3	200	6
4	175	5.5
5	150	4.5
6	225	6.5

Lo — 2   *Hi — 6*   *Diff $'000   Sr. 100   Ae. 4*

Using the high-low method which of the following is the correct equation for linking advertising and sales from the above data?

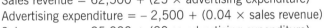 

⊗ Sales revenue = 62,500 + (25 × advertising expenditure)

⊗ Advertising expenditure = – 2,500 + (0.04 × sales revenue)

⊗ Sales revenue = 95,000 + (20 × advertising expenditure)

⊗ Advertising expenditure = – 4,750 + (0.05 × sales revenue)

$\frac{100}{4} = 25$ Vc

225 = fc + 25(6.5)

225 – 162.5 = 62.5

(2 marks)

3b.12 A total cost is described as staying the same over a certain activity range and then increasing but remaining stable over a revised activity range in the short term.

What type of cost is this?

○ A fixed cost

○ A variable cost

○ A semi-variable cost

○ A stepped fixed cost

(2 marks)

3b.13 A company incurs the following costs at various activity levels:

Total cost $	Activity level Units
250,000	5,000
312,500	7,500
400,000	10,000

Lo — 250,000 — 5,000   *Hi* — 400,000 — 10,000

Using the high-low method what is the variable cost per unit (to the nearest whole number)?

$ [   ]

$\frac{150,000}{5,000}$

(2 marks)

3b.14 The following diagram represents the behaviour of one element of cost:

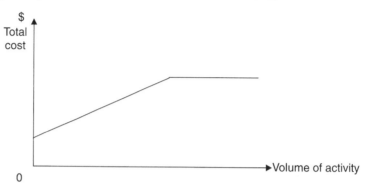

Which of the following statements is consistent with the above diagram?

O   Annual factory power cost where the electricity supplier sets a tariff based on a fixed charge plus a constant unit cost for consumption but subject to a maximum annual charge.

O   Weekly total labour cost when there is a fixed wage for a standard 40 hour week but overtime is paid at a premium rate.

O   Total direct material cost for a period if the supplier charges a lower unit cost on all units once a certain quantity has been purchased in that period.

O   Total direct material cost for a period where the supplier charges a constant amount per unit for all units supplied up to a maximum charge for the period. **(2 marks)**

3b.15 An organisation manufactures a single product. The total cost of making 4,000 units is $20,000 and the total cost of making 20,000 units is $40,000. Within this range of activity the total fixed costs remain unchanged.

What is the variable cost per unit of the product (to 2 dp)?

$ [   ]

(2 marks)

3b.16 When total purchases of raw material exceed 30,000 units in any one period then all units purchased, including the initial 30,000, are invoiced at a lower cost per unit.

Which of the following graphs is consistent with the behaviour of the total materials cost in a period?

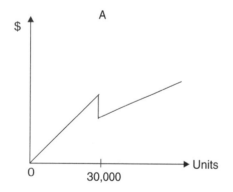

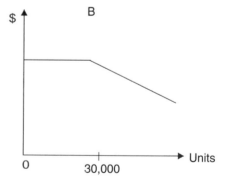

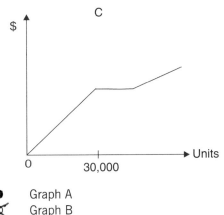

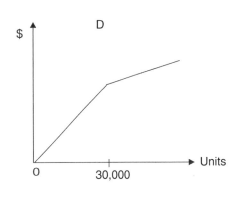

●   Graph A
✗   Graph B
✗   Graph C
✗   Graph D

(2 marks)

3b.17 The total cost of production for two levels of activity is as follows:

	Level 1	Level 2
Production (units)	3,000	5,000
Total cost ($)	6,750	9,250

The variable production cost per unit and the total fixed production cost both remain constant in the range of activity shown.

What is the level of fixed costs (to the nearest whole number)?

$

(2 marks)

3b.18 **The following question is taken from the December 2011 exam.**

The following shows the total overhead costs for given levels of a company's total output.

Cost	Output
$	Units
4,000	1,000
7,000	2,000
10,000	3,000
9,500	4,000

A step up in fixed costs of $500 occurs at an output level of 3,500 units.

What would be the variable overhead cost per unit (to the nearest $0.01) using the high-low technique?

O $1.67 per unit
O $1.83 per unit
O $2.75 per unit
O $3.00 per unit

(2 marks)

3b.19 **The following question is taken from the January to June 2014 exam period.**

A company has prepared flexed budgets at two activity levels. The cost per unit of three costs is given below. All three costs behave in a linear manner with respect to activity.

	Activity level (units)	
	10,000	15,000
Cost		
X	$3.0 per unit	$2.0 per unit
Y	$1.0 per unit	$1.0 per unit
Z	$3.5 per unit	$3.0 per unit

Is each of the costs variable, semi-variable or fixed?

	X	Y	Z
O	Variable	Fixed	Semi-variable
O	Variable	Fixed	Variable
O	Fixed	Variable	Semi-variable
O	Fixed	Variable	Fixed

(2 marks)

3b.20 **The following question is taken from the September to June 2018 exam period.**

The following observations of output and cost have been made:

Output	Cost
Units	$
8,000	39,400
20,000	68,000

It is known that at output levels above 15,000 units, variable cost per unit drops by $1 per unit for all subsequent units produced.

What is the variable cost for each unit of output above 15,000 units?

- O $1.80
- O $0.97
- O $2.80
- O $3.40

(2 marks)

(Total = 40 marks)

Do you know? – Forecasting, summarising and analysing data

Check that you can fill in the blanks in the statements below before you attempt any questions. If in doubt, you should go back to your BPP Interactive Text and revise first.

- A .... is a plan of what the organisation is aiming to achieve and what it has set as a target whereas a .... is an estimate of what is likely to occur in the future.

- The degree of correlation between two variables is measured by the ....

    r = +1 means that the variables are .... correlated.

    r = –1 means that the variables are .... correlated.

    r = 0 means that the variables are ....

    The square of the correlation coefficient is called the .... of .... It measures the .... of the total variation in the value of one variable that can be explained by variations in the value of the other variable.

- Linear regression analysis is one method used for estimating a line of .... As with all forecasting techniques, the results from regression analysis will not be wholly reliable. There are a number of factors which affect the reliability of forecasts made using regression analysis. For example, it assumes that a .... exists between the two variables.

- A time series is a series of figures or values recorded over time. The time series analysis forecasting technique is usually used to ....

- There are four components of a time series: ...., ..., ... and ....

- One way of finding the trend is to use ....

- .... is data where the frequency is shown in terms of a range. .... is data where the frequency is shown in terms of a specific measure or value. .... can only take on a countable number of values. .... can take on any value.

- The arithmetic mean is the best known type of average and is widely understood.

    Arithmetic mean of ungrouped data = ... ÷..........................

    Arithmetic mean of grouped data = ... ÷.......................... or .... ÷..........................

- The average which means 'the most frequently occurring value' is called the ....

- The mode of a grouped frequency distribution can be calculated from a ....

- The .... is the value of the middle member of an array. The middle item of an odd number of items is calculated as ....

- The .... of a grouped frequency distribution can be established from an ....

- The ...., which is the square root of the ...., is the most important measure of spread used in statistics.

- The spreads of two distributions can be compared using the .... of .... calculated as .... ÷..........................

- Properties of the normal distribution are as follows:

    It is .... and .... It has a ...., μ (pronounced mew)

    The area under the curve totals exactly ... The area to the left of μ = area to the right of μ = ...

- *Possible pitfalls*

    Write down the mistakes you know you should avoid.

BPP
LEARNING MEDIA

Did you know? – Forecasting

Could you fill in the blanks? The answers are in bold. Use this page for revision purposes as you approach the exam.

- A **budget** is a plan of what the organisation is aiming to achieve and what it has set as a target whereas a **forecast** is an estimate of what is likely to occur in the future.

- The degree of correlation between two variables is measured by the **correlation coefficient**.

  r = +1 means that the variables are **perfectly positively** correlated

  r = -1 means that the variables are **perfectly negatively** correlated

  r = 0 means that the variables are **uncorrelated**

  The square of the correlation coefficient is called the **coefficient** of **determination**. It measures the **proportion** of the total variation in the value of one variable that can be explained by variations in the value of the other variable.

- Linear regression analysis is one method used for estimating a line of **best fit.** As with all forecasting techniques, the results from regression analysis will not be wholly reliable. There are a number of factors which affect the reliability of forecasts made using regression analysis. For example, it assumes that a **linear relationship** exists between the two variables.

- A time series is a series of figures or values recorded over time. The time series analysis forecasting technique is usually used to **forecast sales**.

- There are four components of a time series: **trend, seasonal variations, cyclical variations and random variations**.

- One way of finding the trend is to use **moving averages**.

- **Grouped data** is data where the frequency is shown in terms of a range. **Ungrouped data** is data where the frequency is shown in terms of a specific measure or value. **Discrete data** can only take on a countable number of values. **Continuous data** can take on any value.

- The arithmetic mean is the best known type of average and is widely understood.

  Arithmetic mean of ungrouped data = **Sum of values of items ÷ Number of items.**

  Arithmetic mean of grouped data = **Σfx ÷ n** or **Σfx ÷ Σf**

- The average which means 'the most frequently occurring value' is called the **mode.**

- The **mode of a grouped frequency distribution** can be calculated from a histogram.

- The **median** is the value of the middle member of an array. The middle item of an odd number of items is calculated as the $\dfrac{(n+1)^{th}}{2}$ item.

- The median of a grouped frequency distribution can be established from an **ogive.**

- The **standard deviation**, which is the square root of the **variance**, is the most important measure of spread used in statistics.

- The spreads of two distributions can be compared using the **coefficient** of **variation** calculated as **standard deviation ÷ mean.**

- Properties of the normal distribution are as follows:

  It is **symmetrical** and **bell-shaped.** It has a **mean,** μ (pronounced mew)

  The area under the curve totals exactly **1.** The area to the left of μ = area to the right of μ = **0.5**

- *Possible pitfalls*

  – Not understanding the meanings of correlation coefficient and coefficient of determination
  – Forgetting that linear regression gives an *estimate* only. It is not wholly reliable

4a Forecasting   82 mins

4a.1   The following four data pairs have been obtained: (1, 5), (2, 6), (4, 9), (5, 11). Without carrying out any calculations, which of the following correlation coefficients best describes the relationship between x and y?

⊠   –0.98
⊠   –0.25
◉   0.98
⊠   0.25   **(2 marks)**

4a.2   A company's management accountant is analysing the reject rates achieved by 100 factory operatives working in identical conditions. Reject rates, Y%, are found to be related to months of experience, X, by this regression equation: Y = 20 – 0.25X. (The correlation coefficient was r = –0.9.)

Using the equation, what is the predicted reject rate for an operative with 12 months' experience?

○   17%
○   19%
○   20%
○   23%   **(2 marks)**

4a.3   A regression equation Y = a + bX is used to forecast the value of Y for a given value of X.

Which TWO of the following increase the reliability of the forecast?

☐   A correlation coefficient numerically close to 1

☐   Working to a higher number of decimal places of accuracy

☐   Forecasting for values of X outside the range of those used in the sample

☐   A large sample is used to calculate the regression equation   **(2 marks)**

4a.4   If $\Sigma x = 12$, $\Sigma y = 42$, $\Sigma x^2 = 46$, $\Sigma y^2 = 542$, $\Sigma xy = 157$ and n = 4, what is the correlation coefficient?

○   0.98
○   –0.98
○   0.26
○   0.008   **(2 marks)**

4a.5   Using data from twelve European countries, it has been calculated that the correlation between the level of car ownership and the number of road deaths is 0.73.

Which TWO of the statements shown follow from this?

☒   High levels of car ownership cause high levels of road deaths

☑   There is a strong relationship between the level of car ownership and the number of road deaths

☒   53% of the variation in the level of road deaths from one country to the next can be explained by the corresponding variation in the level of car ownership

☑   73% of the variation in the level of road deaths from one country to the next can be explained by the corresponding variation in the level of car ownership

                                                                           (2 marks)

4a.6 The regression equation $Y = 3 + 2X$ has been calculated from 6 pairs of values, with X ranging from 1 to 10. The correlation coefficient is 0.8. It is estimated that $Y = 43$ when $X = 20$.

Which TWO of the following are true?

☑ The estimate is not reliable because X is outside the range of the data

☒ The estimate is not reliable because the correlation is low

☒ The estimate is reliable

☑ The estimate is not reliable because the sample is small   **(2 marks)**

4a.7 In calculating the regression equation linking two variables, the standard formulae for the regression coefficients are given in terms of X and Y. Which of the following is true?

○ X must be the variable which will be forecast
○ It does not matter which variable is which
○ Y must be the dependent variable
○ Y must be the variable shown on the vertical axis of a scatter diagram   **(2 marks)**

4a.8 A company uses regression analysis to establish a total cost equation for budgeting purposes.

Data for the past four months is as follows:

Month	Total cost $'000	Quantity produced $'000
1	57.5	1.25
2	37.5	1.00
3	45.0	1.50
4	60.0	2.00
	200.0	5.75

The gradient of the regression line is 17.14.

What is the value of a?

○ 25.36
○ 48.56
○ 74.64
○ 101.45   **(2 marks)**

4a.9 Regression analysis is being used to fine the line of best fit ($y = a + bx$) from eleven pairs of data. The calculations have produced the following information:

$\Sigma x = 440$, $\Sigma y = 330$, $\Sigma x^2 = 17{,}986$, $\Sigma y^2 = 10{,}366$ and $\Sigma xy = 13{,}467$

What is the value of 'a' in the equation for the line of best fit (to 2 decimal places)?

○ 0.63
○ 0.69
○ 2.33
○ 5.33   **(2 marks)**

4a.10 Which of the following is a feasible value for the correlation coefficient?

○ − 2.0
○ − 1.2
○ 0
○ + 1.2   **(2 marks)**

4a.11 Over an 18-month period, sales have been found to have an underlying linear trend of y = 7.112 + 3.949x, where y is the number of items sold and x represents the month. Monthly deviations from trend have been calculated and month 19 is expected to be 1.12 times the trend value.

What is the forecast number of items to be sold in month 19?

- ○ 91
- ○ 92
- ○ 93
- ○ 94 **(2 marks)**

4a.12 Based on the last 15 periods the underlying trend of sales is y = 345.12 – 1.35x. If the 16th period has a seasonal factor of –23.62, assuming an additive forecasting model, what is the forecast for that period, in whole units?

- ○ 300
- ○ 301
- ○ 324
- ○ 325 **(2 marks)**

4a.13 Unemployment numbers actually recorded in a town for the second quarter of the year 2000 were 4,700. The underlying trend at this point was 4,300 people and the seasonal factor is 0.92. Using the multiplicative model for seasonal adjustment, what is the seasonally-adjusted figure (in whole numbers) for the quarter?

(2 marks)

4a.14 Monthly sales have been found to follow a linear trend of y = 9.82 + 4.372x, where y is the number of items sold and x is the number of the month. Monthly deviations from the trend have been calculated and follow an additive model. In month 24, the seasonal variation is estimated to be plus 8.5.

What is the forecast number of items to be sold in month 24? (to the nearest whole number.)

- ○ 106
- ○ 115
- ○ 123
- ○ 152 **(2 marks)**

4a.15 Which TWO of the following are necessary if forecasts obtained from a time series analysis are to be reliable?

- ☐ There must be no unforeseen events
- ☐ The model used must fit the past data
- ☐ The trend must be increasing
- ☐ There must be no seasonal variation

(2 marks)

4a.16 What is the purpose of seasonally adjusting the values in a time series?

- ○ To obtain an instant estimate of the degree of seasonal variation
- ○ To obtain an instant estimate of the trend
- ○ To ensure that seasonal components total zero
- ○ To take the first step in a time series analysis of the data **(2 marks)**

4a.17 The following data represents a time series:

X   36   Y   41   34   38   42

A series of three point moving averages produced from this data has given the first two values as 38 and 39.

What are the values of (X, Y) in the original time series?

- ○ (38, 39)
- ○ (38, 40)
- ○ (40, 38)
- ○ (39, 38) **(2 marks)**

4a.18 Using an additive time series model, the quarterly trend (Y) is given by $Y = 65 + 7t$, where t is the quarter (starting with $t = 1$ in the first quarter of 20X5). If the seasonal component in the fourth quarter is –30, what is the forecast for the actual value for the fourth quarter of 20X6, to the nearest whole number?

- ○ 63
- ○ 546
- ○ 85
- ○ 91 **(2 marks)**

4a.19 The trend for monthly sales ($Y) is related to the month (t) by the equation $Y = 1,500 - 3t$ where $t = 1$ in the first month of 20X8. What are the forecast sales (to the nearest dollar) for the first month of 20X9 if the seasonal component for that month is 0.92 using a multiplicative model?

- ○ $1,377
- ○ $17,904
- ○ $1,344
- ○ $1,462 **(2 marks)**

4a.20 Which TWO of the following are necessary if forecasts obtained from a time series analysis are to be reliable?

- ☐ The trend must not be increasing or decreasing
- ☐ The trend must continue as in the past
- ☐ Extrapolation must not be used
- ☐ The same pattern of seasonal variation must continue as in the past

(2 marks)

4a.21 Under which of the following circumstances would a multiplicative model be preferred to an additive model in time series analysis?

- ○ When a model easily understood by non-accountants is required
- ○ When the trend is increasing or decreasing
- ○ When the trend is steady
- ○ When accurate forecasts are required **(2 marks)**

4a.22 A company's annual profits have a trend line given by $Y = 20t - 10$, where Y is the trend in $'000 and t is the year with $t = 0$ in 20X0.

What are the forecast profits for the year 20X9 using an additive model if the cyclical component for that year is –30?

- ○ $160,000
- ○ $140,000
- ○ $119,000
- ○ $60,000 **(2 marks)**

4a.23 In January, the unemployment in Ruritania is 567,800. If the seasonal factor using an additive time series model is +90,100, what is the seasonally-adjusted level of unemployment (to the nearest whole number)?

    O   90,100
    O   477,700
    O   567,800
    O   657,900   **(2 marks)**

4a.24 The following statements relate to Paasche and Laspeyre indices.

(i)   Constructing a Paasche index is generally more costly than a Laspeyre index

(ii)   With a Laspeyre index, comparisons can only be drawn directly between the current year and the base year

Which statements are true?

    O   Both statements are true
    O   Both statements are false
    O   (i) is true and (ii) is false
    O   (ii) is true and (i) is false   **(2 marks)**

4a.25 The following information is available for the price of materials used at P Co.

Laspeyre index for price in 20X5 (with base year of 20X0)   150.0
Corresponding Paasche index   138.24

What is Fisher's ideal index?

    O   12.00
    O   16.98
    O   144.00
    O   288.24   **(2 marks)**

4a.26 A large bag of cement cost $0.80 in 20X3. The price indices are as follows.

20X3	91
20X4	95
20X5	103
20X6	106

How much does a bag of cement cost in 20X6 (to 2 dp)?

$ _____

        (2 marks)

4a.27 Four years ago material X cost $5 per kg and the price index most appropriate to the cost of material X stood at 150.

The same index now stands at 430.

What is the best estimate of the current cost of material X per kg?

    O $1.74
    O $9.33
    O $14.33
    O $21.50   **(2 marks)**

4a.28 Six years ago material M cost $10 per kg and the price index most appropriate to the cost of material M was 130. The same index now stands at 510.

What is the best estimate of the current cost of material M per kg?

- ○ $2.55
- ○ $29.23
- ○ $39.23
- ○ $51.00 **(2 marks)**

4a.29 Which of the following are common applications of spreadsheets used by management accountants?

- (i) Variance analysis
- (ii) Cash flow budgeting and forecasting
- (iii) Preparation of financial accounts

- ○ (i) and (ii) only
- ○ (i) and (iii) only
- ○ (ii) and (iii) only
- ○ (i), (ii) and (iii) **(2 marks)**

4a.30 A spreadsheet is unlikely to be used for which of the following tasks?

- ○ Cash flow forecasting
- ○ Monthly sales analysis by market
- ○ Writing a memo
- ○ Calculation of depreciation **(2 marks)**

4a.31 The following question is taken from the December 2012 exam.

The following data relates to a company's overhead cost.

Time (units)	Output	Overhead cost ($)	Price index
2 years ago	1,000	3,700	121
Current year	3,000	13,000	155

Using the high low technique, what is the variable cost per unit (to the nearest $0.01) expressed in current year prices?

- ○ $3.22
- ○ $4.13
- ○ $4.65
- ○ $5.06 **(2 marks)**

4a.32 The following question is taken from the June 2013 exam.

An additive time series has the following trend and seasonal variations:

Trend Y=4,000 + 6X where Y= sales in units

X is the number of quarters, with the first quarter of 2014 being 1, the second quarter of 2014 being 2 etc.

Seasonal variation

Quarter	1	2	3	4
Quarterly variation (units)	−4	−2	+1	+5

What is the forecast sales volume for the fourth quarter of 2015?

- ○ 4,029
- ○ 4,043
- ○ 4,048
- ○ 4,053 **(2 marks)**

4a.33 The following question is taken from the July to December 2015 exam period.

The following spreadsheet shows part of a time series analysis of a company's sales.

Year	Quarter	Sales (unit)	Four quarter moving total (unit)
2014	1	1,100	
	2	1,700	
			7,000
	3	1,900	
			9,000
	4	2,300	
			11,000
2015	1	3,100	
			13,200
	2	3,700	
	3	4,100	

What is the four quarter centred moving average of sales units for quarter 4, 2014?

O   2,500
O   5,025
O   5,000
O   10,000   **(2 marks)**

4a.34 The following question is taken from the January to June 2017 exam period.

The following information relates to a company's semi-variable production overheads.

Year	Output units	Overhead $	Relevant price index
2012	1,000	12,000	130
2013	1,200	14,000	140

What is the variable overhead cost per unit, expressed in 2013 prices?

O $5.00
O $5.38
O $10.00
O $11.67   **(2 marks)**

(Total = 68 marks)

4b Summarising and analysing data   67 mins

4b.1   The arithmetic mean of the following ten invoice values is $20:

$X, $15, $22, $14, $21, $15, $20, $18, $27, $X.

What does $X equal?

O $15
O $19
O $24
O $48   **(2 marks)**

4b.2   A factory employs staff in four departments for which the average (mean) wage per employee per week is as follows.

Department	W	X	Y	Z
Mean wage	$50	$100	$70	$80
Number of employees	20	5	10	5

What is the average (mean) wage per employee per week in this factory?

- O $50
- O $65
- O $70
- O $75

(2 marks)

4b.3   A car travels 20 miles at 30 mph, then 10 miles at 60 mph.

What is the mean speed for the whole journey of 30 miles?

- O   36
- O   40
- O   42
- O   45

(2 marks)

4b.4   The following scores are observed for the times taken to complete a task, in minutes.

12, 34, 14, 15, 21, 24, 9, 17, 11, 8

What is the median score?

[   ]

(2 marks)

4b.5   What is the median of the scores 34, 23, 78, 12, 56, 43, 28, 9, 24 and 87?

- O   26
- O   28
- O   31
- O   34

(2 marks)

4b.6   Quality control of four independent production processes reveals the length of certain parts (in mm) to be as follows.

Process	Mean	Standard deviation
W	100	10
X	40	5
Y	80	8
Z	150	12

Which process has the largest relative variation, as measured by the coefficient of variation?

- O   Process W
- O   Process X
- O   Process Y
- O   Process Z

(2 marks)

4b.7   Which of the following sets of data have the widest spread?

	A	B	C	D
Mean	150	175	200	250
Standard deviation	25	20	25	30

- O   Data A
- O   Data B
- O   Data C
- O   Data D

(2 marks)

4b.8 A group of shoppers were interviewed and asked how many loaves of bread they would need to buy from the bakers over a one-week period. The results are as follows.

Number of loaves	Number of shoppers
0	2
1	22
2	32
3	2
4	34
5	6
6	12

What is the mode of the number of loaves needed per shopper in a one-week period?

[   ]

(2 marks)

4b.9 A large publishing company awards a 14% salary increase to every employee.

Which of the following statements about the distribution of the company's salaries is/are correct?

1 The standard deviation will remain unaltered
2 The standard deviation will increase by 14%
3 The coefficient of variation will remain unaltered

O 1 and 2 only
O 1 and 3 only
O 2 and 3 only
O 1, 2 and 3

(2 marks)

4b.10 The coefficient of variation is used to measure which of the following?

O The correlation between two variables.
O The percentage variation in one variable caused by variation in another.
O The strength of a relationship between two variables.
O Relative dispersion.

(2 marks)

4b.11 A company must decide between two projects – Project A and Project B. The profits that might be generated from each project are as follows.

Project A		Project B	
Probability	Profit $	Probability	Profit/(loss) $
0.45	4,000	0.64	8,000
0.55	2,000	0.36	(1,000)

Which project should be chosen and what is the associated expected value of profit?

	Project	Expected profit $
O	A	2,900
O	A	3,000
O	B	4,760
O	B	5,480

(2 marks)

4b.12 A company is bidding for three contracts which are awarded independently of each other. The board estimates its chances of winning Contract A as 50%, of winning Contract B as 1 in 5 and of winning Contract C as 1 in 3. The profits from A, B and C are estimated to be $500,000, $800,000 and $900,000 respectively.

The expected value to the company of the profits from all three contracts will be closest to which of the following?

- O $300,000
- O $710,000
- O $733,000
- O $900,000   **(2 marks)**

4b.13 Singers Co is launching a new sewing machine. With television advertising, sales are estimated to achieve the following levels, with associated probabilities.

Sales Units	Probability
1,000	0.3
4,000	0.5
8,000	0.2

What is the expected level of sales?

- O   4,000
- O   4,333
- O   13,000
- O   3,900   **(2 marks)**

The following information relates to questions 4b.14 – 4b.16

A company sells and manufactures product SX. The selling price of the product is $10 per unit and estimates of demand and variable costs of sales are as follows.

Probability	Demand Units	Probability	Variable cost per unit $
0.1	5,000	0.1	3.00
0.6	6,000	0.5	3.50
0.3	8,000	0.3	4.00
		0.1	4.50

The unit variable costs do not depend on the volume of sales.

Fixed costs will be $30,000.

4b.14 What is the EV of demand? [   ] units   **(2 marks)**

4b.15 What is the EV of unit variable costs? $ [   ] (to 2 decimal places)   **(2 marks)**

4b.16 What is the EV of profit? $ [   ]   **(2 marks)**

4b.17 A normal distribution has a mean of 55 and a variance of 14.44.

The probability of a score of 59 or more is approximately which of the following?

- O   0.15
- O   0.35
- O   0.50
- O   0.85   **(2 marks)**

4b.18 A normal distribution has a mean of 75 and a variance of 25.

What is the upper quartile of this distribution?

O   58.25
O   71.65
O   78.35
O   91.75   **(2 marks)**

4b.19 A normal distribution has a mean of 150, and a standard deviation of 20.

80% of the distribution is below which of the following (approximately)?

O   158
O   170
O   161
O   167   **(2 marks)**

4b.20 A normal distribution is to be split into four equal areas, two to the right of $Z = 0$ and two to the left of $Z = 0$ ($Z = 0$ at the mean).

Using normal distribution tables, the $|Z|$ value that splits the area in this way is closest to which of the following?

O   0.0987
O   0.1915
O   0.3333
O   0.675099   **(2 marks)**

4b.21 Production of aluminium tubes is normally distributed with a mean length of 50 cm and a standard deviation of 5 cm.

The percentage of tubes at least 57 cm long is closest to which of the following?

O   8%
O   42%
O   58%
O   92%   **(2 marks)**

4b.22 A normal distribution has a mean of 60 and a variance of 25.

What is the probability of a score of 72 or more? (to 4 decimal places)

| | **(2 marks)**

4b.23 A normal distribution has a mean of 150 and a variance of 6,944.

What percentage of the population is less than 210? (to two decimal places.)

O   23.58%
O   26.42%
O   72.00%
O   76.42%   **(2 marks)**

4b.24 A normal distribution has a mean of 650 and a variance of 100.

What is the upper quartile of this distribution?

O   643.3
O   656.7
O   717.0
O   812.5   **(2 marks)**

4b.25 A normal distribution is to be split into eight equal areas, four to the right of Z = 0 and four to the left of Z = 0 (Z = 0 at the mean).

Using normal distribution tables, the |Z| value that splits the area in this way is closest to which of the following?

   O   0.28
   O   0.30
   O   0.32
   O   0.34   **(2 marks)**

4b.26 The weights of component X are normally distributed. The mean weight is 5,200kg and the standard deviation is 430kg.

What is the probability of a component X weighing more than 6,000kg?

   O   0.0314
   O   0.2343
   O   0.4686
   O   0.9686   **(2 marks)**

4b.27 Which TWO of the following statements are true?

☐   If a sample is selected using random sampling, it will be free from bias.

☐   A sampling frame is a numbered list of all items in a sample.

☐   In cluster sampling there is very little potential for bias.

☐   In quota sampling, investigators are told to interview all the people they meet up to a certain quota.

            (2 marks)

4b.28 Which of the following explains the essence of quota sampling?

   O   Each element of the population has an equal chance of being chosen
   O   Every nth member of the population is selected
   O   Every element of one definable sub-section of the population is selected
   O   None of the above   **(2 marks)**

                             (Total = 56 marks)

Do you know? – Materials and labour

Check that you can fill in the blanks in the statements below before you attempt any questions. If in doubt, you should go back to your BPP Interactive Text and revise first.

- FIFO prices materials issues at the prices of the newest/oldest items in inventory, and values closing inventory at the value of the most recent/oldest items in inventory. (Delete as appropriate)

- LIFO prices materials issues at the prices of the newest/oldest items in inventory and values closing inventory at the value of the most recent/oldest items. (Delete as appropriate)

- .... is usually carried out annually, when all items of inventory are counted on a specific date. .... involves counting and checking a number of inventory items on a regular basis so that each item is checked at least once a year.

- Inventory control levels are calculated in order to maintain inventory at the optimum level. The four critical control levels are as follows.

   .... (maximum usage × maximum lead time)
   .... (quantity of inventory to be reordered when inventory reaches reorder level)
   .... (reorder level – (average usage × average lead time))
   .... (reorder level + reorder quantity – (min usage × min lead time))

- The .... is the ordering quantity which minimises inventory costs (holding costs and ordering costs), and is calculated as follows.

   $$EOQ = \sqrt{\frac{2C_oD}{C_h}}$$ Where C_h = ...

   C_o = ...
   D = ...
   EOQ = ...

- Labour attendance time is recorded on an .... or on a .... Job time is recorded on the following documents:

   ....
   ....
   ....

- *Possible pitfalls*

   Write down the mistakes you know you should avoid.

Could you fill in the blanks? The answers are in bold. Use this page for revision purposes as you approach the exam.

- FIFO prices materials issues at the prices of the ~~newest~~/**oldest** items in inventory, and values closing inventory at the value of the **most recent**/~~oldest~~ items in inventory.

- LIFO prices materials issues at the prices of the **newest**/~~oldest~~ items in inventory and values closing inventory at the value of the most ~~recent~~/**oldest items**.

- **Periodic inventory taking** is usually carried out annually, when all items of inventory are counted on a specific date. **Continuous inventory taking** involves counting and checking a number of inventory items on a regular basis so that each item is checked at least once a year.

- Inventory control levels are calculated in order to maintain inventory at the optimum level. The four critical control levels are as follows.

  Reorder level (maximum usage × maximum lead time)
  Reorder quantity (quantity of inventory to be reordered when inventory reaches reorder level)
  Minimum inventory level (reorder level – (average usage × average lead time))
  Maximum inventory level (reorder level + reorder quantity – (min usage × min lead time))

- The **economic order quantity** is the ordering quantity which minimises inventory costs (holding costs and ordering costs), and is calculated as follows.

$$EOQ = \sqrt{\frac{2C_0 D}{C_h}}$$

Where	C_h	= **holding costs of one unit of inventory for one year**
	C_0	= **cost of ordering a consignment**
	D	= **annual demand**
	EOQ	= **economic order quantity**

- Labour attendance time is recorded on an **attendance card** or on a **clock card.** Job time is recorded on the following documents.

  Daily time sheets
  Weekly time sheets
  Job cards

- *Possible pitfalls*

  – Confusing FIFO with LIFO.
  – Not being able to reproduce the inventory control formulae.
  – Confusing the meaning of 'c', 'd', and 'h' in the economic order quantity equation.

5 Accounting for materials   53 mins

5.1   Which of the following functions are fulfilled by a goods received note (GRN)?

    (i)   Provides information to update the inventory records on receipt of goods
    (ii)   Provides information to check the quantity on the supplier's invoice
    (iii) Provides information to check the price on the supplier's invoice

    O   (i) and (ii) only
    O   (i) and (iii) only
    O   (ii) and (iii) only
    O   (i) only   **(2 marks)**

5.2   There are 27,500 units of Part Number X35 on order with the suppliers and 16,250 units outstanding on existing customers' orders.

    If the free inventory is 13,000 units, what is the physical inventory? $x + 27,500 - 16,250 = 13,000$

    | 1750 | units $x + 11,250 = 13,500$

                        $13,000 - 11,250 = 1,750$ $11,250$ **(2 marks)**

The following information relates to questions 5.3 and 5.4.

A domestic appliance retailer with multiple outlets sells a popular toaster known as the Autocrisp 2000, for which the following information is available:

Average sales	75 per day
Maximum sales	95 per day
Minimum sales	50 per day
Lead time	12-18 days
Reorder quantity	1,750

5.3   Based on the data above, at what level of inventory would a replenishment order be issued?

    | 1710 | units 95×18

                                          (2 marks)

5.4   Based on the data above, what is the maximum inventory level?

    O   1,750 units
    O   2,275 units
    ●   2,860 units $1710 + 1750 - \left(50 \times 12 \right)$
    O   2,900 units   **(2 marks)**

5.5   The annual demand for an item of inventory is 2,500 units. The cost of placing an order is $80 and the cost of holding an item in stock for one year is $15. What is the economic order quantity, to the nearest unit?

    | 163 | units

                                           (2 marks)

$$\sqrt{\frac{2(80)(2,500)}{15}} = \sqrt{\frac{400\,000}{15}} = 163.$$

5.6   Which of the following is correct with regard to inventories?

    (i)   Stock-outs arise when too little inventory is held.

    (ii)   Safety inventories are the level of units maintained in case there is unexpected demand.

    (iii)   A re-order level can be established by looking at the maximum usage and the maximum lead-time.

    ⊠   (i) and (ii) only
    O   (i) and (iii) only
    O   (ii) and (iii) only
    ●   (i), (ii) and (iii)   **(2 marks)**

5.7   What is the economic batch quantity used to establish?

Optimal

    O   reorder quantity
    O   recorder level
    O   order quantity
    O   inventory level for production   **(2 marks)**

5.8   The demand for a product is 12,500 units for a three month period. Each unit of product has a purchase price of $15 and ordering costs are $20 per order placed.

The annual holding cost of one unit of product is 10% of its purchase price.

What is the Economic Order Quantity (to the nearest unit)?

    O   577
    O   816
    O   866
    O   1,155   **(2 marks)**

5.9   A company determines its order quantity for a raw material by using the Economic Order Quantity (EOQ) model.

What would be the effects on the EOQ and the total annual holding cost of a decrease in the cost of ordering a batch of raw material?

	EOQ	Total annual holding cost
O	Higher	Lower
O	Higher	Higher
O	Lower	Higher
O	Lower	Lower

    (2 marks)

5.10   Data relating to a particular stores item are as follows:

Average daily usage	400 units
Maximum daily usage	520 units
Minimum daily usage	180 units
Lead time for replenishment of inventory	10 to 15 days
Reorder quantity	8,000 units

What is the reorder level (in units) which avoids stockouts (running out of inventory)?

    O   5,000
    O   6,000
    O   7,800
    O   8,000   **(2 marks)**

5.11 The material stores control account for a company for March looks like this:

Material stores control account

	$		$
Balance b/d	12,000	Work in progress	40,000
Suppliers	49,000	Overhead control	12,000
Work in progress	18,000	Balance c/d	27,000
	79,000		79,000
Balance b/d	27,000		

Which of the following statements are correct?

(i)   Issues of direct materials during March were $18,000
(ii)   Issues of direct materials during March were $40,000
(iii)   Issues of indirect materials during March were $12,000
(iv)   Purchases of materials during March were $49,000

- ○ (i) and (iv) only
- ○ (ii) and (iv) only
- ◉ (ii), (iii) and (iv) only
- ○ All of them   **(2 marks)**

5.12 A manufacturing company uses 25,000 components at an even rate during a year. Each order placed with the supplier of the components is for 2,000 components, which is the economic order quantity. The company holds a buffer inventory of 500 components. The annual cost of holding one component in inventory is $2.

What is the total annual cost of holding inventory of the component?

- ○ $2,000
- ○ $2,500
- ○ $3,000
- ○ $4,000   **(2 marks)**

5.13 A company wishes to minimise its inventory costs. Order costs are $10 per order and holding costs are $0.10 per unit per month. Fall Co estimates annual demand to be 5,400 units.

What is the economic order quantity (to the nearest whole unit)?

[ ] units

(2 marks)

5.14 For a particular component, the re-order quantity is 6,000 units and the average inventory holding is 3,400 units.

Using the drop down list, select the level of safety inventory (in whole units).

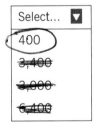

Select... ▼
(400)
~~3,400~~
~~3,000~~
~~6,400~~

$$3400 = x + \tfrac{1}{2} 6000$$

$$3400 - \tfrac{1}{2} 6000 = x$$

$$400 = x$$

(2 marks)

5.15   The following data relates to component L512:

Ordering costs $100 per order
Inventory holding costs $8 per unit per year
Annual demand   1,225 units

What is the economic order quantity (to the nearest whole unit)?

O   175 units
O   62 units
O   44 units
O   124 units

(2 marks)

5.16   The following data relate to inventory item A452:

Average usage   100 units per day
Minimum usage   60 units per day
Maximum usage   130 units per day
Lead time   20-26 days
EOQ   4,000 units

What is the maximum inventory level?

$130 \times 26 = 3380$
Reorder

$3380 + 4,000 - \left(60 \times 20\right)$

$= 7,380 - 1200$

$= 6180$

6180   units

(2 marks)

5.17   ACB Co gradually receives its re-supply of inventory at a rate of 10,000 units a week. Other information is available as follows.

Weekly demand   5,000 units
Set-up costs for each production run $125
Weekly cost of holding one unit $0.0025

What is the economic production run?

O   1,577 units
O   7,071 units
O   31,623 units
O   894,427 units

(2 marks)

5.18

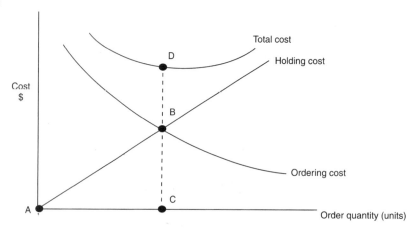

Where on the graph would you read off the value for the economic order quantity?

☒   At point A
●   At point B
☒   At point C
☒   At point D

(2 marks)

5.19 A company uses an item of inventory as follows.

Purchase price $25 per unit
Annual demand   1,800 units
Ordering cost $32
Annual holding cost $4.50 per unit
EOQ   160 units

What is the minimum total cost assuming a discount of 2% applies to the purchase price and to holding costs on orders of 300 and over?

- ○ $45,720.00
- ○ $44,953.50
- ○ $45,000.00
- ○ $44,967.00   **(2 marks)**

The following information relates to questions 5.20 and 5.21.

G Co makes the following purchases and sales.

1 January	Purchases	4,000 units for $10,000
31 January	Purchases	1,000 units for $2,000
15 February	Sales	3,000 units for $13,000
28 February	Purchases	1,500 units for $3,750
14 March	Sales	500 units for $1,200

5.20 At 31 March which of the following closing inventory valuations using FIFO is correct?

- ○ $8,000
- ○ $7,500
- ○ $7,000
- ○ $6,500   **(2 marks)**

5.21 At 31 March which of the following closing inventory valuations using LIFO is correct?

- ○ $6,500
- ○ $7,000
- ○ $7,500
- ○ $8,000   **(2 marks)**

5.22 A wholesaler had opening inventory of 300 units of product Emm valued at $25 per unit at the beginning of January. The following receipts and sales were recorded during January.

Date	2 Jan	12 Jan	21 Jan	29 Jan
Issues	250	400	200	75

The purchase cost of receipts was $25.75 per unit. Using a weighted average method of valuation, calculate the value of closing inventory at the end of January.

- ○ $11,550
- ○ $4,492
- ○ $4,192
- ○ $9,550   **(2 marks)**

(Total = 44 marks)

6 Accounting for labour   29 mins

The following information relates to questions 6.1 and 6.2.

Budgeted and actual production data for the year that has just ended are as follows.

Product	Budgeted production		Actual production
	Units	Standard machine hours	Units
W	15,000	3,000	12,000
X	20,000	8,000	25,000
Y	14,000	7,000	16,000
Z	6,000	9,000	5,000

Total machine hours worked in the period amounted to 29,000 hours.

6.1   What was the capacity ratio in the year, as a percentage to one decimal place?

        [   ] %

                                                                    (2 marks)

6.2   What was the efficiency ratio in the year, as a percentage to one decimal place?

        [   ] %

                                                                    (2 marks)

6.3   What does the labour cost graph below depict?

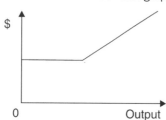

         0   Output

   ○ A piece rate scheme with a minimum guaranteed wage
   ⊗ A straight piece rate scheme
   ⊗ A straight time rate scheme
   ⊗ A differential piece rate scheme   (2 marks)

6.4   The following data relate to work in the finishing department of a certain factory.

7x5=35

Normal working day	7 hours
Basic rate of pay per hour	$5
Standard time allowed to produce 1 unit	4 minutes
Premium bonus payable at the basic rate	60% of time saved

420 mins
in 1 day

On a particular day one employee finishes 180 units. What is his gross pay for the day?

$ [50]

                                                                    (2 marks)

4 x 180 = 720 mins = 12 hrs
        8hrs over.

6.5 An employee is paid on a piecework basis. The basis of the piecework scheme is as follows:

1 to 100 units	–	$0.20 per unit
101 to 200 units	–	$0.30 per unit
201 to 299 units	–	$0.40 per unit

with only the additional units qualifying for the higher rates. <u>Rejected units do not qualify for payment.</u>

During a particular day the employee produced <u>210 units</u> of which 17 were rejected as faulty.

What did the employee earn for their day's work?   *210 − 17 = 193*

- ● $47.90
- ⊗ $54.00
- ⊗ $57.90
- ⊗ $63.00

100 × 0.2
93 × 0.3

(2 marks)

6.6 Employee A is a carpenter and normally works 36 hours per week. The standard rate of pay is $3.60 per hour. A premium of 50% of the basic hourly rate is paid for all overtime hours worked. During the last week of October, Employee A worked for 42 hours. The overtime hours worked were for the following reasons:

| Machine breakdown: | 4 hours |
| To complete a special job at the request of a customer: | 2 hours |

How much of Employee A's earnings for the last week of October would have been treated as direct wages?

$ 159.30   *3.60*   *38 × 3.60 136.80*
4 × 1.80 = 22.50

(2 marks)

6.7 Which TWO of the following statements about group bonus schemes are true?

- ☐ Group bonus schemes are appropriate when increased output depends on a number of people all making extra effort
- ☐ With a group bonus scheme, it is easier to award each individual's performance
- ☐ Non-production employees can be rewarded as part of a group incentive scheme
- ☐ Compared with individual schemes, group bonus schemes are difficult to administer

(2 marks)

6.8   X Co has recorded the following wages costs for direct production workers for November.

	$	
Basic pay	70,800	– Direct
Overtime premium	2,000	– ~~Direct~~ Indirect
Holiday pay	500	– Indirect
Gross wages incurred	73,300	

The overtime was not worked for any specific job.

What are the accounting entries for these wages costs?

	Debit	Credit
	$	$
A Work in progress account	72,800	
Overhead control account	500	
Wages control account		73,300
B Work in progress account	70,800	
Overhead control account	2,500	
Wages control account		73,300
C Wages control account	73,300	
Work in progress account		70,800
Overhead control account		2,500
D Wages control account	73,300	
Work in progress account		72,800
Overhead control account		500

(2 marks)

6.9   A company had 30 direct production employees at the beginning of last year and 20 direct production employees at the end of the year. During the year, a total of 15 direct production employees had left the company to work for a local competitor. What is the labour turnover rate for last year?

○   16.7%
○   20.0%
○   25.0%
○   60.0%

(2 marks)

6.10   Jane works as a member of a three-person team in the assembly department of a factory. The team is rewarded by a group bonus scheme whereby the team leader receives 40 per cent of any bonus earned by the team, and the remaining bonus is shared evenly between Jane and the other team member. Details of output for one day are given below.

Hours worked by team	8 hours
Team production achieved	80 units
Standard time allowed to produce one unit	9 minutes
Group bonus payable at $6 per hour	70% of time saved

What is the bonus element of Jane's pay for this particular day?

○ $5.04
○ $7.20
○ $10.08
○ $16.80

(2 marks)

6.11 In a typical cost ledger, what is the double entry for indirect labour cost incurred?

    Ⓐ   DR   Wages control   CR   Overhead control
    Ⓑ   DR   Admin overhead control   CR   Wages control
    Ⓒ   DR   Overhead control   CR   Wages control
    Ⓓ   DR   Wages control   CR   Admin overhead control

(2 marks)

6.12 A company has 4,000 staff at the start of 20X6 and at the end this had reduced to 3,800 due to redundancies being made. 210 staff took voluntary redundancy which was 10 more than the company had anticipated and these 10 employees were replaced.

What is the labour turnover rate per year (to two decimal places)?

    | 0.26 | %

(2 marks)

(Total = 24 marks)

$$\frac{\text{replaced}}{\text{average}} \times 100$$

           down
4000 → 3,800

$$\frac{7800}{2} = 3900 \qquad \frac{10}{3900} \times 100 = \frac{1000}{3900}$$

$$\frac{4000 + 3,800}{2} = 3900 \quad — \text{average no. of employees}$$

Do you know? – Absorption costing and marginal costing

Check that you can fill in the blanks in the statements below before you attempt any questions. If in doubt, you should go back to your BPP Interactive Text and revise first.

- Costs incurred during production or while providing a service that cannot be traced directly and in full to the product or service are known as ...., and the four main types of .... are production, administration, ... and distribution.

- The three stages of calculating the costs of overheads to be charged to manufactured output are as follows: .... ; .... ; and ....

- The procedure whereby indirect costs (overheads) are spread fairly between cost centres is known as .... Service cost centres may be apportioned to production cost centres by the .... method or by the .... method of reapportionment.

- The three main types of overhead absorption rate are as follows.

  .... (calculated by dividing budgeted overhead by budgeted level of activity)

  .... (or blanket overhead absorption rate, which is used throughout a factory for all jobs and units of output irrespective of the department in which they were produced)

  .... (a fairer rate which is representative of the costs of the resources put into making products)

- Under and over absorption of overhead occurs when actual overhead incurred is different to absorbed overhead. ....-absorbed overhead occurs when actual overhead is less than absorbed overhead, and therefore too .... overhead has been charged to production. ....-absorbed overhead occurs when actual overhead is greater than absorbed overhead, and therefore too .... overhead has been charged to production. Under or over absorption of overheads occurs because the predetermined overhead absorption rates are based on forecasts (estimates).

- Marginal cost is the .... cost of one unit of product or service. .... is the difference between the sales value and the marginal cost of one unit of product or service.

- In marginal costing, fixed production costs are treated as .... costs and are written off as they are incurred. In absorption costing fixed production costs are .... the cost of units and are carried forward in inventory to be charged against the sales revenue for the next period. Inventory values using absorption costing are therefore .... than those calculated using marginal costing.

- Marginal costing and absorption costing will report different profit figures if there is any change in the volume of inventory during the period. If closing inventory is greater than opening inventory, absorption costing will report a .... profit than marginal costing. If opening inventory is greater than closing inventory (ie inventory levels ....), then absorption costing will report a .... profit than marginal costing.

- *Possible pitfalls*

  Write down the mistakes you know you should avoid.

49

Did you know? – Absorption costing and marginal costing

Could you fill in the blanks? The answers are in bold. Use this page for revision purposes as you approach the exam.

- Costs incurred during production or while providing a service that cannot be traced directly and in full to the product or service are known as **overheads**, and the four main types of **overhead** are production, administration, **selling** and distribution.

- The three stages of calculating the costs of overheads to be charged to manufactured output are as follows: **allocation; apportionment;** and **absorption.**

- The procedure whereby indirect costs (overheads) are spread fairly between cost centres is known as **apportionment**. Service cost centres may be apportioned to production cost centres by the **direct** method or by the **step down** method of reapportionment.

- The three main types of overhead absorption rate are as follows.

  Predetermined overhead absorption rate (calculated by dividing budgeted overhead by budgeted level of activity)

  Single factory-wide absorption rate (or blanket overhead absorption rate, which is used throughout a factory for all jobs and units of output irrespective of the department in which they were produced)

  Separate departmental overhead absorption rate (a fairer rate which is representative of the costs of the resources put into making products)

- Under and over absorption of overhead occurs when actual overhead incurred is different to absorbed overhead. **Over**-absorbed overhead occurs when actual overhead is less than absorbed overhead, and therefore too **much** overhead has been charged to production. **Under**-absorbed overhead occurs when actual overhead is greater than absorbed overhead, and therefore too **little** overhead has been charged to production. Under or overabsorption of overheads occurs because the predetermined overhead absorption rates are based on forecasts (estimates).

- Marginal cost is the **variable** cost of one unit of product or service. **Contribution** is the difference between the sales value and the marginal cost of one unit of product or service.

- In marginal costing, fixed production costs are treated as **period** costs and are written off as they are incurred. In absorption costing fixed production costs are **absorbed into** the cost of units and are carried forward in inventory to be charged against the sales revenue for the next period. Inventory values using absorption costing are therefore **greater** than those calculated using marginal costing.

- Marginal costing and absorption costing will report different profit figures if there is any change in the volume of inventory during the period. If closing inventory is greater than opening inventory, absorption costing will report a **higher** profit than marginal costing. If opening inventory is greater than closing inventory (ie inventory levels **decrease**), then absorption costing will report a **lower** profit than marginal costing.

- *Possible pitfalls*

  - Including an element of fixed overheads in the inventory valuation in marginal costing statements
  - Selecting inappropriate bases when calculating overhead absorption rates
  - Confusing under recovery and over recovery of overheads

7a   Accounting for overheads   62 mins

7a.1   The following extract of information is available concerning the four cost centres of EG Co.

	Production cost centres			Service cost centre
	Machinery	Finishing	Packing	Canteen
Number of direct employees	7	6	2	–
Number of indirect employees	3	2	1	4
Overhead allocated and apportioned	$28,500	$18,300	$8,960	$8,400

The overhead cost of the canteen is to be re-apportioned to the production cost centres on the basis of the number of employees in each production cost centre. After the re-apportionment, what is the total overhead cost of the packing department, to the nearest $?

- ○ $1,200
- ○ $9,968
- ◉ $10,080
- ○ $10,160   **(2 marks)**

The following information relates to questions 7a.2 and 7a.3.

Budgeted information relating to two departments in a company for the next period is as follows.

Department	Production overhead $	Direct material cost $	Direct labour cost $	Direct labour hours	Machine hours
1	27,000	67,500	13,500	2,700	45,000
2	18,000	36,000	100,000	25,000	300

Individual direct labour employees within each department earn differing rates of pay, according to their skills, grade and experience.

7a.2   What is the most appropriate production overhead absorption rate for department 1?

- ◉   40% of direct material cost
- ⊗   200% of direct labour cost
- ⊗ $10 per direct labour hour
- ○ $0.60 per machine hour   **(2 marks)**

7a.3   What is the most appropriate production overhead absorption rate for department 2?

- ○   50% of direct material cost
- ○   18% of direct labour cost
- ◉ $0.72 per direct labour hour
- ○ $60 per machine hour   **(2 marks)**

7a.4   Which TWO of the following statements about predetermined overhead absorption rates are true?

- ☐   Using a predetermined absorption rate avoids fluctuations in unit costs caused by abnormally high or low overhead expenditure or activity levels
- ☐   Using a predetermined absorption rate offers the administrative convenience of being able to record full production costs sooner
- ☑   Using a predetermined absorption rate avoids problems of under/over absorption of overheads because a constant overhead rate is available
- ☑   Using a predetermined absorption rate avoids the problems associated with choosing an appropriate absorption base

(2 marks)

7a.5   Over-absorbed overheads occur when

     O   Absorbed overheads exceed actual overheads
     O   Absorbed overheads exceed budgeted overheads
     O   Actual overheads exceed absorbed overheads
     O   Actual overheads exceed budgeted overheads   **(2 marks)**

The following information relates to questions 7a.6 and 7a.7.

A company has the following actual and budgeted data for year 4.

	Budget	Actual
Production	8,000 units	9,000 units
Variable production overhead per unit	$3	$3
Fixed production overheads	$360,000	$432,000
Sales	6,000 units	8,000 units

Overheads are absorbed using a rate per unit, based on budgeted output and expenditure.

7a.6   What was the fixed production overhead absorbed amount during year 4?

    $ [   ]

          (2 marks)

7a.7   Using the drop down list select how much the fixed production overhead was under or over absorbed.

Select...   ▼
Under absorbed by $27,000
Under absorbed by $72,000
Under absorbed by $75,000
Over absorbed by $27,000

          (2 marks)

7a.8   Which of the following would be the most appropriate basis for apportioning machinery insurance costs to cost centres within a factory?

     ⊠   The number of machines in each cost centre
     ⊠   The floor area occupied by the machinery in each cost centre
     ◉   The value of the machinery in each cost centre
     ⊠   The operating hours of the machinery in each cost centre   **(2 marks)**

7a.9   Factory overheads can be absorbed by which of the following methods?

    (i)   Direct labour hours
    (ii)   Machine hours
    (iii)   As a percentage of prime cost
    (iv) $x per unit

     O   (i), (ii), (iii) and (iv)
     O   (i) and (ii) only
     O   (i), (ii) and (iii) only
     O   (ii), (iii) and (iv) only   **(2 marks)**

7a.10 The production overhead control account for R Co at the end of the period looks like this.

Production overhead control account

	$		$
Stores control	22,800	Work in progress	404,800
Wages control	180,400	Statement of profit or loss	8,400
Expense creditors	210,000		
	413,200		413,200

Which TWO of the following statements are correct?

☐ Indirect material issued from inventory was $22,800

☐ Overhead absorbed during the period was $210,000

☐ Overhead for the period was over absorbed by $8,400

☐ Indirect wages costs incurred were $180,400

(2 marks)

7a.11 Which of the following is correct when considering the allocation, apportionment and reapportionment of overheads in an absorption costing situation?

○ Only production related costs should be considered

◉ Allocation is the situation where part of an overhead is assigned to a cost centre

☒ Costs may only be reapportioned from production centres to service centres

☒ Any overheads assigned to a single department should be ignored **(2 marks)**

7a.12 A company has over-absorbed fixed production overheads for the period by $6,000. The fixed production overhead absorption rate was $8 per unit and is based on the normal level of activity of 5,000 units. Actual production was 4,500 units.

What was the actual fixed production overheads incurred for the period?

○ $30,000
○ $36,000
○ $40,000
○ $42,000 **(2 marks)**

7a.13 A company manufacturers two products, X and Y, in a factory divided into two production cost centres, Primary and Finishing. The following budgeted data are available:

Cost centre	Primary	Finishing
Allocated and apportioned fixed overhead costs	$96,000	$82,500
Direct labour minutes per unit:		
– Product X	36	25
– Product Y	48	35

Budgeted production is 6,000 units of product X and 7,500 units of product Y. Fixed overhead costs are to be absorbed on a direct labour hour basis.

What is the budgeted fixed overhead cost per unit for product Y?

○ $11
○ $12
○ $14
○ $15 **(2 marks)**

83 mins per unit

83× 7,500 = 622500 mins

7a.14 A company uses an overhead absorption rate of $3.50 per machine our, based on 32,000 budgeted machine hours for the period. During the same period the actual total overhead expenditure amounted to $108,875 and 30,000 machine hours were recorded on actual production.

By how much was the total overhead under or over absorbed for the period?

○   Under absorbed by $3,875
○   Under absorbed by $7,000
○   Over absorbed by $3,875
○   Over absorbed by $7,000   **(2 marks)**

7a.15 A factory consists of two production cost centres (P and Q) and two service cost centres (X and Y). The total allocated and apportioned overhead for each is as follows:

P	Q	X	Y
$95,000	$82,000	$46,000	$30,000

It has been estimated that each service cost centre does work for the other cost centres in the following proportions:

	P	Q	X	Y
Percentage of service cost centre X to	40	40	–	20
Percentage of service cost centre Y to	30	60	10	–

After the reapportionment of service cost centre costs has been carried out using a method that fully recognises the reciprocal service arrangements in the factory, what is the total overhead for production cost centre P?

○ $122,400
○ $124,716
○ $126,000
○ $127,000   **(2 marks)**

7a.16 The following data is available for a paint department for the latest period.

Budgeted production overhead	$150,000
Actual production overhead	$150,000
Budgeted machine hours	60,000
Actual machine hours	55,000

Which of the following statements is correct?

○   There was no under or over absorption of overhead
○   Overhead was $13,636 over absorbed
○   Overhead was $12,500 over absorbed
○   Overhead was $12,500 under absorbed   **(2 marks)**

7a.17

Actual overheads	$496,980
Actual machine hours	16,566
Budgeted overheads	$475,200

Based on the data above, and assuming that the budgeted overhead absorption rate was $32 per hour, what were the budgeted number of hours (to the nearest hour) budgeted to be worked?

☐ hours

                           (2 marks)

7a.18

Budgeted overheads	$690,480
Budgeted machine hours	15,344
Actual machine hours	14,128
Actual overheads	$679,550

Based on the data above, what is the machine hour absorption rate (to the nearest $)?

- ○ $44 per machine hour
- ○ $45 per machine hour
- ○ $48 per machine hour
- ○ $49 per machine hour **(2 marks)**

7a.19 A company absorbs overheads on machine hours. In a period, actual machine hours were 22,435, actual overheads were $496,500 and there was over absorption of $64,375.

What was the budgeted overhead absorption rate per machine hour (to the nearest $)?

$ _____

(2 marks)

7a.20 A company absorbs fixed production overheads in one of its departments on the basis of machine hours. There were 100,000 budgeted machine hours for the forthcoming period. The fixed production overhead absorption rate was $2.50 per machine hour.

During the period, the following actual results were recorded:

Standard machine hours	110,000
Fixed production overheads	$300,000

What was the fixed production overhead under/over absorption amount?

- ○ Over absorbed by $25,000
- ○ Under absorbed by $50,000
- ○ Over absorbed by $50,000
- ○ Under absorbed by $25,000 **(2 marks)**

7a.21 Consider the following statements, regarding the reapportionment of service cost centre overheads to production cost centres, where reciprocal services exist.

Which TWO statements are correct?

☒ The direct method results in costs being reapportioned between service cost centres

☑ If the direct method is used, the order in which the service cost centre overheads are reapportioned is irrelevant

☑ The step down method results in costs being reapportioned between service cost centres

☒ If the step down method is used, the order in which the service cost centre overheads are reapportioned is irrelevant

(2 marks)

7a.22 CTF Co has two service centres serving two production departments. Overhead costs apportioned to each department are as follows.

	Production departments		Service centres	
	Mixing $	Stirring $	Stores $	Canteen $
Allocated and apportioned overheads	216,400	78,800	181,600	47,200
Estimated work done by the service centres for other departments				
Stores	50%	30%	–	20%
Canteen	45%	40%	15%	–

The business uses the direct method of apportionment.

After the apportionment of the service centres to the production departments, what will the total overhead cost be for the mixing department?

O $328,440
O $342,041
O $351,416
● $354,888   **(2 marks)**

7a.23 HMF Co has two service centres serving two production departments. Overhead costs apportioned to each department are as follows.

	Production departments		Service centres	
	Mixing $	Stirring $	Stores $	Canteen $
Allocated and apportioned overheads	216,400	78,800	181,600	47,200
Estimated work done by the service centres for other departments				
Stores	50%	30%	–	20%
Canteen	45%	40%	15%	–

The business uses the step down method of apportionment.

After the apportionment of the service centres to the production departments, what will the total overhead cost be for the mixing department?

O $325,968
O $344,784
O $351,416
O $354,888   **(2 marks)**

7a.24 **The following question is taken from the June 2012 exam.**

A company uses standard absorption costing to value inventory. Its fixed overhead absorption rate is $12 per labour hour and each unit of production should take four hours. In a recent period where there was no opening inventory of finished goods, 20,000 units were produced using 100,000 labour hours. 18,000 units were sold. The actual profit was $464,000.

What profit would have been earned under a standard marginal costing system?

O $368,000
O $440,000
O $344,000
O $560,000   **(2 marks)**

7a.25 **The following question is taken from the January to June 2015 exam period.**

A company uses a blanket overhead absorption rate of $5 per direct labour hour. Actual overhead expenditure in a period was as budgeted.

The under/over absorbed overhead account for the period have the following entries:

	DR $		CR $
Production overhead	4,000	Profit or loss account	4,000
	4,000		4,000

Which of the following statements is true?

- ○ Actual direct labour hours were 800 less than budgeted
- ○ Actual direct labour hours were 800 more than budgeted
- ○ Actual direct labour hours were 4,000 less than budgeted
- ○ Production overhead was over absorbed by $4,000   **(2 marks)**

7a.26 **The following question is taken from the January to June 2016 exam period.**

An accountant is using the repeated distribution method to reapportion service department costs. The following table shows the work she has done so far. Figures that are yet to be calculated are shown as "???"

	Production department 1 $	Production department 2 $	Service department X $	Service department Y $
Apportioned and allocated				
Production overheads	60,000	80,000	20,000	10,000
Service department X	8,000	10,000	–20,000	2,000
Service department Y	7,200	4,200	600	–12,000
Service department X	???	???	–600	
Total production overhead	???	???	0	

What is the total production overhead for production department 1 after the remaining reapportionment of the overheads of service department X?

- ○ $74,600
- ○ $75,200
- ○ $75,440
- ○ $75,467   **(2 marks)**

(Total = 52 marks)

7b Absorption and marginal costing   48 mins

7b.1 The following data is available for period 9.

Opening inventory   10,000 units
Closing inventory   8,000 units
Absorption costing profit $280,000

What would be the profit for period 9 using marginal costing?

○ $278,000
○ $280,000
○ $282,000
○   Impossible to calculate without more information   **(2 marks)**

7b.2 The overhead absorption rate for product T is $4 per machine hour. Each unit of T requires 3 machine hours. Inventories of product T last period were:

	Units
Opening inventory	2,400
Closing inventory	2,700

 ⌡ ≈ +3⊙○

Compared with the marginal costing profit for the period, the absorption costing profit for product T will be which of the following?

✗ $1,200 higher
● $3,600 higher ⟵   —
✗ $1,200 lower
✗ $3,600 lower   **(2 marks)**

7b.3 In a period where opening inventories were 15,000 units and closing inventories were 20,000 units, a firm had a profit of $130,000 using absorption costing. If the fixed overhead absorption rate was $8 per unit, the profit using marginal costing would be which of the following?

○ $90,000
○ $130,000
○ $170,000
○   Impossible to calculate without more information   **(2 marks)**

The following information relates to questions 7b.4 and 7b.5.

Cost and selling price details for product Z are as follows.

	$ per unit
Direct materials	6.00
Direct labour	7.50
Variable overhead	2.50
Fixed overhead absorption rate	5.00
	21.00
Profit	9.00
Selling price	30.00

Budgeted production for the month was 5,000 units although the company managed to produce 5,800 units, selling 5,200 of them and incurring fixed overhead costs of $27,400.

7b.4 What is the marginal costing profit for the month?

● $45,400
✗ $46,800
✗ $53,800
✗ $72,800   **(2 marks)**

7b.5 What is the absorption costing profit for the month?

   ○ $45,200
   ○ $45,400
   ○ $46,800
   ○ $48,400   **(2 marks)**

7b.6 In a period, a company had opening inventory of 31,000 units and closing inventory of 34,000 units. Profits based on marginal costing were $850,500 and on absorption costing were $955,500.

   If the budgeted total fixed costs for the company was $1,837,500, what was the budgeted level of activity in units?

   ○   32,500
   ●   52,500
   ○   65,000
   ○   105,000   **(2 marks)**

7b.7 A company had opening inventory of 48,500 units and closing inventory of 45,500 units. Profits based on marginal costing were $315,250 and on absorption costing were $288,250. What is the fixed overhead absorption rate per unit?

   ○ $5.94
   ○ $6.34
   ○ $6.50
   ● $9.00   **(2 marks)**

7b.8 Which of the following are acceptable bases for absorbing production overheads?

   (i)   Direct labour hours
   (ii)   Machine hours
   (iii) As a percentage of the prime cost
   (iv)   Per unit

   ○   Methods (i) and (ii) only
   ○   Methods (iii) and (iv) only
   ●   Methods (i), (ii), (iii) and (iv)
   ○   Methods (i), (ii) or (iii) only   **(2 marks)**

7b.9 Under absorption costing, the total cost of a product will include:

   ○   Direct costs only
   ○   Variable costs only
   ○   All direct and indirect costs excluding a share of fixed overhead
   ○   All direct and indirect costs   **(2 marks)**

7b.10 A company has established a marginal costing profit of $72,300. Opening inventory was 300 units and closing inventory is 750 units. The fixed production overhead absorption rate has been calculated as $5/unit.

   What was the profit under absorption costing?

   $ [   ]

                                                                 (2 marks)

7b.11 A company produces and sells a single product whose variable cost is $6 per unit.

Fixed costs have been absorbed over the normal level of activity of 200,000 units and have been calculated as $2 per unit.

The current selling price is $10 per unit.

How much profit is made under marginal costing if the company sells 250,000 units?

○ $500,000
○ $600,000
○ $900,000
○ $1,000,000   **(2 marks)**

7b.12 A company which uses marginal costing has a profit of $37,500 for a period. Opening inventory was 100 units and closing inventory was 350 units.

The fixed production overhead absorption rate is $4 per unit.

What is the profit under absorption costing?

○ $35,700
○ $35,500
○ $38,500
○ $39,300   **(2 marks)**

7b.13 A company manufactures and sells a single product. For this month the budgeted fixed production overheads are $48,000, budgeted production is 12,000 units and budgeted sales are 11,720 units.

The company currently uses absorption costing.

If the company used marginal costing principles instead of absorption costing for this month, what would be the effect on the budgeted profit?

○ $1,120 higher
○ $1,120 lower
○ $3,920 higher
○ $3,920 lower   **(2 marks)**

7b.14 A company operates a standard marginal costing system. Last month its actual fixed overhead expenditure was 10% above budget resulting in a fixed overhead expenditure variance of $36,000.

What was the actual expenditure on fixed overheads last month?

○ $324,000
○ $360,000
○ $396,000
○ $400,000   **(2 marks)**

7b.15 Last month, when a company had an opening inventory of 16,500 units and a closing inventory of 18,000 units, the profit using absorption costing was $40,000. The fixed production overhead rate was $10 per unit.

What would the profit for last month have been using marginal costing?

$ ☐

                                                                                           (2 marks)

7b.16 Last month a manufacturing company's profit was $2,000, calculated using absorption costing principles. If marginal costing principles has been used, a loss of $3,000 would have occurred. The company's fixed production cost is $2 per unit. Sales last month were 10,000 units.

What was last month's production (in units)?

○   7,500
○   9,500
○   10,500
○   12,500   **(2 marks)**

7b.17 HMF Co produces a single product. The budgeted fixed production overheads for the period are $500,000. The budgeted output for the period is 2,500 units. Opening inventory at the start of the period consisted of 900 units and closing inventory at the end of the period consisted of 300 units. If absorption costing principles were applied, the profit for the period compared to the marginal costing profit would be which of the following?

○ $125,000 higher
○ $125,000 lower
○ $120,000 higher
○ $120,000 lower   **(2 marks)**

7b.18 **The following question is taken from the June 2013 exam.**

A company has the following budgeted costs and revenues:

	$ per unit
Sales price	50
Variable production cost	18
Fixed production cost	10

In the most recent period, 2,000 units were produced and 1,000 units were sold. Actual sales price, variable production cost per unit and total fixed production costs were all as budgeted. Fixed production costs were over-absorbed by $4,000. There was no opening inventory for the period.

What would be the reduction in profit for the period if the company has used marginal costing rather than absorption costing?

○   4,000
○   6,000
○   10,000
○   14,000   **(2 marks)**

7b.19 **The following question is taken from the July to December 2014 exam period.**

The following data is available on the production and sales for the first three years of a company's new product.

	Year 1	Year 2	Year 3
Production units	5,000	6,000	4,000
Sales units	4,000	6,000	5,000

Variable costs per unit, selling price and total fixed costs per year were constant over the three-year period. The company is considering the use of either marginal or absorption costing.

Which of the following statements is/are true?

(1)   Absorption costing will show a lower profit than marginal costing in Year 1
(2)   Marginal costing will show a lower closing inventory valuation than absorption costing in Year 2
(3)   Total profit over the three-year period will be the same under both methods

○   1 only
○   2 only
○   3 only
○   2 and 3   **(2 marks)**

7b.20 **The following question is taken from the July to December 2015 exam period.**

A company's total operating cost is semi variable. It flexes its profit budget from an output level of 1,000 units to an output level of 2,000 units?

Which of the following statements is true?

- ○ Operating profit will double between the two output levels
- ○ Fixed cost per unit at the two output levels will be the same
- ○ Total contribution will double between the two output levels
- ○ Contribution per unit will increase between the two output levels **(2 marks)**

(Total = 40 marks)

Do you know? – Process, job, batch, service and alternative costing

Check that you can fill in the blanks in the statements below before you attempt any questions. If in doubt, you should go back to your BPP Interactive Text and revise first.

- Process costing is a costing method used where it is not possible to identify separate units of production usually because of the continuous nature of the production processes involved.

- .... loss is the loss expected during a process and it is not given a cost. If it has a scrap value then it is valued at this amount.

- .... loss is the extra loss resulting when actual loss is greater than the loss anticipated. It is given a cost.

- Loss may have a scrap value. Revenue from normal scrap is treated as a reduction in costs.

- When there is closing work in progress at the end of a period, it is necessary to calculate the .... of production in order to determine the cost of a completed unit.

- The costs of labour and overhead are sometimes referred to as .... costs.

- .... products are two or more products separated in a process, each of which has a significant value compared to the other.

- A .... is an incidental product from a process which has an insignificant value compared to the main product.

- The point at which joint and by-products become separately identifiable is known as the .... or the .... point.

- Job costing is the costing method used where each cost unit is separately identifiable. Costs for each job are collected on a .... or .... Overhead is absorbed into the cost of jobs using the .... rate.

- Batch costing is similar to job costing in that each batch of similar articles is separately identifiable. The cost per unit manufactured in a batch is calculated by dividing the .... by the .... in the batch.

- Service costing is used by companies operating in a service industry or by companies wishing to establish the cost of services carried out by some of their departments.

- Characteristics of services ─┤ ....
....
....
....

- If a service is a function of two activity variables, a .... cost unit might be appropriate.

- A difficulty with service costing is the selection of an appropriate cost unit. The cost per unit is calculated by dividing the .... for the period by the .... in the period.

- Activity based costing involves the identification of factors, called cost ...., which cause costs.

- .... costing tracks and accumulates costs and revenues attributable to each product over the entire ....

- *Possible pitfalls*

  Write down the mistakes you know you should avoid.

Did you know? – Process, job, batch, service and alternative costing

Could you fill in the blanks? The answers are in bold. Use this page for revision purposes as you approach the exam.

- Process costing is a costing method used where it is not possible to identify separate units of production usually because of the continuous nature of the production processes involved.

- **Normal** loss is the loss expected during a process and it is not given a cost. If it has a scrap value then it is valued at this amount.

- **Abnormal** loss is the extra loss resulting when actual loss is greater than the loss anticipated. It is given a cost.

- Loss may have a scrap value. Revenue from normal scrap is treated as a reduction in costs.

- When there is closing work in progress at the end of a period, it is necessary to calculate the **equivalent units** of production in order to determine the cost of a completed unit.

- The costs of labour and overhead are sometimes referred to as **conversion** costs.

- **Joint** products are two or more products separated in a process, each of which has a significant value compared to the other.

- A **by-product** is an incidental product from a process which has an insignificant value compared to the main product.

- The point at which joint and by-products become separately identifiable is known as the **point of separation** or the **split-off** point.

- Job costing is the costing method used where each cost unit is separately identifiable. Costs for each job are collected on a **job cost sheet** or **job card**. Overhead is absorbed into the cost of jobs using the **predetermined overhead absorption** rate.

- Batch costing is similar to job costing in that each batch of similar articles is separately identifiable. The cost per unit manufactured in a batch is calculated by dividing the **total batch cost** by the **number of units** in the batch.

- Service costing is used by companies operating in a service industry or by companies wishing to establish the cost of services carried out by some of their departments.

- Characteristics of services**: Intangibility, Simultaneity, Perishability, Heterogeneity**

- If a service is a function of two activity variables, a **composite** cost unit might be appropriate.

- A difficulty with service costing is the selection of an appropriate cost unit. The cost per unit is calculated by dividing the **total costs** for the period by the **number of service units** in the period.

- Activity based costing involves the identification of factors, called cost **drivers**, which cause costs.

- **Life cycle** costing tracks and accumulates costs and revenues attributable to each product over the entire **product life cycle**

- *Possible pitfalls*

  - Forgetting that units arising from abnormal loss are included as equivalent units, whereas those arising from normal loss are not.

  - Not using the suggested four-step approach when answering process costing questions.

8a   Process costing   41 mins

8a.1   A chemical process has a normal wastage of 10% of input. In a period, 2,500 kg of material were input and there was an abnormal loss of 75 kg.

What quantity of good production was achieved?

$2500 = 4175 + 250 + 75$

[2175] kg

(2 marks)

The following information relates to questions 8a.2 and 8a.3.

A company manufactures Chemical X, in a single process. At the start of the month there was no work-in-progress. During the month 300 litres of raw material were input into the process at a total cost of $6,000. Conversion costs during the month amounted to $4,500. At the end of the month 250 litres of Chemical X were transferred to finished goods inventory. The remaining work-in-progress was 100% complete with respect to materials and 50% complete with respect to conversion costs. There were no losses in the process and there is no scrap value available during months when losses occur.

8a.2   What are the equivalent units for closing work-in-progress at the end of the month?

	Material	Conversion costs
O	25 litres	25 litres
O	25 litres	50 litres
☑	50 litres	25 litres
O	50 litres	50 litres

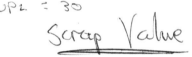

$300 = 250 + 0 + 50$

$WiP = 50$

(2 marks)

8a.3   If there had been a normal process loss of 10% of input during the month what would the value of this loss have been?

- ☑ Nil
- O $450
- O $600
- O $1,050

$NPL = 30$

Scrap Value

(2 marks)

8a.4   In a particular process, the input for the period was 2,000 units. There were no inventories at the beginning or end of the process. Normal loss is 5% of input. In which of the following circumstances is there an abnormal gain?

(i)   Actual output = 1,800 units
(ii)   Actual output = 1,950 units
(iii)   Actual output = 2,000 units

$2000 = + 100 +$

- O   (i) only
- O   (ii) only
- O   (i) and (ii) only
- ☑   (ii) and (iii) only

(2 marks)

8a.5   In a process account, how are abnormal losses valued?

   At their scrap value
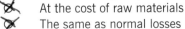   The same as good production
☒   At the cost of raw materials
☒   The same as normal losses

(2 marks)

8a.6 A company needs to produce 340 litres of Chemical X. There is a normal loss of 10% of the material input into the process. During a given month the company did produce 340 litres of good production, although there was an abnormal loss of 5% of the material input into the process.

How many litres of material were input into the process during the month?

$\boxed{400}$ litres

$x = 340 + 10\% x + 5\% x$

(2 marks)

The following information relates to questions 8a.7 and 8a.8.

A company produces a certain food item in a manufacturing process. On 1 November, there was no opening inventory of work in process. During November, 500 units of material were input to the process, with a cost of $9,000. Direct labour costs in November were $3,840. Production overhead is absorbed at the rate of 200% of direct labour costs. Closing inventory on 30 November consisted of 100 units which were 100% complete as to materials and 80% complete as to labour and overhead. There was no loss in process.

8a.7 What is the full production cost of completed units during November?

Input

See notepad for Workings.

- ○ ~~$10,400~~
- ○ $16,416
- ⦿ $16,800
- ○ $20,520

$500 \leq 1400 + 100$

~~9000~~ 9000 ÷ 500

(2 marks)

8a.8 What is the value of the closing work in progress on 30 November?

- ○ $2,440
- ⦿ $3,720
- ○ $4,104
- ○ $20,520

(2 marks)

The following information relates to questions 8a.9 and 8a.10.

A company makes a product in two processes. The following data is available for the latest period, for process 1.

Opening work in progress of 200 units was valued as follows.

Material	$2,400
Labour	$1,200
Overhead	$400

No losses occur in the process.

$500 + 200 = 650 + 30 + 70$

700 $700.$

Units added and costs incurred during the period:

Material	$6,000 (500 units)
Labour	$3,350
Overhead	$1,490

Open 200
Raw 2,400
Labour 1,200
Over 400

Closing work in progress of 100 units had reached the following degrees of completion:

Material	100%
Labour	50%
Overhead	30%

The company uses the weighted average method of inventory valuation.

To complete = 70% × 100 = 70.
30 complete.

✱ 8a.9 How many equivalent units are used when calculating the cost per unit in relation to overhead?

- ○ 500
- ○ 600
- ⦿ 630
- ○ 700

(2 marks)

BPP
LEARNING MEDIA

✳ 8a.10 What is the value of the units transferred to process 2?

2400   *1200*   *400*

- ○ $7,200
- ● $13,200
- ○ $14,840
- ○ $15,400

(2 marks)

8a.11 A company uses <u>process costing</u> to establish the cost per unit of its output.

The following information was available for the last month:

Input units	10,000
Output units	9,850
Opening inventory *open WIP?*	300 units, 100% complete for materials and 70% complete for conversion costs
Closing inventory *Close WIP*	450 units, 100% complete for materials and 30% complete for conversion costs

The company uses the weighted average method of valuing inventory.

300 + 10,000 = 450 + 9850

What were the equivalent units for conversion costs?

materials   conversion

- ○ 9,505 units
- ○ 9,715 units
- ○ 9,775 units
- ◉ 9,985 units

open WIP 300
Input 10,000   10,000   10,000
Output 9,850   9850   9850
Close WIP 450   135   450

(2 marks)

30% = 450

8a.12 A company uses process costing to value its output. The following was recorded for the period:

Input materials	2,000 units at $4.50 per unit
Conversion costs	13,340
Normal loss	5% of input valued at $3 per unit
Actual loss	150 units

There were no opening or closing inventories.

2000 = 1900 + 100 + 450
9000   7425   300   675

What was the valuation of one unit of output to one decimal place?

- ○ $11.8
- ◉ $11.6
- ○ $11.2
- ○ $11.0

$$\frac{9000 + 13,340 - 300}{1900} = 11.60$$

(2 marks)

8a.13 A company operates a continuous process into which <u>3,000</u> units of material costing $9,000 was input in a period. Conversion costs for this period were $11,970 and losses, which have a scrap value of $1.50, are expected at a rate of 10% of input. There were no <u>opening or closing inventories</u> and output for the period was <u>2,900 units</u>.

3000 = 2900 + 300
1
9000

What was the output valuation?

- ○ $20,271
- ○ $20,520
- ○ $20,970
- ◉ $22,040

Loss = 3000 × 0.1 × 1.50
= 450

(2 marks)

$$\frac{9000 + 11,970 - 450}{2,900} = 7.60 \text{ per unit}$$
× 2900

8a.14 The following information relates to a company's polishing process for the previous period.

Output to finished goods	5,408 units valued at $29,744
Normal loss	276 units
Actual loss	112 units

All losses have a scrap value of $2.50 per unit and there was no opening or closing work in progress.

What was the value of the input during the period?

- ○ $28,842
- ⦿ $29,532
- ○ $29,744
- ○ $30,434

(2 marks)

Handwritten:
24,532   29,744
902   640
――――――― ―――――
30,434 = 30,434

29,744 / 5408 = 5.50

5496 → 5,408 + 276 + 112
29,744
164 × 2.50 = 902
164 × 5.50 = 902
(164 / 388 × 3.50 = 470)
Abnormal gain
276 × 2.50 = 690

8a.15 Which of the following statements about process losses are correct?

(i) Units of normal loss should be valued at full cost per unit — *scrap value*
(ii) Units of abnormal loss should be valued at their scrap value — *good output value*

- ○ (i) only
- ○ (ii) only
- ○ Both of them
- ⦿ Neither of them

(2 marks)

8a.16 The following question is taken from the January to June 2015 exam period.

Normally no losses are expected from a process. Any abnormal losses are sold for scrap.

Which of the following calculates the net cost to the company of one unit of abnormal loss?

- ○ Total input cost ÷ actual output units
- ○ Total input cost ÷ expected output units
- ⦿ (Total input cost – total scrap value) ÷ expected output units
- ○ (Total input cost ÷ expected output units) – scrap value per unit   *← correct answer*

(2 marks)

8a.17 The following question is taken from the September to June 2018 exam period.

A process is subject to a normal loss of 12% of input. Losses can be sold for $5 per kg. In the last period 10,000 kg of material costing $100,000 was input to the process. Conversion costs for the period were $50,000 and output was 9,200 kg.

What is the credit to the statement of profit or loss from the abnormal gain account in the last period?

- ○ $4,260
- ○ $4,818
- ⦿ $4,545
- ○ $6,818

(2 marks)

(Total = 34 marks)

Handwritten:
Normal loss   10,000 × 0.12 × 5 = 6000
Conversion = 50,000
4200
10,000 = 4,200 + 800
100,000
+ 50,000
– 6,000
――――――
144,000

CALCULATE EXPECTED OUTPUT
= 10,000 – (10,000 × 0.12)
= 10,000 – 8,800
= 8,800

(10,000 × 0.12) 144,000 / 10,000   8,800 ÷ 9,200   16.36
16.36 – 5 = 5.87   11.36

800 × 5.87 = 4544

8b Process costing, joint products and by-products   26 mins

The following data relates to questions 8b.1 and 8b.2.

A company manufactures two joint products, P and R, in a common process. Data for June are as follows.

	$
Opening inventory	1,000
Direct materials added	10,000
Conversion costs	12,000
Closing inventory	3,000
	20,000

	Production Units	Sales Units	Sales price $ per unit
P	4,000 ×5 = 20,000	5,000 = 25,000	5
R	6,000 ×10 = 60,000	5,000 = 50,000	10
	80,000		

8b.1 If costs are apportioned between joint products on a sales value basis, what was the cost per unit of product R in June?

- ○ $1.25
- ○ $2.22
- ⊘ $2.50
- ○ $2.75

P 20,000 × (20/80) = 5000
R 20,000 × (60/80) = 45000
20,000
R = 15,000 / 6000 = 2.50
P = 5000 / 4,000 = 1.25

(2 marks)

8b.2 If costs are apportioned between joint products on a physical unit basis, what was the total cost of product P production in June?

- ⊘ $8,000
- ○ $8,800
- ○ $10,000
- ○ $12,000

Units $
P: 4000   ∴ 20 000 × 4/10 = 8000
R: 6000   ∴ 20 000 × 6/10 = 12,000
*   20 000*

(2 marks)

8b.3 Which of the following statements is/are correct?

(i) A by-product is a product produced at the same time as other products which has a relatively low volume compared with the other products

(ii) Since a by-product is a saleable item it should be separately costed in the process account, and should absorb some of the process costs

(iii) Costs incurred prior to the point of separation are known as common or joint costs

- ○ (i) and (ii)
- ○ (i) and (iii)
- ○ (ii) and (iii)
- ● (iii) only

(2 marks)

8b.4 A company manufactures two joint products and one by-product in a single process. Data for November are as follows.

	$
Raw material input	216,000
Conversion costs	72,000

288 000 − 4000 = 284,000

There were no inventories at the beginning or end of the period.

	Output Units	Sales price $ per unit
Joint product E	21,000 ×15 = 315 000	15
Joint product Q	18,000 × 10 = 180 000	10
By-product X	2,000 × 2 = 4 0002	2
	495,000	

E : 284,000 × 315/495 = 180,804
Q: " × 180/495 = 103,888

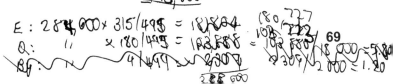

69

By-product sales revenue is credited to the process account. Joint costs are apportioned on a sales value basis. What were the full production costs of product Q in November (to the nearest $)?

- ○ $102,445
- ☞ $103,273
- ○ $104,727
- ○ $180,727

(2 marks)

8b.5 A company manufactures three joint products and one by-product from a single process.

Data for May are as follows.

Opening and closing inventories	Nil
Raw materials input	$180,000
Conversion costs	$50,000
	230 000 = 20000 = 210 000

Output

		Units	Sales price $ per unit
Joint product	L	3,000 × 32 = 96,000	32
	M	2,000 × 42 = 84,000	42
	N	4,000 × 38 = 152,000	38
By product R		1,000 332,000	2

By-product sales revenue is credited to the sales account. Joint costs are apportioned on a sales value basis.

What were the full production costs of product M in May (to the nearest $)?

66,506

230,000 × 46/332 = 60,723

230 000 × 84/332 = 58,193

230,000 × 152/332 = 96,146
105,301

- ○ $57,687
- ○ $57,844
- ☞ $58,193
- ○ $66,506

(2 marks)
230,000

8b.6 Two products G and H are created from a joint process. G can be sold immediately after split-off. H requires further processing before it is in a saleable condition. There are no opening inventories and no work in progress. The following data are available for last period:

	$
Total joint production costs	384,000
Further processing costs (product H)	159,600

Product	Selling price per unit	Sales Units	Production Units
G	$0.84	400,000	412,000
H	$1.82	200,000	228,000

Using the physical unit method for apportioning joint production costs, what was the cost value of the closing inventory of product H for last period?

- ○ $36,400
- ○ $37,520
- ○ $40,264
- ○ $45,181

(2 marks)

8b.7 Two products (W and X) are created from a joint process. Both products can be sold immediately after split-off. There are no opening inventories or work in progress. The following information is available for last period:

Total joint production costs $776,160

Product	Production units	Sales units	Selling price per unit
W	12,000	10,000	$10
X	10,000	8,000	$12

Using the sales value method of apportioning joint production costs, what was the value of the closing inventory of product X for last period?

- ○ $310,464
- ○ $388,080
- ○ $155,232
- ○ $77,616

(2 marks)

8b.8 **The following question is taken from the July to December 2013 exam period.**

Two joint products A and B are produced in a process. Data for the process for the last period are as follows:

Product	A Tonnes	B Tonnes	Total
Sales	480	320	800
Production	600	400	1,000

Handwritten: Pro A : 12,000 × 600/1000 = 7,200

Sales A : 7,200 × 480/600 = 5,76

Common production costs in the period were $12,000. There was no opening inventory. Both products had a gross profit margin of 40%. Common production costs were apportioned on a physical basis.

What was the gross profit for product A in the period?

Handwritten: Gross profit A: 5760 × 40/60 = 3840

- ○ $2,304
- ○ $2,880
- ⊘ $3,840
- ○ $4,800

(2 marks)

8b.9 **The following question is taken from the July to December 2015 exam period.**

A process produces two joint products A and B in equal physical quantities. A and B are sold at split off point for $5 per kg and $8 per kg respectively. There are no further costs after the split off point.

If joint costs are apportioned on a relative sales value basis, which of the following statements is true?

- ⊘ Both products will have the same return on sales ratio (operating margin)
- ○ Product A will have the higher return on sales ratio (operating margin)
- ○ The cost per kg will be the same for both products
- ○ The cost per kg of product A will be higher than that of product B

(2 marks)

8b.10 **The following question is taken from the July to December 2016 exam period.**

Which of the following is NOT an acceptable method of accounting for by-products?

- ○ Net realisable value of the by-product is deducted from the cost of the main product
- ⊘ Pre-separation costs are apportioned to the by-product to calculate its profit
- ○ Sales value of the by-product is deducted from the cost of the main product
- ○ By-product income less post-separation costs is added to the sales of the main product

(2 marks)

8b.11 **The following question is taken from the January to June 2017 exam period.**

In a period, a process produced 2,000 kg of a main product and 400 kg of a by-product. The cost of production was $5,000. 1,800 kg of the main product were sold at $10 per kg and all of the by-product produced was sold for $1 per kg. There was no opening inventory.

If the sales income of the by-product is deducted from the cost of production, what is the profit for the period?

Handwritten: (5000 − 400 × 1) / 2000 = 2.30   400 × 1 = 400 − by product   1800 × 10 = 18,000

- ○ $13,400
- ⊘ $13,860
- ○ $13,900
- ○ $15,860

(2 marks)

(Total = 22 marks)

Handwritten: (10 − 2.30) × 1,800 = 13,860

9a Job, batch and service costing
36 mins

9a.1 Which of the following costing methods is most likely to be used by a company involved in the manufacture of liquid soap?

- ~~Batch costing~~
- ~~Service costing~~
- ~~Job costing~~
- Process costing

(2 marks)

9a.2 A company calculates the prices of jobs by adding overheads to the prime cost and adding 30% to total costs as a mark up. Job number Y256 was sold for $1,690 and incurred overheads of $694. What was the prime cost of the job? *working backwards*

$ 606

(2 marks)

9a.3 A company operates a job costing system.

The estimated costs for job 173 are as follows.

Direct materials   5 metres @ $20 per metre = 100
Direct labour   14 hours @ $8 per hour   = 112

Variable production overheads are recovered at the rate of $3 per direct labour hour. $42 – 14hrs

Fixed production overheads for the year are budgeted to be $200,000 and are to be recovered on the basis of the total of 40,000 direct labour hours for the year.

Other overheads, in relation to selling, distribution and administration, are recovered at the rate of $80 per job.

What is the total cost of job 173?

80 x 173 = 13,840

$ 504

$\frac{\$200,000}{40,000} = 5$

$ 5 per hour ×14

add.

(2 marks)

The following information relates to questions 9a.4 and 9a.5.

A firm makes special assemblies to customers' orders and uses job costing.

The data for a period are:

	Job number AA10 $	Job number BB15 $	Job number CC20 $
Opening WIP	26,800	42,790	0
Material added in period	17,275	0	18,500
Labour for period	14,500	3,500	24,600

The budgeted overheads for the period were $126,000.
Job number BB15 was completed on the last day of the period.

9a.4 What overhead should be added to job number CC20 for the period?

$ [   ]

(2 marks)

9a.5 What was the approximate value of closing work-in-progress at the end of the period?

- $58,575
- $101,675
- $217,323
- $227,675

(2 marks)

9a.6 The following items may be used in costing batches.

(i)   Actual material cost
(ii)   Actual manufacturing overheads
(iii) Absorbed manufacturing overheads
(iv)   Actual labour cost

Which of the above are contained in a typical batch cost?

○   (i), (ii) and (iv) only
○   (i) and (iv) only
◉   (i), (iii) and (iv) only
○   (i), (ii), (iii) and (iv)   (2 marks)

9a.7 Which of the following would be appropriate cost units for a passenger coach company?

(i)   Vehicle cost per passenger-kilometre
(ii)   Fuel cost for each vehicle per kilometre
(iii) Fixed cost per kilometre

○   (i) only
◉   (i) and (ii) only
○   (i) and (iii) only
○   (ii) and (iii) only   (2 marks)

9a.8 The following information is available for a hotel company for the latest thirty day period.

Number of rooms available per night   40   26 rooms occupied
Percentage occupancy achieved   65%
Room servicing cost incurred $3,900   x 26 = 101,400

What was the room servicing cost per occupied room-night last period, to the nearest cent?

$ [101,400]
   5

(2 marks)

9a.9 Annie is to set up a small hairdressing business at home. She anticipates working a 35-hour week and taking four weeks' holiday per year. Her expenses for materials and overheads are expected to be $3,000 per year, and she has set herself a target profit of $18,000 for the first year.

Assuming that only 90% of her working time will be chargeable to clients, what price should she charge for a 'colour and cut' which would take 3 hours?

○ $13.89
○ $35.71
○ $37.50
◉ $41.67

35 52 − 4 = 48 Days weeks
Hours   48 x 35 = 1680 x 90% = 1512
cost per   18 000 + 3 000 / 1512 = 13.89 x 3 = 41.67
hour   (2 marks)
cost for 3 hours.

9a.10 Which of the following are likely to use service costing?

(i)   A college
(ii)   A hotel
(iii) A plumber

○   (i), (ii) and (iii)
◉   (i) and (ii)
○   (ii) only
○   (ii) and (iii) only   (2 marks)

9a.11 Which of the following would be considered a service industry?

(i)   An airline company
(ii)   A railway company
(iii) A firm of accountants

O̶ ̶ ̶(i) and (ii) only̶
O̶ ̶ ̶(i) and (iii) only
⊙ (i), (ii) and (iii)
O̶ ̶ ̶(ii) and (iii) only̶

(2 marks)

9a.12 The following information relates to a management consultancy organisation:

	$
Salary cost per hour for senior consultants	40
Salary cost per hour for junior consultants	25
Overhead absorption rate per hour applied to all hours	20

The organisation adds 40% to total cost to arrive at the final fee to be charged to a client.

Assignment number 789 took 54 hours of a senior consultant's time and 110 hours of junior consultants' time.

What is the final fee to be charged for Assignment 789?

O $6,874
O $10,696
O $11,466
O $12,642

(2 marks)

9a.13 A company operates a job costing system. Job number 1012 requires $45 of direct materials and $30 of direct labour. Direct labour is paid at the rate of $7.50 per hour. Production overheads are absorbed at a rate of $12.50 per direct labour hour and non-production overheads are absorbed at a rate of 60% of prime cost.

What is the total cost of job number 1012?

$ [   ]

(2 marks)

9a.14 Last year, Bryan Air carried excess baggage of 250,000 kg over a distance of 7,500 km at a cost of $3,750,000 for the extra fuel.

What is the cost per kg-km?

O $0.002 per kg-km
O $2.00 per kg-km
O $33.33 per kg-km
O $500.00 per kg-km

(2 marks)

9a.15 **The following question is taken from the December 2012 exam.**

A truck delivered sand to two customers in a week. The following details are available.

Customer	Weight of goods delivered (kilograms)	Distance covered (kilometres)
X	500	200
Y	180	1,200
	680	1,400

The truck cost $3,060 to operate in the week. Each customer delivery was carried out separately, and the truck made no other deliveries in the week.

What is the cost per kilogram/kilometre of sand delivered in the week (to the nearest $0.001)?

O $0.003
◑ $0.010
O $2.186
O $4.500

$\frac{3060}{316,000}$

(2 marks)

(Total = 30 marks)

9b   Alternative costing principles   17 mins

9b.1   A product is in the stage of its life cycle which is typified by falling prices but good profit margins due to high sales volumes. What stage is it in?

    O   Growth
    O   Maturity
    O   Introduction
    O   Decline   **(2 marks)**

9b.2   In what stage of the product life cycle are initial costs of the investment in the product typically recovered?

    O   Introduction
    O   Decline
    O   Growth
    O   Maturity   **(2 marks)**

9b.3   How is target cost calculated?

    O   Desired selling price – actual profit margin
    O   Market price – desired profit margin
    O   Desired selling price – desired profit margin
    O   Market price – standard profit margin   **(2 marks)**

9b.4   Which stage of the product life cycle do the following characteristics refer to?

New competitors
Customer feedback received
New distribution outlets being found
Product quality improvements made

    O   Growth
    O   Decline
    O   Maturity
    O   Introduction   **(2 marks)**

9b.5   A new product is being developed. The development will take one year and the product is expected to have a life cycle of two years before it is replaced.

Which of the following statements are true of life cycle costing?

Statement 1: It is useful for assessing whether new products have been successful.
Statement 2: The individual profitability for products is less accurate.

    O   Both statements are true
    O   Both statements are false
    O   Statement 1 is true and statement 2 is false
    O   Statement 2 is true and statement 1 is false   **(2 marks)**

9b.6   A chain of coffee shops has implemented a Total Quality Management system to ensure high quality and consistency across all outlets. As part of the scheme, the chain offers a free replacement drink to any customer not completely satisfied with their purchase.

Which of the following BEST describes the cost of providing replacement drinks?

    O   An external failure cost
    O   An internal failure cost
    O   A prevention cost
    O   An appraisal cost   **(2 marks)**

9b.7   Which costing method is based around a calculation involving a desired profit margin and a competitive market price?

- O   Activity Based Costing
- O   Total Quality Management
- O   Target costing
- O   Life cycle costing

(2 marks)

(Total = 14 marks)

Do you know? – Budgeting

Check that you can fill in the blanks in the statements below before you attempt any questions. If in doubt, you should go back to your BPP Interactive Text and revise first.

- Management accountants will use spreadsheet software in activities such as budgeting, forecasting, reporting performance and variance analysis. Spreadsheet packages have the facility to perform ......-... calculations at great speed.

- The .... should be identified at the beginning of the budgetary process and the budget for this is prepared before all others.

- .... budgets include production budgets, marketing budgets, sales budgets, personnel budgets, purchasing budgets and research and development budgets.

- *Possible pitfalls*

  Write down the mistakes you know you should avoid.

Did you know? – Forecasting and budgeting

Could you fill in the blanks? The answers are in bold. Use this page for revision purposes as you approach the exam.

- Management accountants will use spreadsheet software in activities such as budgeting, forecasting, reporting performance and variance analysis. Spreadsheet packages have the facility to perform **what-if** calculations at great speed.

- The **principal budget factor** should be identified at the beginning of the budgetary process and the budget for this is prepared before all others.

- **Functional** budgets include production budgets, marketing budgets, sales budgets, personnel budgets, purchasing budgets and research and development budgets.

- *Possible pitfalls*

    - Not understanding the meanings of correlation coefficient and coefficient of determination
    - Forgetting that linear regression gives an *estimate* only. It is not wholly reliable

10a Budgeting   34 mins

10a.1 Which of the following may be considered to be objectives of budgeting?

- (i)   Co-ordination
- (ii)   Communication
- (iii) Expansion
- (iv)   Resource allocation

- O   All of them
- O   (i), (ii) and (iv)
- O   (ii), (iii) and (iv)
- O   (ii) and (iv)   **(2 marks)**

10a.2 What does the statement 'sales is the principal budget factor' mean?

- O   The level of sales will determine the level of cash at the end of the period
- O   The level of sales will determine the level of profit at the end of the period
- O   The company's activities are limited by the level of sales it can achieve
- O   Sales is the largest item in the budget   **(2 marks)**

10a.3 QT Co manufactures a single product and an extract from their flexed budget for production costs is as follows.

	Activity level	
	80%	90%
	$	$
Direct material	2,400	2,700
Labour	2,120	2,160
Production overhead	4,060	4,080
	8,580	8,940

(handwritten annotations: VC + 30, Sʋ, Sʋ)

What would the total production cost allowance be in a budget flexed at the 83% level of activity? (to the nearest $)

$ [8688]

(handwritten: 2,400 x 80% =, 2,120 x 90%, 4060 x 80% =)

                                                                          (2 marks)

10a.4 Which of these statements is untrue?

- O   Spreadsheets make the calculation and manipulation of data easier and quicker
- O   Spreadsheets are very useful for word-processing
- O   Budgeting can be done very easily using spreadsheets
- O   Spreadsheets are useful for plotting graphs   **(2 marks)**

The following data applies to questions 10a.5 to 10a.7.

	A	B	C	D	F	G
1		Jan	Feb	Mar	Apr	May
2	Sales	15,000	13,400	16,100	17,200	15,300
3	Cost of sales	11,090	10,060	12,040	13,000	11,100
4	Gross profit	3,910	3,340	4,060	4,200	4,200
5	Expenses	1,500	1,500	1,500	1,500	1,500
6	Net profit	2,410	1,840	2,560	2,700	2,700
7						
8	Net profit %					

10a.5 The formula =C2-C3 will give the contents of which cell in the drop down list?

Select... ▼
C6
C4
C5
C1

(2 marks)

10a.6 What would be the formula for March net profit?

○   =D2–D3
○   =B6+C6
○   =D4–D5
○   =D3*D8

(2 marks)

10a.7 What will be the formula to go in G8?

○   =G6/G2*100
○   =G4/100*G6
○   =G2/G6*100
○   =G6/G4*100

(2 marks)

10a.8 A company manufactures a single product. In a computer spreadsheet the cells F1 to F12 contain the budgeted monthly sales units for the twelve months of next year in sequence, with January sales in cell F1 and finishing with December sales in cell F12. The company policy is for the closing inventory of finished goods each month to be 10% of the budgeted sales units for the following month.

Which of the following formulae will generate the budgeted production (in units) for March next year?

○   =[F3 + (0.1*F4)]
○   =[F3 – (0.1*F4)]
○   =[(1.1*F3) – (0.1*F4)]
○   =[(0.9*F3) + (0.1*F4)]

(2 marks)

10a.9 Misty Co's budgetary control report for last month is as follows:

	Fixed budget $	Flexed budget $	Actual results $
Direct costs	61,100	64,155	67,130
Production overhead	55,000	56,700	54,950
Other overhead	10,000	10,000	11,500
	126,100	130,855	133,580

What was the volume variance for last month?

☑ $4,755 (A)
○ $2,725 (A)
○ $4,755 (F)
○ $2,725 (F)

Handwritten annotations:
67,130 - 61,100 = 6,030
Direct   54,950 - 55,000 =
Production   6,030
other   -5.50
  1,500
133 580
-126 100

(2 marks)

10a.10 Misty Co's budgetary control report for last month is as follows:

	Fixed budget $	Flexed budget $	Actual results $
Direct costs	61,100	64,155	67,130
Production overhead	55,000	56,700	54,950
Other overhead	10,000	10,000	11,500
	126,100	130,855	133,580

What was the expenditure variance for last month?

○ $7,480 (F)
○ $2,725 (F)
○ $7,480 (A)
○ $2,725 (A)

(2 marks)

10a.11 **The following question is taken from the July to December 2014 exam period.**

The standard cost card for a company's only product is given below:

	$ per unit
Selling price	118
Direct labour 4 hours at $20 per hour	80
Direct material 3 kg at $7 per hour	21
Fixed production overhead	5
Profit	12

(handwritten: 17 × 6000 = 102,000)
(handwritten next to Fixed production overhead: shouldn't change)
(handwritten: = OAR)

For a period, budgeted production and sales were 8,000 units, whilst actual production and sales were 6,000 units.

What is the flexed budget profit?

- ○ $62,000 *(handwritten: Answer)*
- ○ $72,000
- ○ $96,000
- ○ $102,000

(2 marks)

10a.12 **The following question is taken from the January to June 2016 exam period.**

Budgeted costs and revenues for an output level of 4,000 units are given below. It is known that after an output level of 5,000 units there is a step up in fixed costs of $1,000:

	$ per unit
Selling price	30
Variable cost	18
Fixed cost	4
Profit	8

What is the flexed budget profit at an output level of 6,000 units?

- ○ $47,000
- ○ $48,000
- ○ $55,000
- ○ $56,000

(2 marks)

10a.13 **The following question is taken from the July to December 2016 exam period.**

The following spreadsheet shows the calculation of a company's profit.

	A	B
1		$
2	Sales revenue	20,000
3	Variable production costs	5,000
4	Fixed production costs	3,000
5	Gross profit	12,000
6	Variable selling costs	1,000
7	Fixed selling costs	500
8	Profit	10,500

Which formula would calculate contribution?

- ○ B2 – B3
- ○ B5 – B6 *(handwritten tick)*
- ○ B8 + B7
- ○ B8 + B7 + B4

(2 marks)

10a.14 **The following question is taken from the July to December 2017 exam period.**

The following spreadsheet shows a profit centre's variances against budget for a period. Some figures have been omitted (omitted figures are labelled ????).

	A	B	C	D	E
1		Fixed budget	Flexed budget	Actual	Variance
2	Sales/production units	1,200	1,500	1,500	300
3		$	$	$	$
4	Sales revenue	60,000	75,000	74,000	-1,000
5	Direct material	21,600	???	24,000	???
6	Direct labour	14,400	18,000	22,000	-4,000
7	Contribution	24,000	???	28,000	???
8	Fixed costs	17,000	17,000	16,500	500
9	Profit	7,000	13,000	11,500	na

What figure should appear in cell E5?

○   -2,400
○   2,400
○   -3,000
○   3,000

(2 marks)

(Total = 28 marks)

10b The budgetary process   60 mins

10b.1 What does a master budget comprise?

○   The budgeted statement of profit or loss

○   The budgeted cash flow, budgeted statement of profit or loss and budgeted statement of financial position

○   The budgeted cash flow

○   The entire set of budgets prepared   **(2 marks)**

10b.2 If a company has no production resource limitations, in which order would the following budgets be prepared?

(i)	Material usage budget	(iv)	Finished goods inventory budget
(ii)	Sales budget	(v)	Production budget
(iii)	Material purchase budget	(vi)	Material inventory budget

○   (v), (iv), (i), (vi), (iii), (ii)
○   (ii), (iv), (v), (i), (vi), (iii)
○   (ii), (iv), (v), (i), (iii), (vi)
○   (ii), (v), (iv), (i), (vi), (iii)

(2 marks)

10b.3 In a situation where there are no production resource limitations, which TWO of the following items of information must be available for the production budget to be completed?

☐   Sales volume from the sales budget

☐   Material purchases from the purchases budget

☐   Budgeted change in finished goods inventory

☐   Standard direct labour cost per unit   **(2 marks)**

10b.4 When preparing a production budget, what does the quantity to be produced equal?

    O   Sales quantity + opening inventory of finished goods + closing inventory of finished goods

    O   Sales quantity − opening inventory of finished goods + closing inventory of finished goods

    O   Sales quantity − opening inventory of finished goods − closing inventory of finished goods

    O   Sales quantity + opening inventory of finished goods − closing inventory of finished goods

(2 marks)

10b.5 The quantity of material in the material purchases budget is greater than the inferred from quantity of material in the material usage budget. Which of the following statements can be this situation?

    O   Wastage of material occurs in the production process

    O   Finished goods inventories are budgeted to increase

    O   Raw materials inventories are budgeted to increase

    O   Raw materials inventories are budgeted to decrease

(2 marks)

10b.6 A company plans to sell 24,000 units of product R next year. Opening inventory of R is expected to be 2,000 units and PQ Co plans to increase inventory by 25 per cent by the end of the year. How many units of product R should be produced next year?

    [   ] units

(2 marks)

10b.7 Each unit of product Alpha requires 3 kg of raw material. Next month's production budget for product Alpha is as follows.

Opening inventories:

Raw materials	15,000 kg
Finished units of Alpha	2,000 units
Budgeted sales of Alpha	60,000 units

Planned closing inventories:

Raw materials	7,000 kg
Finished units of Alpha	3,000 units

How many kilograms of raw materials should be purchased next month?

    [   ] kgs

(2 marks)

10b.8 Budgeted sales of X for December are 18,000 units. At the end of the production process for X, 10% of production units are scrapped as defective. Opening inventories of X for December are budgeted to be 15,000 units and closing inventories will be 11,400 units. All inventories of finished goods must have successfully passed the quality control check. What is the production budget for X for December?

    [   ] units

(2 marks)

10b.9 A company manufactures a single product, M. Budgeted production output of product M during August is 200 units. Each unit of product M requires 6 labour hours for completion and PR Co anticipates 20 per cent idle time. Labour is paid at a rate of $7 per hour. What is the direct labour cost budget for August?

    O $6,720

    O $8,400

    O $10,080

    O $10,500

(2 marks)

10b.10 Each unit of product Echo takes five direct labour hours to make. Quality standards are high, and 8% of units are rejected after completion as sub-standard. Next month's budgets are as follows.

Opening inventories of finished goods	3,000 units
Planned closing inventories of finished goods	7,600 units
Budgeted sales of Echo	36,800 units

All inventories of finished goods must have successfully passed the quality control check.

What is the direct labour hours budget for the month?

- ○   190,440 hours
- ○   207,000 hours
- ○   223,560 hours
- ○   225,000 hours   **(2 marks)**

10b.11 Budgeted production in a factory for next period is 4,800 units. Each unit requires five labour hours to make. Labour is paid $10 per hour. Idle time represents 20% of the total labour time.

What is the budgeted total labour cost for the next period?

- ○ $192,000
- ○ $240,000
- ○ $288,000
- ○ $300,000   **(2 marks)**

10b.12 Which of the following statements are true?

(i)   A flexed budget allows businesses to evaluate a manager's performance more fairly
(ii)   A fixed budget is useful for defining the broad objectives of the organisation
(iii)   Relying on fixed budgets alone would usually give rise to massive variances

- ○   (i) and (iii) only
- ○   (i) and (ii) only
- ○   (ii) and (iii) only
- ○   (i), (ii) and (iii)   **(2 marks)**

10b.13 The following details have been extracted from the receivables collection records of C Co.

Invoices paid in the month after sale	60%
Invoices paid in the second month after sale	25%
Invoices paid in the third month after sale	12%
Bad debts	3%

Invoices are issued on the last day of each month.
Customers paying in the month after sale are entitled to deduct a 2% settlement discount.
Credit sales values for June to September are budgeted as follows.

June	July	August	September
$35,000	$40,000	$60,000	$45,000

What is the amount budgeted to be received from credit sales in September?

- ○ $46,260
- ○ $49,480
- ○ $50,200
- ○ $50,530   **(2 marks)**

10b.14 BDL plc is currently preparing its cash budget for the year to 31 March 20X8. An extract from its sales budget for the same year shows the following sales values.

	$
March	60,000
April	70,000
May	55,000
June	65,000

40% of its sales are expected to be for cash. Of its credit sales, 70% are expected to pay in the month after sale and take a 2% discount; 27% are expected to pay in the second month after the sale, and the remaining 3% are expected to be bad debts.

What is the value of sales receipts to be shown in the cash budget for May 20X7?

- ○ $60,532
- ○ $61,120
- ○ $66,532
- ○ $86,620 **(2 marks)**

The following information relates to questions 10b.15 and 10b.16.

Each unit of product Zeta requires 3 kg of raw material and 4 direct labour hours. Material costs $2 per kg and the direct labour rate is $7 per hour.

The production budget for Zeta for April to June is as follows.

	April	May	June
Production units	7,800	8,400	8,200

10b.15 Raw material opening inventories are budgeted as follows.

	April	May	June
	3,800 kg	4,200 kg	4,100 kg

The closing inventory budgeted for June is 3,900 kg.

Material purchases are paid for in the month following purchase. What is the figure to be included in the cash budget for June in respect of payments for purchases?

- ○ $25,100
- ○ $48,800
- ○ $50,200
- ○ $50,600 **(2 marks)**

10b.16 Wages are paid 75% in the month of production and 25% in the following month. What is the figure to be included in the cash budget for May in respect of wages?

$ [   ]

(2 marks)

10b.17 An extract from a company's sales budget is as follows:

	$
October	224,000
November	390,000
December	402,000

Ten per cent of sales are paid for immediately in cash. Of the credit customers, 30 per cent pay in the month following the sale and are entitled to a one per cent discount. The remaining customers pay two months after the sale is made.

What is the value of sales receipts shown in the company's cash budget for December?

- ○ $285,567
- ○ $286,620
- ○ $290,430
- ○ $312,830 **(2 marks)**

10b.18 Extracts from a company's budget are as follows:

	August	September
Production units	12,600	5,500
Fixed production overhead cost incurred	$9,440	$7,000

The standard variable production overhead cost per unit is $5. Variable production overhead is paid 70 per cent in the month incurred and 30 per cent in the following month.

Fixed production overhead cost is paid in the month following that in which it is incurred and includes depreciation of $2,280 per month.

What is the payment for total production overhead cost shown in the cash budget for September?

- ○ $32,220
- ○ $42,870
- ○ $45,310
- ○ $47,590 **(2 marks)**

10b.19 The following extract is taken from the production cost budget of S Co.

Production (units)	2,000	3,000
Production cost ($)	11,100	12,900

What is the budget cost allowance for an activity level of 4,000 units?

- ○ $7,200
- ○ $7,500
- ○ $13,460
- ○ $14,700 **(2 marks)**

10b.20 The following details have been extracted from the payables' records of X Co:

Invoices paid in the month of purchase	25%
Invoices paid in the first month after purchase	70%
Invoices paid in the second month after purchase	5%

Purchases for July to September are budgeted as follows:

July	$250,000
August	$300,000
September	$280,000

For suppliers paid in the month of purchase, a settlement discount of 5% is received. What is the amount budgeted to be paid to suppliers in September?

- ○ $278,500
- ○ $280,000
- ○ $289,000
- ○ $292,500 **(2 marks)**

10b.21 Which of the following control actions could be taken to help eliminate an adverse direct labour efficiency variance?

(i)   Employ more highly skilled labour
(ii)   Ensure stricter supervision of labour workers
(iii)   Ask employees to work paid overtime

- ○ (i) and (iii) only
- ○ (i) and (ii) only
- ○ (i), (ii) and (iii)
- ○ (ii) and (iii) only **(2 marks)**

10b.22 X department is a division of W Plc. X department usually has a quarterly wages cost of $4,500,000. Quarterly material costs are usually around $2,000,000. W Plc made a central decision to award all employees a wages increase of 2%.

Which of the following variances for the latest quarter are worth investigating?

(i) Direct material price variance $400 (A)
(ii) Labour rate variance $90,000 (A)
(iii) Sales volume variance $4,000,000 (F)

○ (i) and (iii) only
○ (i) and (ii) only
○ (i), (ii) and (iii)
○ (iii) only   **(2 marks)**

10b.23 Which of the following BEST describes the purpose of a flexible budget?

○ To ensure managers are motivated
○ To facilitate control by establishing a budget relevant to actual activity levels
○ To facilitate control by preventing discretionary expenditure
○ To enable accurate reforecasting when actual costs are known   **(2 marks)**

10b.24 The following statements relate to fixed budgets and flexible budgets.

(i) If production levels far exceed those anticipated, relying on a fixed budget is likely to result in massive variances

(ii) Flexible budgets assist management control by providing dynamic, comparable information

(iii) Flexible budgets are always superior to fixed budgets

Which statements are true?

○ (i) only
○ (i) and (ii) only
○ (ii) and (iii) only
○ (i), (ii) and (iii)   **(2 marks)**

10b.25 **The following question is taken from the January to June 2014 exam period.**

An accountant wishes to use the following spreadsheet to calculate budgeted production units.

	A	B	C	D
1		Jul	Aug	Sep
2		units	units	units
3	Sales	1,000	2,000	3,000
4	Opening inventory finished goods	100	200	300
5	Production			
6				

Which formula should be entered in cell B5?

○ =B3-C4+B4
○ =B3-B4
○ =B3+C4
○ =B3+C4-B4   **(2 marks)**

(Total = 50 marks)

11 Making budgets work   12 mins

11.1 Participation by staff in the budgeting process is often seen as an aid to the creation of a realistic budget and to the motivation of staff. There are, however, limitations to the effectiveness of such participation.

Which of the following illustrates one of these limitations?

- ○ Participation allows staff to buy into the budget
- ○ Staff suggestions may be ignored leading to de-motivation
- ○ Staff suggestions may be based on local knowledge
- ○ Budgetary slack can be built in by senior manager as well as staff   **(2 marks)**

11.2 Which of the following statements about budgeting and motivation are true?

- (i)   A target is more motivating than no target at all
- (ii) The problem with a target is setting an appropriate degree of difficulty
- (iii) Employees who are challenged tend to withdraw their commitment

- ○ All of them
- ○ (ii) and (iii) only
- ○ (i) and (ii) only
- ○ (iii) only   **(2 marks)**

11.3 Which of the following best describes a top-down budget?

- ○ A budget which has been set by scaling down individual expenditure items until the total budgeted expenditure can be met from available resources

- ○ A budget which is set by delegating authority from top management, allowing budget holders to participate in setting their own budgets

- ○ A budget which is set without permitting the ultimate budget holder to participate in the budgeting process

- ○ A budget which is set within the framework of strategic plans determined by top management   **(2 marks)**

11.4 In which of the following circumstances is the use of a participative budgeting process appropriate?

- (i)   In decentralised organisations
- (ii) When acceptance of the budget as fair and equitable is essential
- (iii) When an organisation's different units act autonomously

- ○ All of (i), (ii) and (iii)
- ○ (ii) and (iii) only
- ○ (i) and (ii) only
- ○ (iii) only   **(2 marks)**

11.5 Which of the following best describes a controllable cost?

- ○ A cost which can be easily forecast and is therefore readily controllable using budgetary control techniques

- ○ A cost which can be specifically identified with a particular cost object

- ○ A cost which is easily controlled because it is not affected by fluctuations in the level of activity

- ○ A cost which can be influenced by its budget holder   **(2 marks)**

(Total = 10 marks)

Check that you can fill in the blanks in the statements below before you attempt any questions. If in doubt, you should go back to your BPP Interactive Text and revise first.

- The basic principle of .... involves calculating the present value of an investment. The present value of an investment is the amount of money which must be invested now (for a number of years) in order to earn a future sum (at a given rate of interest).

- A constant sum of money received or paid each year for a given number of years is known as an .... If this constant sum lasts forever, then it is known as a ....

- Annuity × annuity factor = ...

- Annuity ÷ interest rate = ...

- The two main discounted cash flow methods ⎡— NPV ⎣— IRR

    - **Net present value (NPV) method**. If an investment has a .... NPV then it is acceptable. An investment with a .... NPV should be rejected.

    - **Internal rate of return (IRR) method**. This method determines the rate of interest at which the NPV of the investment = ... The project is viable if the IRR exceeds the minimum acceptable return.

- The IRR formula is as follows.

$$IRR = a\% + \left[\frac{A}{A-B} \times (b-a)\right]\%$$

    Where   a = ...

            b = ...

            A = ...

            B = ...

- The time that is required for the cash inflows from a capital investment project to equal the cash outflows is known as the ....

- *Possible pitfalls*

    Write down the mistakes you know you should avoid.

Did you know? – Capital investment appraisal

Could you fill in the blanks? The answers are in bold. Use this page for revision purposes as you approach the exam.

- The basic principle of **discounting** involves calculating the present value of an investment. The present value of an investment is the amount of money which must be invested now (for a number of years) in order to earn a future sum (at a given rate of interest).

- A constant sum of money received or paid each year for a given number of years is known as an **annuity**. If this constant sum lasts forever, then it is known as a **perpetuity**.

- Annuity × annuity factor = **present value of an annuity**

- Annuity ÷ interest rate = **present value of a perpetuity**

- The two main discounted cash flow methods
  - NPV
  - IRR

    - **Net present value (NPV) method**. If an investment has a **positive** NPV then it is acceptable. An investment with a **negative** NPV should be rejected.

    - **Internal rate of return (IRR) method**. This method determines the rate of interest at which the NPV of the investment = **zero**. The project is viable if the IRR exceeds the minimum acceptable return.

- The IRR formula is as follows.

$$\text{IRR} = a\% + \left[\frac{A}{A-B} \times (b-a) \right] \%$$

  Where
  - a = **one interest rate**
  - b = **the other interest rate**
  - A = **NPV at rate a**
  - B = **NPV at rate b**

- The time that is required for the cash inflows from a capital investment project to equal the cash outflows is known as the **payback period**.

- *Possible pitfalls*

    - Not being able to calculate and distinguish between the nominal rate of interest and the effective annual rate of interest.

    - Not being able to calculate the IRR of an investment, even when given the IRR formula. (You must remember what the symbols in the formula mean so that you can use the correct figures in your calculations.)

12a Capital expenditure budgeting   10 mins

12a.1 You are currently employed as a Management Accountant in an insurance company. You are
contemplating starting your own business. In considering whether or not to start your own business,
what would your current salary level be?

- O   A sunk cost
- O   ~~An incremental cost~~
- ⬤   An irrelevant cost   — relevent cost.
- O   An opportunity cost

(2 marks)

12a.2 In decision making, costs which need to be considered are said to be relevant costs. Which of the
following are characteristics associated with relevant costs?

- (i)   Future costs
- (ii)   ~~Unavoidable costs~~
- (iii) Incremental costs
- (iv)   Differential costs   — relevent cost feature of.

- ⬤   (i) and (iii) only
- O   (i) and (ii) only
- O   (i), (iii) and (iv) only
- O   All of them

(2 marks)

12a.3 A machine owned by a company has been idle for some months but could now be used on a one year
contract which is under consideration. The net book value of the machine is $1,000. If not used on this
contract, the machine could be sold now for a net amount of $1,200. After use on the contract, the
machine would have no saleable value and the cost of disposing of it in one year's time would be $800.

What is the total relevant cost of the machine to the contract?

$ [   ]

(2 marks)

12a.4 Which of the following would be part of the capital expenditure budget?

- (i)   Purchase of a new factory premises
- (ii)   ~~Replacement of existing machinery~~
- (iii) Refurbishment of existing factory premises
- (iv)   ~~Purchases of raw materials~~

- O   (i) and (ii) only
- ⬤   (iii) and (iv) only
- O   (i), (ii) and (iii) only
- O   (ii) and (iv) only

(2 marks)

(Total = 8 marks)

12b Methods of project appraisal   55 mins

12b.1 A building society adds interest monthly to investors' accounts even though interest rates are expressed
in annual terms. The current rate of interest is 6% per year.

An investor deposits $1,000 on 1 January. How much interest will have been earned by 30 June?

$ [   ]

$$1000 + \left(1 + 0.03\right)^{6}$$

(2 marks)

= 1000.52

Interest 0.52

12b.2 A one-year investment yields a return of 15%. The cash returned from the investment, including principal and interest, is $2,070. What is the interest?

- ○ $250
- ○ $270
- ○ $300
- ○ $310.50 (2 marks)

12b.3 If a single sum of $12,000 is invested at 8% per year with interest compounded quarterly, what is the amount to which the principal will have grown by the end of year three? (approximately)

- ○ $15,117
- ○ $9,528
- ○ $15,219
- ○ $30,924 (2 marks)

12b.4 Which is worth most, at present values, assuming an annual rate of interest of 8%?

- ○ $1,200 in exactly one year from now
- ○ $1,400 in exactly two years from now
- ○ $1,600 in exactly three years from now
- ○ $1,800 in exactly four years from now (2 marks)

12b.5 A bank offers depositors a nominal 4% pa, with interest payable quarterly. What is the effective annual rate of interest?

- ○ 1%
- ○ 4%
- ○ 1.025%
- ○ 4.06% (2 marks)

12b.6 A project requiring an investment of $1,200 is expected to generate returns of $400 in years 1 and 2 and $350 in years 3 and 4. If the NPV = $22 at 9% and the NPV = –$4 at 10%, what is the IRR for the project?

- ○ 9.15%
- ● 9.85%
- ○ 10.15%
- ○ 10.85%

$$IRR = a + \left(\frac{NPV_a \times (a - b)}{NPV_a - NPV_b} \right)$$

$$0.09 + \frac{22 \times (0.09 - 0.1)}{22 + 4} =$$

(2 marks)

12b.7 A sum of money was invested for 10 years at 7% per year and is now worth $2,000. What was the original amount invested (to the nearest $)?

- ○ $1,026
- ○ $1,017
- ○ $3,937
- ○ $14,048 (2 marks)

12b.8 House prices rise at 2% per calendar month. What is the annual rate of increase correct to one decimal place?

- ○ 24%
- ○ 26.8%
- ○ 12.7%
- ○ 12.2% (2 marks)

12b.9 What is the present value of ten annual payments of $700, the first paid immediately and discounted at 8%, giving your answer to the nearest $?

- ○ $4,697
- ○ $1,050
- ○ $4,435
- ○ $5,073 (2 marks)

12b.10 An investor is to receive an annuity of $19,260 for six years commencing at the end of year 1. It has a present value of $86,400.

What is the rate of interest (to the nearest whole percent)?

○   4%
○   7%
○   9%
○   11%   **(2 marks)**

12b.11 How much should be invested now (to the nearest $) to receive $24,000 per year in perpetuity if the annual rate of interest is 5%?

○ $1,200
○ $25,200
○ $120,000
○ $480,000   **(2 marks)**

12b.12 The net present value of an investment at 12% is $24,000, and at 20% is –$8,000. What is the internal rate of return of this investment?

☐ %

State your answer to the nearest whole percent.   **(2 marks)**

The following data is relevant for questions 12b.13 and 12b.14.

Diamond Co has a payback period limit of three years and is considering investing in one of the following projects. Both projects require an initial investment of $800,000. Cash inflows accrue evenly throughout the year.

Project Alpha		Project Beta	
Year	Cash inflow	Year	Cash inflow
	$		$
1	250,000	1	250,000
2	250,000	2	350,000
3	400,000	3	400,000
4	300,000	4	200,000
5	200,000	5	150,000
6	50,000	6	150,000

The company's cost of capital is 10%.

12b.13 What is the non-discounted payback period of Project Beta?

○   2 years and 2 months
○   2 years and 4 months
○   2 years and 5 months
○   2 years and 6 months   **(2 marks)**

12b.14 What is the discounted payback period of Project Alpha?

○   Between 1 and 2 years
○   Between 3 and 4 years
○   Between 4 and 5 years
○   Between 5 and 6 years   **(2 marks)**

12b.15 A capital investment project has an initial investment followed by constant annual returns.

How is the payback period calculated?

O   Initial investment ÷ annual profit
O   Initial investment ÷ annual net cash inflow
O   (Initial investment – residual value) ÷ annual profit
O   (Initial investment – residual value) ÷ annual net cash inflow   **(2 marks)**

12b.16 A machine has an investment cost of $60,000 at time 0. The present values (at time 0) of the expected net cash inflows from the machine over its useful life are:

Discount rate	Present value of cash inflows
10%	$64,600
15%	$58,200
20%	$52,100

What is the internal rate of return (IRR) of the machine investment?

O   Below 10%
O   Between 10% and 15%
O   Between 15% and 20%
O   Over 20%   **(2 marks)**

12b.17 An investment project has a positive net present value (NPV) of $7,222 when its cash flows are discounted at the cost of capital of 10% per year. Net cash inflows from the project are expected to be $18,000 per year for five years. The cumulative discount (annuity) factor for five years at 10% is 3.791.

What is the investment at the start of the project?

O $61,016
O $68,238
O $75,460
O $82,778   **(2 marks)**

12b.18 Which of the following accurately defines the internal rate of return (IRR)?

O   The average annual profit from an investment expressed as a percentage of the investment sum

O   The discount rate (%) at which the net present value of the cash flows from an investment is zero

O   The net present value of the cash flows from an investment discounted at the required rate of return

O   The rate (%) at which discounted net profits from an investment are zero   **(2 marks)**

12b.19 An investment project has the following discounted cash flows ($'000):

Year		Discount rate	
	0%	10%	20%
0	(90)	(90)	(90)
1	30	27.3	25.0
2	30	24.8	29.8
3	30	22.5	17.4
4	30	20.5	14.5
	30	5.1	(12.3)

The required rate of return on investment is 10% per year.

What is the discounted payback period of the investment project?

O   Less than 3.0 years
O   3.0 years
O   Between 3.0 years and 4.0 years
O   More than 4.0 years   **(2 marks)**

12b.20 What is the effective annual rate of interest of 2.1% compounded every three months?

- O 6.43%
- O 8.40%
- O 8.67%
- O 10.87%   **(2 marks)**

12b.21 If the interest rate is 8%, what would you pay for a perpetuity of $1,500 starting in one year's time? (to the nearest $)

$ [   ]

(2 marks)

12b.22 **The following question is taken from the June 2012 exam.**

An investor has the choice between two investments. Investment Exe offers interest of 4% per year compounded semi-annually for a period of three years. Investment Wye offers one interest payment of 20% at the end of its four-year life.

What is the annual effective interest rate offered by the two investments?

Investment Exe	*Investment Wye*
O 4.00%	4.66%
O 4.00%	5.00%
O 4.04%	4.66%
O 4.04%	5.00%

(2 marks)

12b.23 **The following question is taken from the June 2013 exam.**

A project has an initial outflow of $12,000 followed by six equal annual cash inflows, commencing in one year's time. The payback period is exactly four years. The cost of capital is 12% per year.

What is the project's net present value (to the nearest $)?

- O $333
- O −$2,899
- O −$3,778
- O −$5,926   **(2 marks)**

(Total = 46 marks)

Important note

You have now reached the end of the multiple choice questions for Budgeting (Chapters 4, and 10a to 12b). Make sure that you practise the multi-task questions on Budgeting in Section 23. The real exam will contain three 10-mark multi-task questions on Budgeting, Standard costing and Performance measurement.

Do you know? – Standard costing

Check that you can fill in the blanks in the statements below before you attempt any questions. If in doubt, you should go back to your BPP Interactive Text and revise first.

- If an organisation uses standard marginal costing instead of standard absorption costing, there will be no .... variance and the ..../............ variances will be valued at the standard contribution per unit (as opposed to standard profit per unit).

- There are many possible reasons for variances arising including efficiencies and inefficiencies of operations, errors in standard setting and changes in exchange rates.

- Individual variances should not be looked at in isolation. They might be interdependent/ interrelated. One may be .... and one ....

- An .... provides a reconciliation between budgeted and actual profit.

- .... , ... and .... should be considered before a decision about whether or not to investigate a variance is taken. One way of deciding whether or not to investigate a variance is to investigate only those variances which exceed pre-set tolerance limits.

- A variance should only be investigated if the expected value of .... from investigation and any control action exceed the ....of investigation.

- If the cause of a variance is controllable, action can be taken to bring the system back under control in future. If the variance is uncontrollable, but not simply due to chance, it will be necessary to review .... of expected results, and perhaps to revise the ....

- *Possible pitfalls*

  Write down a list of mistakes you know you should avoid.

Did you know? – Standard costing

Could you fill in the blanks? The answers are in bold. Use this page for revision purposes as you approach the exam.

- If an organisation uses standard marginal costing instead of standard absorption costing, there will be no **fixed overhead volume** variance and the **sales volume/quantity** variances will be valued at the standard contribution per unit (as opposed to standard profit per unit).

- There are many possible reasons for variances arising including efficiencies and inefficiencies of operations, errors in standard setting and changes in exchange rates.

- Individual variances should not be looked at in isolation. They might be interdependent/ interrelated. One may be **adverse** and one **favourable**.

- An **operating statement** provides a reconciliation between budgeted and actual profit.

- **Materiality**, **controllability** and **variance trend** should be considered before a decision about whether or not to investigate a variance is taken. One way of deciding whether or not to investigate a variance is to investigate only those variances which exceed pre-set tolerance limits.

- A variance should only be investigated if the expected value of **benefits** from investigation and any control action exceed the **costs** of investigation.

- If the cause of a variance is controllable, action can be taken to bring the system back under control in future. If the variance is uncontrollable, but not simply due to chance, it will be necessary to review **forecasts** of expected results, and perhaps to revise the **budget**.

- *Possible pitfalls*

    - Forgetting to state whether the variance is adverse or favourable
    - Not learning how to calculate each type of variance

13 Standard costing   17 mins

13.1 A company is in the process of setting standard unit costs for next period. Product J uses two types of material, P and S. 7 kg of material P and 3 kg of material S are needed, at a standard price of $4 per kg and $9 per kg respectively.

Direct labour will cost $7 per hour and each unit of J requires 5 hours of labour.

Production overheads are to be recovered at the rate of $6 per direct labour hour, and general overhead is to be absorbed at a rate of ten per cent of production cost.

What is the standard prime cost for one unit of product J?

$ [   ]

(2 marks)

13.2 What is an attainable standard?

- ○ A standard which includes no allowance for losses, waste and inefficiencies. It represents the level of performance which is attainable under perfect operating conditions

- ○ A standard which includes some allowance for losses, waste and inefficiencies. It represents the level of performance which is attainable under efficient operating conditions

- ○ A standard which is based on currently attainable operating conditions

- ○ A standard which is kept unchanged, to show the trend in costs   **(2 marks)**

13.3 Which of the following statements is correct?

- ○ The operating standards set for production should be the most ideal possible
- ○ The operating standards set for production should be the minimal level
- ○ The operating standards set for production should be the attainable level
- ○ The operating standards set for production should be the maximum level   **(2 marks)**

13.4 A company manufactures a carbonated drink, which is sold in 1 litre bottles. During the bottling process there is a 20% loss of liquid input due to spillage and evaporation. What is the standard usage of liquid per bottle (to two decimal places)?

[   ] litres

(2 marks)

13.5 Which of the following best describes management by exception?

- ○ Using management reports to highlight exceptionally good performance, so that favourable results can be built upon to improve future outcomes

- ○ Sending management reports only to those managers who are able to act on the information contained within the reports

- ○ Focusing management reports on areas which require attention and ignoring those which appear to be performing within acceptable limits

- ○ Focusing management reports on areas which are performing just outside acceptable limits

(2 marks)

13.6 Standard costing provides which of the following?

(i) Targets and measures of performance
(ii) Information for budgeting
(iii) Simplification of inventory control systems
(iv) Actual future costs

○ (i), (ii) and (iii) only
○ (ii), (iii) and (iv) only
○ (i), (iii) and (iv) only
○ (i), (ii) and (iv) only   **(2 marks)**

13.7 A unit of product L requires 9 active labour hours for completion. The performance standard for product L allows for ten per cent of total labour time to be idle, due to machine downtime. The standard wage rate is $9 per hour. What is the standard labour cost per unit of product L?

$ [   ]

(2 marks)

(Total = 14 marks)

14a Cost variances   46 mins

✱ 14a.1 A company manufactures a single product L, for which the standard material cost is as follows.

	$ per unit
Material 14 kg × $3	42

During July, 800 units of L were manufactured, 12,000 kg of material were purchased for $33,600, of which 11,500 kg were issued to production.

SM Co values all inventory at standard cost.

What are the material price and usage variances for July?

Price   *£*

12 000
12 000   (33 600)

	Price	Usage
○	$2,300 (F)	$900 (A)
✔	$2,300 (F)	$300 (A)
○	$2,400 (F)	$900 (A)
○	$2,400 (F)	$840 (A)

Usage
should 11,200
did (11,500)

(300) A **(2 marks)**

× 3.

The following information relates to questions 14a.2 and 14a.3.

A company expected to produce 200 units of its product, the Bone, in 20X3. In fact 260 units were produced. The standard labour cost per unit was $70 (10 hours at a rate of $7 per hour). The actual labour cost was $18,600 and the labour force worked 2,200 hours although they were paid for 2,300 hours.

14a.2 What is the direct labour rate variance for the company in 20X3?

○ $400 (A)
○ $2,500 (F)
○ $2,500 (A)
○ $3,200 (A)   **(2 marks)**

14a.3 What is the direct labour efficiency variance for the company in 20X3?

○ $400 (A)
○ $2,100 (F)
○ $2,800 (A)
○ $2,800 (F)   **(2 marks)**

14a.4 Extracts from a company's records from last period are as follows.

	Budget	Actual
Production	1,925 units	2,070 units
Variable production overhead cost	$11,550	$14,904
Labour hours worked	5,775	8,280

What are the variable production overhead variances for last period?

	Expenditure	Efficiency	
O	$1,656 (F)	$2,070 (A)	
O	$1,656 (F)	$3,726 (A)	
O	$1,656 (F)	$4,140 (A)	
O	$3,354 (A)	$4,140 (A)	**(2 marks)**

14a.5 A company has budgeted to make and sell 4,200 units of product X during the period.

The standard fixed overhead cost per unit is $4.

During the period covered by the budget, the actual results were as follows.

Production and sales	5,000 units
Fixed overhead incurred	$17,500

What are the fixed overhead variances for the period?

	Fixed overhead expenditure variance	Fixed overhead volume variance
O	$700 (F)	$3,200 (F)
O	$700 (F)	$3,200 (A)
O	$700 (A)	$3,200 (F)
O	$700 (A)	$3,200 (A)
		(2 marks)

14a.6 A company manufactures a single product, and relevant data for December is as follows.

	Budget/standard	Actual
Production units	1,800	1,900
Labour hours	9,000	9,400
Fixed production overhead	$36,000	$39,480

What are the fixed production overhead capacity and efficiency variances for December?

	Capacity	Efficiency	
O	$1,600 (F)	$400 (F)	
O	$1,600 (A)	$400 (A)	
O	$1,600 (A)	$400 (F)	
O	$1,600 (F)	$400 (A)	**(2 marks)**

14a.7 Which of the following would help to explain a favourable direct labour efficiency variance?

(i)	Employees were of a lower skill level than specified in the standard
(ii)	Better quality material was easier to process
(iii)	Suggestions for improved working methods were implemented during the period

O	(i), (ii) and (iii)	
O	(i) and (ii) only	
O	(ii) and (iii) only	
O	(i) and (iii) only	**(2 marks)**

14a.8 Which of the following statements is correct?

    O   An adverse direct material cost variance will always be a combination of an adverse material price variance and an adverse material usage variance

    O   An adverse direct material cost variance will always be a combination of an adverse material price variance and a favourable material usage variance

    O   An adverse direct material cost variance can be a combination of a favourable material price variance and a favourable material usage variance

    O   An adverse direct material cost variance can be a combination of a favourable material price variance and an adverse material usage variance   **(2 marks)**

The following information relates to Questions 14a.9 and 14a.10.

A company has a budgeted material cost of $125,000 for the production of 25,000 units per month. Each unit is budgeted to use 2 kg of material. The standard cost of material is $2.50 per kg.

Actual materials in the month cost $136,000 for 27,000 units and 53,000 kg were purchased and used.

14a.9 What was the adverse material price variance?

$ [   ]

(2 marks)

14a.10 What was the favourable material usage variance?

$ [   ]

(2 marks)

14a.11 The following information relates to labour costs for the past month:

Budget		
Labour rate	$10 per hour
Production time	15,000 hours
Time per unit	3 hours
Production units	5,000 units

Actual		
Wages paid	$176,000
Production	5,500 units
Total hours worked	14,000 hours

There was no idle time.

What were the labour rate and efficiency variances?

	Rate variance	Efficiency variance
O	$26,000 Adverse	$25,000 Favourable
O	$26,000 Adverse	$10,000 Favourable
O	$36,000 Adverse	$2,500 Favourable
O	$36,000 Adverse	$25,000 Favourable

(2 marks)

14a.12 A manufacturing company operates a standard absorption costing system. Last month 25,000 production hours were budgeted and the budgeted fixed production overhead cost was $125,000. Last month the actual hours worked were 24,000 and the standard hours for actual production were 27,000.

What was the fixed production overhead capacity variance for last month?

- ⊘ $5,000 Adverse
- ○ $5,000 Favourable
- ○ $10,000 Adverse
- ○ $10,000 Favourable

(handwritten notes:) f O/H capacity.
24000 should 125 000
24 000 did (125, 000)
(5,000) A

(2 marks)

The following information relates to questions 14a.13 to 14a.15.

Number of units produced	2,200	2,000
	Budget	*Actual*
	$	$
Direct materials	110,000	110,000
Direct labour	286,000	280,000
Variable overhead	132,000	120,000

The actual number of units produced was 2,000.

14a.13 What was the total direct materials variance?

- ○ Nil
- ○ $10,000 Adverse
- ○ $10,000 Favourable
- ○ $11,000 Adverse

(2 marks)

14a.14 What was the total direct labour variance?

- ○ $6,000 Favourable
- ○ $20,000 Adverse
- ○ $22,000 Favourable
- ○ Nil

(2 marks)

14a.15 What was the total direct variable overheads variance?

- ○ Nil
- ○ $12,000 Favourable
- ○ $12,000 Adverse
- ○ $11,000 Adverse

(2 marks)

14a.16 Which of the following statements are true?

(i) A favourable fixed overhead volume capacity variance occurs when actual hours of work are greater than budgeted hours of work

(ii) A labour force that produces 5,000 standard hours of work in 5,500 actual hours will give a favourable fixed overhead volume efficiency variance

- ⊘ (i) is true and (ii) is false
- ○ Both are true
- ○ Both are false
- ⊘ (i) is false and (ii) is true

(2 marks)

14a.17   Which of the following statements are true?

(i)   The fixed overhead volume capacity variance represents part of the over/under absorption of
         overheads

(ii)   A company works fewer hours than budgeted. This will result in an adverse fixed overhead
         volume capacity variance

○   (i) is true and (ii) is false
○   Both are true
○   Both are false
○   (i) is false and (ii) is true   **(2 marks)**

14a.18   The costs below relate to the month of June.

	Fixed budget 2,200 units	Flexed budget 2,000 units	Actual 2,000 units
Total direct materials	$165,000	$150,000	$140,000

What was the total direct material variance?

○ $10,000 Adverse
○ $10,000 Favourable
○ $25,000 Adverse
○ $25,000 Favourable   **(2 marks)**

14a.19   The graph below shows the standard fixed overhead cost per unit, the total budgeted fixed overhead
         cost and the actual fixed overhead cost for the month of December. The actual number of units
         produced in June was 2,500 units.

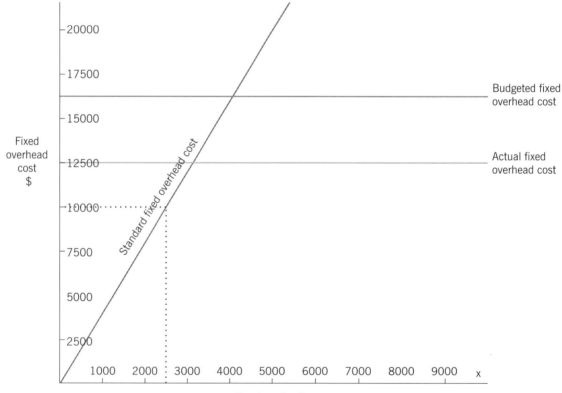

What is the total fixed overhead variance?

○ $2,500 Adverse
○ $3,750 Favourable
○ $5,000 Adverse
○ $6,250 Favourable   **(2 marks)**

(Total = 38 marks)

14b   Sales variances and operating statements   70 mins

14b.1 A company currently uses a standard absorption costing system. The fixed overhead variances extracted from the operating statement for November are:

	$
Fixed production overhead expenditure variance	5,800 adverse
Fixed production overhead capacity variance	4,200 favourable
Fixed production overhead efficiency variance	1,400 adverse

PQ Co is considering using standard marginal costing as the basis for variance reporting in future. What variance for fixed production overhead would be shown in a marginal costing operating statement for November?

O   No variance would be shown for fixed production overhead
O   Expenditure variance: $5,800 adverse
O   Volume variance: $2,800 favourable
O   Total variance: $3,000 adverse   **(2 marks)**

14b.2 Which of the following situations is most likely to result in a favourable selling price variance?

O   The sales director decided to change from the planned policy of market skimming pricing to one of market penetration pricing.

O   Fewer customers than expected took advantage of the early payment discounts offered.

O   Competitors charged lower prices than expected, therefore selling prices had to be reduced in order to compete effectively.

O   Demand for the product was higher than expected and prices could be raised without adverse effects on sales volumes.   **(2 marks)**

The following information relates to questions 14b.3 to 14b.6.

A company manufactures a single product. An extract from a variance control report together with relevant standard cost data is shown below.

Standard selling price per unit	$70
Standard direct material cost (5 kg × $2 per kg)	$10 per unit
Budgeted total material cost of sales	$2,300 per month
Budgeted profit margin	$6,900 per month
Actual results for February	
Sales revenue	$15,200
Total direct material cost	$2,400
Direct material price variance	$800 adverse
Direct material usage variance	$400 favourable

There was no change in inventory levels during the month.

14b.3 What was the actual production in February?

|_____| units

      (2 marks)

14b.4 What was the actual usage of direct material during February?

|_____| kg

      (2 marks)

14b.5 What was the selling price variance for February?

○ $120 (F)
○ $900 (A)
○ $1,200 (A)
○ $1,200 (F)   (2 marks)

14b.6 What was the sales volume profit variance for February?

○ $900 (F)
○ $1,200 (F)
○ $900 (A)
○ $2,100 (A)   (2 marks)

14b.7 A company uses a standard absorption costing system. The following details have been extracted from its budget for April.

Fixed production overhead cost	$48,000
Production (units)	4,800

In April the fixed production overhead cost was under absorbed by $8,000 and the fixed production overhead expenditure variance was $2,000 adverse.

What was the actual number of units produced?

☐ units

(2 marks)

14b.8 A company purchased 6,850 kgs of material at a total cost of $21,920. The material price variance was $1,370 favourable. What was the standard price per kg?

$ ☐

(2 marks)

14b.9 The following data relates to one of a company's products.

	$ per unit	$ per unit
Selling price		27.00
Variable costs	12.00	
Fixed costs	9.00	
		21.00
Profit		6.00

Budgeted sales for control period 7 were 2,400 units, but actual sales were 2,550 units. The revenue earned from these sales was $67,320.

Profit reconciliation statements are drawn up using marginal costing principles. What sales variances would be included in such a statement for period 7?

	Price	Volume
○	$1,530 (A)	$900 (F)
○	$1,530 (A)	$2,250 (F)
○	$1,530 (A)	$2,250 (A)
○	$1,530 (F)	$2,250 (F)

(2 marks)

14b.10 A company uses variance analysis to control costs and revenues.

Information concerning sales is as follows:

Budgeted selling price $15 per unit
Budgeted sales units   10,000 units
Budgeted profit per unit $5 per unit

Actual sales revenue $151,500
Actual units sold   9,800 units

What is the sales volume profit variance?

O $500 Favourable
O $1,000 Favourable
O $1,000 Adverse
O $3,000 Adverse   **(2 marks)**

The following information relates to questions 14b.11 and 14b.12.

The standard direct material cost per unit for a product is calculated as follows:

10.5 litres at $2.50 per litre

Last month the actual price paid for 12,000 litres of material used was 4% above standard and the direct material usage variance was $1,815 favourable. No stocks of material are held.

14b.11 What was the adverse direct material price variance for last month?

O $1,000
O $1,200
O $1,212
O $1,260   **(2 marks)**

14b.12 What was the actual production last month (in units)?

O   1,074
O   1,119
O   1,212
O   1,258   **(2 marks)**

14b.13 Last month a company budgeted to sell 8,000 units at a price of $12.50 per unit. Actual sales last month were 9,000 units giving a total sales revenue of $117,000.

What was the sales price variance for last month?

O $4,000 Favourable
O $4,000 Adverse
O $4,500 Favourable
O $4,500 Adverse   **(2 marks)**

14b.14 A company uses a standard absorption costing system. Last month budgeted production was 8,000 units and the standard fixed production overhead cost was $15 per unit. Actual production last month was 8,500 units and the actual fixed production overhead cost was $17 per unit.

What was the total adverse fixed production overhead variance for last month?

$ [   ]

                                                                              (2 marks)

14b.15 A cost centre had an overhead absorption rate of $4.25 per machine hour, based on a budgeted activity level of 12,400 machine hours.

In the period covered by the budget, actual machine hours worked were 2% more than the budgeted hours and the actual overhead expenditure incurred in the cost centre was $56,389.

What was the total over or under absorption of overheads in the cost centre for the period?

- O $1,054 over absorbed
- O $2,635 under absorbed
- O $3,689 over absorbed
- O $3,689 under absorbed **(2 marks)**

14b.16 A company uses standard marginal costing. Last month the standard contribution on actual sales was $10,000 and the following variances arose:

	$
Total variable costs variance	2,000 Adverse
Sales price variance	500 Favourable
Sales volume contribution variance	1,000 Adverse

What was the actual contribution for last month?

$ [   ]

(2 marks)

14b.17 AD Co manufactures and sells a single product, E, and uses a standard absorption costing system. Standard cost and selling price details for product E are as follows.

	$ per unit
Variable cost	8
Fixed cost	2
	10
Standard profit	5
Standard selling price	15

The sales volume variance reported for last period was $9,000 adverse.

AD Co is considering using standard marginal costing as the basis for variance reporting in future. What would be the correct sales volume variance to be shown in a marginal costing operating statement for last period?

- O $6,428 (A)
- O $6,428 (F)
- O $12,600 (F)
- O $12,600 (A) **(2 marks)**

14b.18 When comparing the profits reported under absorption costing and marginal costing during a period when the level of inventory increased, which of the following is true?

- O Absorption costing profits will be higher and closing inventory valuations lower than those under marginal costing.

- O Absorption costing profits will be higher and closing inventory valuations higher than those under marginal costing.

- O Marginal costing profits will be higher and closing inventory valuations lower than those under absorption costing.

- O Marginal costing profits will be higher and closing inventory valuations higher than those under absorption costing. **(2 marks)**

14b.19 PH Co produces a single product and currently uses absorption costing for its internal management accounting reports. The fixed production overhead absorption rate is $34 per unit. Opening inventories for the year were 100 units and closing inventories were 180 units. The company's management accountant is considering a switch to marginal costing as the inventory valuation basis.

If marginal costing were used, the marginal costing profit for the year, compared with the profit calculated by absorption costing, would be which of the following?

○ $2,720 lower
○ $2,720 higher
○ $3,400 lower
○ $3,400 higher   **(2 marks)**

14b.20 The budgeted contribution for HMF Co for June was $290,000. The following variances occurred during the month.

	$	
Fixed overhead expenditure variance	6,475	Favourable
Total direct labour variance	11,323	Favourable
Total variable overhead variance	21,665	Adverse
Selling price variance	21,875	Favourable
Fixed overhead volume variance	12,500	Adverse
Sales volume variance	36,250	Adverse
Total direct materials variance	6,335	Adverse

What was the actual contribution for the month?

○ $252,923
○ $258,948
○ $321,052
○ $327,077   **(2 marks)**

14b.21 **The following question is taken from the December 2011 exam.**

A company calculates the following under a standard absorption costing system.

(i)   The sales volume margin variance
(ii)   The total fixed overhead variance
(iii) The total variable overhead variance

If a company changed to a standard marginal costing system, which variances could change in value?

○   (i) only
○   (ii) only
○   (i) and (ii) only
○   (i), (ii) and (iii)   **(2 marks)**

14b.22 **The following question is taken from the December 2012 exam.**

A company uses a standard absorption costing system. The following figures are available for the last accounting period in which actual profit was $108,000.

	$
Sales volume profit variance	6,000 adverse
Sales price variance	5,000 favourable
Total variable cost variance	7,000 adverse
Fixed cost expenditure variance	3,000 favourable
Fixed cost volume variance	2,000 adverse

What was the standard profit for actual sales in the last accounting period?

○ $101,000
○ $107,000
○ $109,000
○ $115,000   **(2 marks)**

14b.23 **The following question is taken from the July to December 2013 exam period.**

A company uses a standard absorption costing system. Last month the actual profit was $500,000. The only variances recorded for the month were as follows:

	$'000
Sales volume profit variance	10 adverse
Fixed production overhead capacity variance	30 favourable
Fixed production overhead efficiency variance	40 adverse
Fixed production overhead volume variance	10 adverse
Fixed production overhead expenditure variance	50 favourable
Direct labour efficiency variance	15 adverse

What was the budgeted profit for last month?

- O $485,000
- O $495,000
- O $505,000
- O $515,000

(2 marks)

14b.24 **The following question is taken from the January to June 2014 exam period.**

A company uses a standard absorption costing system. Actual profit last period was $25,000, which was $5,000 less than budgeted profit. The standard profit on actual sales for the period was $15,000. Only three variances occurred in the period: a sales volume profit variance, a sales price variance and a direct material price variance.

Which of the following is a valid combination of the three variances?

	Sales volume profit variance	Sales price variance	Direct material price variance
O	$15,000 A	$2,000 F	$8,000 F
O	$5,000 A	$2,000 A	$2,000 F
O	$15,000 A	$2,000 A	$8,000 A
O	$5,000 A	$5,000 F	$5,000 A

(2 marks)

14b.25 **The following question is taken from the July to December 2014 exam period.**

A company's actual profit for a period was $27,000. The only variances for the period were:

	$
Sales price	5,000 adverse
Fixed overhead volume	3,000 favourable.
Fixed overhead capacity	4,000 favourable
Fixed overhead efficiency	1,000 adverse

What was the budgeted profit for the period?

- O $25,000
- O $26,000
- O $28,000
- O $29,000

(2 marks)

14b.26 **The following question is taken from the January to June 2015 exam period.**

A company uses standard marginal costing. Its budgeted contribution for the last month was $20,000. The actual contribution for the month was $15,000, and the following variances have been calculated:

Sales volume contribution variance $5,000 adverse
Sales price variance $9,000 favourable
Fixed overhead expenditure variance $3,000 favourable

What was the total variable cost variance?

O $9,000 adverse
O $9,000 favourable
O $12,000 adverse
O $12,000 favourable   **(2 marks)**

14b.27 **The following question is taken from the January to June 2016 exam period.**

The following variances occurred last period.

Sales volume contribution $20,000 favourable
Sales price $5,000 adverse
Total variable cost $18,000 favourable
Fixed cost expenditure $12,000 adverse

If the flexed budget contribution was $200,000, what was the actual contribution?

O $213,000
O $218,000
O $221,000
O $233,000   **(2 marks)**

14b.28 **The following question is taken from the January to June 2017 exam period.**

A firm uses standard marginal costing. Last period the following results were recorded:

Actual sales units   5,000
Standard contribution per unit $60
Sales price variance $5,000 Adverse
Sales volume contribution variance $8,000 Favourable
No other variances arose last period.

What was the actual contribution for the period?

O $295,000
O $305,000
O $303,000
O $297,000   **(2 marks)**

14b.29 **The following question is taken from the July to December 2017 exam period.**

A company uses standard marginal costing to monitor performance. The budgeted profit and budgeted fixed overhead for a month were $25,000 and $12,000 respectively. In the month, the following variances occurred:

	$
Sales volume contribution	1,000 Adverse
Sales price	2,000 Favourable
Total variable costs	4,000 Adverse
Fixed production overhead expenditure	500 Adverse

What was the actual profit for the month?

○ $9,500
○ $21,500
○ $33,500
○ $40,000

(2 marks)

(Total = 58 marks)

Important note

You have now reached the end of the multiple choice questions for Standard costing (Chapters 13 to 14b). Make sure that you practise the multi-task questions on Standard costing in Section 24. The real exam will contain three 10-mark multi-task questions on Budgeting, Standard costing and Performance measurement.

Do you know? – Performance measurement

Check that you can fill in the blanks in the statements below before you attempt any questions. If in doubt, you should go back to your BPP Interactive Text and revise first.

- A .... is a formal statement of the business' aim. It can play an important point in the .... process. Cascading downwards from this is a hierarchy of goals and .... These may be split into operational, tactical and strategic. Cascading downwards from this are the critical success factors. A critical success factor is a performance requirement that is fundamental to competitive success. .... are quantifiable measurements which reflect the critical success factors.

- The 3 Es which are generally desirable features of organisational performance are ...., ..., and ....

- The formula for return on capital employed = (............./..................) × 100%.

  Capital employed = ... + ... + ... – ....

- The ....ratio is the standard test of liquidity and is the ratio of .... to ....

- Performance of non-profit-making organisations can be measured:

  ....
  ....
  ....

- The balanced scorecard measures performance in four perspectives: ...., ..., ... and ....

- .... is a planned and positive approach to reducing expenditure. Measures should be planned programmes rather than crash programmes to cut spending levels.

- Work study is a means of raising the .... of an operating unit by the .... of work. There are two main parts to work study: .... and ....

- Value analysis considers four aspects of value: .... value, ... value, ... value and .... value.

- *Possible pitfalls*

  - Write down a list of mistakes you know you should avoid.

Did you know? – Performance measurement

Could you fill in the blanks? The answers are in bold. Use this page for revision purposes as you approach the exam.

- A **mission statement** is a formal statement of the business' aim. It can play an important point in the **planning** process. Cascading downwards from this is a hierarchy of goals and **objectives**. These may be split into operational, tactical and strategic. Cascading downwards from this are the critical success factors. A critical success factor is a performance requirement that is fundamental to competitive success. **Key performance indicators** are quantifiable measurements which reflect the critical success factors.

- The 3 Es which are generally desirable features of organisational performance are **economy, efficiency** and **effectiveness**.

- The formula for return on capital employed = (**profit/capital employed**) × 100%.

   Capital employed = **non-current assets** + **investments** + **current assets** – **current liabilities**

- The **current** ratio is the standard test of liquidity and is the ratio **current assets** to **current liabilities**.

   Performance of non-profit-making organisations can be measured:

   In terms of inputs and outputs

   By judgement

   By comparison

- The balanced scorecard measures performance in four perspectives: **customer satisfaction, financial success, process efficiency** and **growth**.

- **Cost reduction** is a planned and positive approach to reducing expenditure. Measures should be planned programmes rather than crash programmes to cut spending levels.

- Work study is a means of raising the **productivity** of an operating unit by the **reorganisation** of work. There are two main parts to work study: **method study** and **work measurement**.

- Value analysis considers four aspects of value: **cost** value, **exchange** value, **use value** and **esteem** value.

- *Possible pitfalls*
   - Not realising that mission statements feed into objectives which feed into critical success factors which are quantified by key performance indicators.
   - Not knowing the performance measures which are appropriate for service industries.
   - Not knowing the meaning of the efficiency, capacity and activity ratios.
   - Not knowing the formulae for measuring profitability, liquidity and gearing.

15 Target setting   38 mins

15.1 All of the following, except one, are sound principles for devising objectives in order to enact the corporate mission. Which is the exception?

- ○ They should be observable or measurable
- ○ They should be easily achievable
- ○ They should relate to a specified time period
- ○ They should be specific   **(2 marks)**

15.2 In order for a business's strength to have a real benefit, it has to be linked to critical success factors. What are critical success factors?

- ○ Factors contributing to reduced costs
- ○ Factors necessary to match strengths to opportunities
- ○ Factors necessary to build on strengths
- ○ Factors fundamental to strategic success   **(2 marks)**

15.3 In general terms, which of the following elements should organisations include in their mission statements?

- (i)   Policies and standards of behaviour
- (ii)   Values – a description of the culture, assumptions and beliefs regarded as important to those managing the business
- (iii) Profitability
- (iv)   Strategy – the commercial logic for the business, defining the nature of the business

- ○ (i) and (ii) only
- ○ (ii) and (iv) only
- ○ (i), (ii) and (iv) only
- ○ (iii) and (iv) only   **(2 marks)**

15.4 Which of the following short-term objectives may involve the sacrifice of longer-term objectives?

- (i)   Reducing training costs
- (ii)   Increasing quality control
- (iii) Increasing capital expenditure projects

- ○ (i) only
- ○ (i), (ii) and (iii)
- ○ (ii) and (iii) only
- ○ (i) and (ii) only   **(2 marks)**

15.5 What is short-termism?

- ○ It is when non-financial performance indicators are used for measurement
- ○ It is when organisations sacrifice short term objectives
- ○ It is when there is a bias towards short term rather than long term performance
- ○ It is when managers' performance is measured on long term results   **(2 marks)**

15.6 Which of the performance measures in the drop down list below is most likely to be recorded because of government regulations?

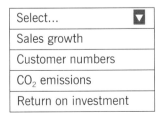

Select... ▼
Sales growth
Customer numbers
CO_2 emissions
Return on investment

(2 marks)

15.7 Market conditions and economic conditions can impact on performance measurement. Which of the following statements are true?

(i)   The entry of a new competitor in the market will cause a business to examine sales performance measures more closely

(ii)   General economic conditions can raise or lower overall demand and supply

○   (i) and (ii) are true
○   (i) and (ii) are false
○   (i) is true and (ii) is false
○   (i) is false and (ii) is true   **(2 marks)**

15.8 Which of the following BEST explains the relationship between mission statements and performance measurement.

○   Mission statements are a marketing tool and have no part to play in performance measurement

○   To be of value, a performance measure must have an obvious link to the mission statement

○   Performance measurement involves comparing actual performance against a target and the mission statement represents the organisation's overall target

○   Mission statements include detailed performance standards that actual performance can be measured against   **(2 marks)**

15.9 Which of the following describes the role of tactical objectives?

○   'Middle tier' objectives to facilitate the planning and control of individual functions within the organisation

○   Day-to-day performance targets related to the organisation's operations

○   A clear vision of the organisation's reason for existing

○   Long-term objectives for the organisation as a whole   **(2 marks)**

15.10 A company sells new, high quality motor vehicles in many countries around the world. Half way through the company's current financial year, the global economy unexpectedly goes in to recession.

What impact would the unexpected recession have on performance measurement relating to sales and revenue?

○   The impact of a recession on the sales of new, high quality motor vehicles cannot be predicted

○   Sales and revenue are likely to decrease in the second half of the year and performance should be measured in that context

○   No impact as a recession is unlikely to impact the sales and revenue of motor vehicles

○   Sales and revenue are likely to increase in the second half of the year and performance should be measured in that context   **(2 marks)**

15.11 Which of the following describes the role of strategic objectives?

○   'Middle tier' objectives to facilitate the planning and control of individual functions within the organisation

○   Day-to-day performance targets related to the organisation's operations

○   A clear vision of the organisation's reason for existing

○   Long-term objectives for the organisation as a whole   **(2 marks)**

15.12 The following statements relate to benchmarking.

Which TWO statements are true?

☐ A danger of benchmarking is that inappropriate comparisons lead to incorrect conclusions

☐ Benchmarking must involve competitors to be effective

☐ The ultimate aim of benchmarking is to improve performance

☐ Benchmarking is essentially a cost cutting exercise

(2 marks)

15.13 A financial services company benchmarks the performance of its IT department with that of a leading IT outsource company.

What type of benchmarking is the company using?

○ Strategic
○ Competitive
○ Functional
○ Internal

(2 marks)

15.14 Company A manufactures mobile phones. Staff employed within the Research & Development function at Company A have purchased a mobile phone manufactured by Company B for the purpose of reverse engineering.

What type of benchmarking is Company A using?

○ Strategic
○ Competitive
○ Functional
○ Internal

(2 marks)

15.15 Which of the following are suitable measures of performance at the strategic level?

(i)   Machine idle time
(ii)   Employee sick days
(iii)   Return on capital employed

○ (i) and (ii)
○ (ii) only
○ (ii) and (iii)
○ (iii) only

(2 marks)

15.16 What is 'short-termism'?

○ A legitimate focus on short-term results
○ A belief that senior management have a duty to maximise profit
○ Prioritising short-term results above the organisation's long-term prospects
○ A management philosophy linked to TQM

(2 marks)

(Total = 32 marks)

16 Financial performance measurement   46 mins

16.1 Which of the following performance indicators is a financial performance measure?

○ Quality rating
○ Number of customer complaints
○ Cash flow
○ System (machine) down time

(2 marks)

16.2 The following summarised statement of financial position is available for L Co.

	$'000	$'000
Non-current assets		31,250
Current assets		
Inventory	35,000	
Receivables	40,000	
Cash	1,250	
		107,500
EQUITY AND LIABILITIES		
Capital and reserves		47,500
Current liabilities (payables only)		60,000
		107,500

What is the value of the acid test ratio?

- ○ 0.6875
- ○ 0.7093
- ○ 1.2708
- ○ 2.000   **(2 marks)**

16.3 **The following question is taken from the December 2011 exam.**

A company has current assets of $1.8m, including inventory of $0.5m, and current liabilities of $1.0m.

What would be the effect on the value of the current and acid test ratios if the company bought more raw material inventory on three months' credit?

	Current ratio	*Acid test*
○	Increase	Increase
○	Decrease	Increase
○	Increase	Decrease
○	Decrease	Decrease

(2 marks)

16.4 **The following question is taken from the June 2012 exam.**

An investment centre earns a return on investment of 18% and a residual income of $300,000. The cost of capital is 15%. A new project offers a return on capital employed of 17%.

If the new project were adopted, what would happen to the investment centre's return on investment and residual income?

	Return on investment	*Residual income*
○	Increase	Decrease
○	Increase	Increase
○	Decrease	Decrease
○	Decrease	Increase

(2 marks)

16.5   An extract from a company's financial results for 20X6 are shown below.

| | 20X6 |
	$'000
Sales	5,400
Less cost of sales:	1,950
	3,450
Less expenses:	
Wages	1,700
Repairs and maintenance	240
All other expenses	490
Net profit	1,020

What is the gross profit percentage for 20X6, to one decimal place?

[   ] %

(2 marks)

16.6   A company's financial results for 20X4 are shown below.

| | 20X4 |
	$'000
Sales	7,200
Less cost of sales:	2,900
Gross profit	4,300
Less expenses:	
Wages	1,600
Repairs and maintenance	360
Directors' salaries	150
Directors' bonuses	55
Other costs (including depreciation)	400
Net profit	1,735

What is the net profit percentage for 20X4, to one decimal place?

[   ] %

(2 marks)

16.7   What is the main focus of the current ratio?

○   Profitability
○   Efficiency
○   Liquidity
○   Productivity

(2 marks)

16.8   The following information has been extracted from the statement of financial position of X Company.

EQUITY AND LIABILITIES	
Capital and reserves	585,000
Long term liabilities (long-term loan)	670,000
Current liabilities (payables only)	84,000
	1,339,000

What is the capital gearing ratio, expressed as a percentage to one decimal place? (Use the formula

$$\frac{D}{D+E}.)$$

[   ] %

(2 marks)

16.9 What is the main focus of the acid test ratio?

○ Profitability
○ Efficiency
○ Liquidity
○ Productivity **(2 marks)**

16.10 The following information is available for company X.

	20X7	20X8
	$	$
Profit	7,500	9,000
Sales	500,000	450,000
Capital employed	37,500	60,000

Calculate the change in ROI from 20X7 to 20X8?

○ Decrease from 20% to 15%
○ Increase from 1.5% to 2%
○ Increase from 7.5% to 13.3%
○ Decrease from 100% to 90% **(2 marks)**

16.11 Using the figures in the question above, what is the asset turnover for 20X8, to one decimal place?

[   ] times

(2 marks)

16.12 Division A of Aigburth Co is considering a project which will increase annual net profit after tax by $30,000 but will require average inventory levels to increase by $200,000. The current target rate of return on investments is 13% and the imputed interest cost of capital is 12%.

Based on the ROI and/or RI criteria would the project be accepted?

○ ROI – yes, RI – no
○ ROI – yes RI – yes
○ ROI – no, RI – yes
○ ROI – no, RI – no **(2 marks)**

16.13 Which of the following statements are valid criticisms of return on investment (ROI) as a performance measure?

(i) It is misleading if used to compare departments with different levels of risk
(ii) It is misleading if used to compare departments with assets of different ages
(iii) Its use may discourage investment in new or replacement assets
(iv) The figures needed are not easily available

○ (ii) and (iii) only
○ (ii) and (iv) only
○ (i) and (iii) only
○ (i), (ii) and (iii) **(2 marks)**

16.14 A means of raising the production efficiency of an operating unit by the reorganisation of work is known as which of the following?

○ Work measurement
○ Work study
○ Method study
○ Method measurement **(2 marks)**

16.15 Value analysis can achieve which TWO of the following?

☐ Eliminate costs

☑ Reduce costs

☐ Increase quantity sold

☐ Increase sales price

(2 marks)

16.16 Value analysis considers four aspects of value. What are they?

○ Cost value, exchange value, use value and esteem value
○ Cost value, trade value, use value and esteem value
○ Cost value, exchange value, use value and retail value
○ Competitive value, exchange value, use value and esteem value

(2 marks)

16.17 **The following question is taken from the July to December 2013 exam period.**

A division currently earns a return on investment (ROI) of 20%. It is considering investing in a project which has a residual income (RI) of $1,000 at an imputed interest charge of 20%.

What is the effect on the division's ROI if the project is undertaken?

○ Increase
○ Decrease
○ Remain the same
○ No possible to tell from this information

(2 marks)

16.18 **The following question is taken from the July to December 2016 exam period.**

A retailer has two divisions, North and South. Both sell similar products and all prices are set centrally. All shop premises are rented. Shop rental costs in the South division are lower than in the North division due to a government subsidy given to landlords.

Which of the following measures would NOT provide a fair comparison of the performance of the management of the two divisions?

○ Gross profit
○ Return on capital employed
○ Turnover per square metre of shop floor space
○ Asset turnover

(2 marks)

16.19 **The following question is taken from the September to June 2018 exam period.**

A company borrows $10,000 repayable in five years' time and immediately uses the loan to repay its overdraft.

What will be the effect on the company's capital gearing and current ratios?

Capital gearing	Current ratio
Increase	Increase
Increase	Decrease
Decrease	Increase
Decrease	Decrease

(2 marks)

(Total = 38 marks)

17   Assessing non-financial performance   29 mins

17.1   A government body uses measures based upon the 'three Es' to the measure value for money generated by a publicly funded hospital. It considers the most important performance measure to be 'cost per successfully treated patient'.

Which of the three E's best describes the above measure?

○   Economy
○   Effectiveness
○   Efficiency
○   Externality   **(2 marks)**

17.2   Which of the following statements are true?

(i)   Non-financial performance indicators are less likely to be manipulated than financial ones
(ii)   Non-financial performance indicators offer a means of counteracting short-termism

○   (i) and (ii) are true
○   (i) and (ii) are false
○   (i) is true and (ii) is false
○   (i) is false and (ii) is true   **(2 marks)**

17.3   Which of the following best describes the advantage of a balanced scorecard approach?

○   The balanced scorecard approach enables organisations that are struggling financially to emphasise other areas

○   The balanced scorecard approach enables organisations to consider all areas of performance relevant to achieving their strategic goals

○   The balanced scorecard approach enables organisations to more easily benchmark their performance against others

○   The balanced scorecard approach enables organisations to demonstrate their ethical credentials   **(2 marks)**

17.4   Why would an organisation use non-financial performance measures?

○   To appear socially responsible
○   To prevent a narrow focus on short-term financial performance
○   To prevent scrutiny of financial performance
○   To encourage short termism   **(2 marks)**

17.5   The balanced scorecard measures performance from four perspectives. What are they?

○   Customer satisfaction, growth, financial stability and process efficiency
○   Customer retention, growth, financial stability and process efficiency
○   Customer satisfaction, growth, financial success and process effectiveness
○   Customer satisfaction, growth, financial success and process efficiency   **(2 marks)**

17.6   In not for profit businesses and state-run entities, a value-for-money audit can be used to measure performance. It covers three key areas: economy, efficiency and effectiveness. Which of the following could be used to describe effectiveness in this context?

○   Avoiding waste of inputs
○   Achieving agreed targets
○   Achieving a given level of profit
○   Obtaining suitable quality inputs at the lowest price   **(2 marks)**

17.7 Balance Co is looking to introduce a balanced scorecard and is finalising the measures to use for the 'innovation and learning' perspective. Which one of the following is not relevant for this perspective?

    ○   Number of ideas from staff

    ○   Percentage of sales from new products

    ○   Number of new products introduced

    ○   Level of refunds given   **(2 marks)**

17.8 Qual Co is keen to increase the use they make of non-financial performance measures in their overall performance measurement activities. In particular, they are keen to improve customer retention and so want to focus on the quality of service they provide to their customers. Which of the following measures would be most appropriate as a measure of service quality?

    (i)   Number of customer complaints

    (ii)   Number of repeat orders as a proportion of total orders

    (iii)   Sales volume growth

    ○   (i) and (ii)

    ○   (i), (ii) and (iii)

    ○   (i) and (iii)

    ○   (ii) and (iii)   **(2 marks)**

17.9 Which of the following are non-financial objectives?

    (i)   Growth of sales

    (ii)   Diversification

    (iii)   Contented workforce

    (iv)   Increase earnings per share

    ○   (ii) and (iii)

    ○   (i), (ii) and (iii)

    ○   (ii), (iii) and (iv)

    ○   (i), (iii) and (iv)   **(2 marks)**

17.10 Which TWO of the following performance measures would be helpful for a service industry company?

    ☐   Net profit margins

    ☐   Standard costs and variance analysis

    ☐   Employee absentee rates

    ☐   Number of defective units   **(2 marks)**

17.11 Which of the following would be suitable for measuring resource utilisation?

    (i)   Efficiency

    (ii)   Productivity

    (iii)   Relative market share

    ○   (i) and (ii) only

    ○   (ii) and (iii) only

    ○   (i) and (iii) only

    ○   (i), (ii) and (iii)   **(2 marks)**

17.12 Which of the following would be suitable for measuring resource utilisation in a parcel delivery company?

    ○   Number of customer complaints

    ○   Cost per consignment

    ○   Depot profit league tables

    ○   Client evaluation interview   **(2 marks)**

(Total = 24 marks)

Important note

You have now reached the end of the multiple choice questions for Performance measurement (Chapters 15 to 17). Make sure that you practise the multi-task questions on Performance measurement in Section 25. The real exam will contain three 10-mark multi-task questions on Budgeting, Standard costing and Performance measurement.

18   Mixed Bank 1   48 mins

18.1 The following data relate to Product D.

Material cost per unit	$20.00
Labour cost per unit	$69.40
Production overhead cost per machine hour	$12.58
Machine hours per unit	14
General overhead absorption rate	8% of total production cost

What is the total cost per unit of Product D, to the nearest $0.01?

$ [   ]

(2 marks)

18.2 A product is made in two consecutive processes. Data for the latest period are as follows:

	Process 1	Process 2
Input (kg)	47,000	42,000
Normal loss (% of input)	8	5
Output (kg)	42,000	38,915

No work in progress is held at any time in either process.

Was there an abnormal loss or abnormal gain arising in each process during the period?

	Process 1	Process 2
O	Abnormal loss	Abnormal loss
O	Abnormal loss	Abnormal gain
O	Abnormal gain	Abnormal loss
O	Abnormal gain	Abnormal gain

(2 marks)

18.3 The following information is available for a company in the latest period.

	Original budget	Flexed budget	Actual results
Sales and production (units)	11,200	9,500	9,500
	$'000	$'000	$'000
Sales revenue	224.0	190.0	209.0
Direct material	56.0	47.5	57.0
Direct labour	66.0	57.5	56.1
Overhead	27.4	24.0	28.0
Profit	74.6	61.0	67.9

Which of the following statements is correct?

O   Budgeted production volumes were achieved during the period.
O   Direct labour is a variable cost.
O   The actual selling price per unit exceeded the standard selling price per unit.
O   Direct material cost savings were achieved against the budget cost allowance.   **(2 marks)**

18.4 Variable costs are conventionally deemed to:

O   Be constant per unit of output
O   Vary per unit of output as production volume changes
O   Be constant in total when production volume changes
O   Vary, in total, from period to period when production is constant   **(2 marks)**

18.5 Which of the following criticisms of standard costing apply in all circumstances?

(i) Standard costing can only be used where all operations are repetitive and output is homogeneous.

(ii) Standard costing systems cannot be used in environments which are prone to change. They assume stable conditions.

(iii) Standard costing systems assume that performance to standard is acceptable. They do not encourage continuous improvement.

- O Criticism (i)
- O Criticism (ii)
- O Criticism (iii)
- O None of them   **(2 marks)**

18.6 Which of the following relates to capital expenditure?

- O Cost of acquiring or enhancing non-current assets
- O Expenditure on the manufacture of goods or the provision of services
- O Recorded as an asset in the statement of profit or loss
- O Recorded as a liability in the statement of financial position   **(2 marks)**

18.7 Overheads in a factory are apportioned to four production cost centres (A, B, C and D). Direct labour hours are used to absorb overheads in A and B and machine hours are used in C and D. The following information is available:

	Production cost centre			
	A	B	C	D
Overhead expenditure ($)	18,757	29,025	46,340	42,293
Direct labour hours	3,080	6,750	3,760	2,420
Machine hours	580	1,310	3,380	2,640

Which cost centre has the highest hourly overhead absorption rate?

- O Production Cost Centre A
- O Production Cost Centre B
- O Production Cost Centre C
- O Production Cost Centre D   **(2 marks)**

18.8 A company sold 56,000 units of its single product in a period for a total revenue of $700,000. Finished inventory increased by 4,000 units in the period. Costs in the period were:

Variable production	$3.60 per unit
Fixed production	$258,000 (absorbed on the actual number of units produced)
Fixed non-production	$144,000

Using absorption costing, what was the profit for the period?

- O $82,000
- O $96,400
- O $113,600
- O $123,200   **(2 marks)**

18.9 A company with a single product sells more units than it manufactures in a period.

Which of the following correctly describes the use of marginal costing in comparison with absorption costing in the above situation?

- O Both profit and inventory values will be higher
- O Both profit and inventory values will be lower
- O Profit will be higher; inventory values will be lower
- O Profit will be lower; inventory values will be higher   **(2 marks)**

18.10 What is a by-product?

○ A product produced at the same time as other products which has no value

○ A product produced at the same time as other products which requires further processing to put it in a saleable state

○ A product produced at the same time as other products which has a relatively low volume compared with the other products

○ A product produced at the same time as other products which has a relatively low value compared with the other products **(2 marks)**

18.11 CA Co manufactures a single product and has drawn up the following flexed budget for the year.

	60%	70%	80%
	$	$	$
Direct materials	120,000	140,000	160,000
Direct labour	90,000	105,000	120,000
Production overhead	54,000	58,000	62,000
Other overhead	40,000	40,000	40,000
Total cost	304,000	343,000	382,000

What would be the total cost in a budget that is flexed at the 77% level of activity?

○ $330,300
○ $370,300
○ $373,300
○ $377,300 **(2 marks)**

18.12 An investment project has net present values as follows:

At a discount rate of 10% $2,700 positive
At a discount rate of 15% $3,740 negative

Using the above figures, what is the BEST approximation of the internal rate of return of the investment project?

○ 2.1%
○ 7.9%
○ 12.1%
○ 13.0% **(2 marks)**

18.13 A company has decided to lease a machine. Six annual payments of $8,000 will be made with the first payment on receipt of the machine. Below is an extract from an annuity table:

Year	Annuity factor
	10%
1	0.909
2	1.736
3	2.487
4	3.170
5	3.791
6	4.355

What is the present value of the lease payments at an interest rate of 10%?

○ $30,328
○ $34,840
○ $38,328
○ $48,000 **(2 marks)**

18.14 Which of the following would be best described as a short term tactical plan?

    O   Reviewing cost variances and investigate as appropriate
    O   Comparing actual market share to budget
    O   Lowering the selling price by 15%
    O   Monitoring actual sales to budget   **(2 marks)**

18.15 A company made 17,500 units at a total cost of $16 each. Three quarters of the costs were variable and one quarter fixed. 15,000 units were sold at $25 each. There were no opening inventories.

By how much will the profit calculated using absorption costing principles differ from the profit if marginal costing principles had been used?

    O   The absorption costing profit would be $10,000 less
    O   The absorption costing profit would be $10,000 greater
    O   The absorption costing profit would be $30,000 greater
    O   The absorption costing profit would be $40,000 greater   **(2 marks)**

18.16 A company uses the Economic Order Quantity (EOQ) model to establish reorder quantities. The following information relates to the forthcoming period:

Order costs   = $25 per order

Holding costs   = 10% of purchase price = $4/unit

Annual demand   = 20,000 units

Purchase price   = $40 per unit

EOQ   = 500 units

No safety inventory are held.

What are the total annual costs of inventory (ie the total purchase cost plus total order cost plus total holding costs)?

    O $22,000
    O $33,500
    O $802,000
    O $803,000   **(2 marks)**

18.17 If $\Sigma X = 100$, $\Sigma Y = 400$, $\Sigma X^2 = 2,040$, $\Sigma Y^2 = 32,278$, $\Sigma XY = 8,104$ and $n = 5$ which of the following values for a and b are correct in the formula $Y = a + bX$?

	a	b
O	28	–2.6
O	28	+2.6
O	–28	–2.6
O	–28	+2.6

    (2 marks)

18.18 A company is considering accepting a one-year contract which will require four skilled employees. The four skilled employees could be recruited on a one-year contract at a cost of $40,000 per employee. The employees would be supervised by an existing manager who earns $60,000 per year. It is expected that supervision of the contract would take 10% of the manager's time.

Instead of recruiting new employees the company could retrain some existing employees who currently earn $30,000 per year. The training would cost $15,000 in total. If these employees were used they would need to be replaced at a total cost of $100,000.

What is the relevant labour cost of the contract?

    O $115,000
    O $135,000
    O $160,000
    O $275,000   **(2 marks)**

18.19 For a set of six data pairs for the variable x (profit) and y (sales) the following values have been found.

$\Sigma x = 2$

$\Sigma y = 15$

$\Sigma x^2 = 30$

$\Sigma y^2 = 130$

$\Sigma xy = 14$

What is the correlation coefficient?

○ 0.0006 (to 4 dp)

○ 0.02 (to 2 dp)

○ 0.17 (to 2 dp)

○ 1.9973 (to 4 dp) **(2 marks)**

18.20 A company wants to calculate the total cost of a job. The estimated cost for the job is as follows.

Direct materials	10 kg @ $10 per kg
Direct labour	20 hours @ $5 per hour

Variable production overheads are recovered at the rate of $2 per labour hour.

Fixed production overheads for the company are budgeted to be $100,000 each year and are recovered on the basis of labour hours. There are 10,000 budgeted labour hours each year.

Other costs in relation to selling, distribution and administration are recovered at the rate of $50 per job.

What is the total production cost of the job?

○ $200

○ $400

○ $440

○ $490 **(2 marks)**

(Total = 40 marks)

19 Mixed Bank 2   48 mins

19.1 A division of a service company is aware that its recent poor performance has been attributable to a low standard of efficiency amongst the workforce, compared to rival firms. The company is adopting a balanced scorecard approach to setting performance targets. As part of its objective of closing the skills gap between itself and rival companies, the division's management has set a target of providing at least 40 hours of training each year for all its employees.

What does this performance target reflect?

- ○ A customer perspective
- ○ A learning and growth perspective
- ○ An internal process perspective
- ○ A finance perspective   **(2 marks)**

19.2 Which of the following could be included in a time series based sales forecast?

- (i) Trend
- (ii) Seasonal variation
- (iii) Cyclical variation
- (iv) Random fluctuation

- ○ (i) only
- ○ (ii) only
- ○ (i), (ii) and (iii) only
- ○ (i), (ii), (iii) and (iv)   **(2 marks)**

19.3 Which of the following is the best definition of return on capital employed?

- ○ Profit before interest and tax ÷ Ordinary shareholders' funds × 100
- ○ Profit before interest and tax ÷ (Ordinary shareholders' funds + Non-current liabilities) × 100
- ○ Profit after interest and tax ÷ Ordinary shareholders' funds × 100
- ○ Profit after interest and tax ÷ (Ordinary shareholders' funds + Non-current liabilities) × 100
                                                       (2 marks)

19.4 Good quality saves money but the cost of quality can be analysed into cost of conformance and cost of non-conformance.

Which one of the following costs is classed as a quality-related appraisal cost?

- ○ Re-inspection cost
- ○ Administration of customer complaints section
- ○ Performance testing
- ○ Training in quality control   **(2 marks)**

19.5 Which TWO of the following costs would be considered to be the responsibility of the manager of a profit centre?

- ☐ Direct labour
- ☐ Variable production overhead
- ☐ Imputed interest on capital invested
- ☐ Depreciation on machinery

                                                       (2 marks)

19.6 In a period 12,250 units were made and there was a favourable labour efficiency variance of $11,250. If 41,000 labour hours were worked and the standard wage rate was $6 per hour, how many standard hours (to two decimal places) were allowed per unit?

[ ] hours

(2 marks)

19.7 In its first year of operations a company produced 100,000 units of a product and sold 80,000 units at $9 per unit. It earned a marginal costing profit of $200,000. It calculates that its fixed production overhead per unit is $5.

What profit would it have earned under an absorption costing system?

$ [ ]

(2 marks)

19.8 The table below contains details of an airline's expenditure on aviation fuel.

Year	Total expenditure on aviation fuel $ million	Total distance flown km million	Fuel price index
20X8	600	4,200	120
20X9	1,440	4,620	240

The following statements relate to the changes between 20X8 and 20X9.

(i)   The quantity of fuel consumed increased by 140%
(ii)   The quantity of fuel consumed increased by 20%
(iii) The quantity of fuel consumed per km flown increased by 20%
(iv) The quantity of fuel consumed per km flown increased by 109%

Which statements are true?

O   (i) only
O   (ii) only
O   (ii) and (iii) only
O   (ii) and (iv) only

(2 marks)

19.9 The following statements relate to spreadsheets.

Which statement is false?

O   They are an efficient method of storing text based files
O   They facilitate 'what if' analysis
O   They allow data to be displayed graphically
O   They allow the font, size and colour of text to be changed

(2 marks)

19.10 A company budgeted to sell 5,000 units of a product in November at a standard price of $30 per unit and to earn a profit of $25,000. It actually sold 6,000 units at $28 per unit and earned a profit of $32,000.

What was the favourable sales volume profit variance for November?

O $5,000
O $7,000
O $12,000
O $30,000

(2 marks)

19.11 Which of the following are benefits of using activity based costing?

(i)   It recognises that overhead costs are not always driven by the volume of production
(ii)   It does not result in under or over absorption of foxed overheads
(iii)   It avoids all arbitrary cost apportionments
(iv)   It is particularly useful in single product businesses

O   (i) only
O   (i) and (ii) only
O   (ii) and (iii) only
O   (i) and (iv) only   **(2 marks)**

19.12 An investment project has net present values as follows.

At a discount rate of 5%	$69,700 positive
At a discount rate of 14%	$16,000 positive
At a discount rate of 20%	$10,500 negative

Using the above figures what is the best approximation of the internal rate of return of the investment project?

O   17.6%
O   17.9%
O   18.0%
O   22.7%   **(2 marks)**

19.13 A company uses production labour hours to absorb its fixed production overheads. A strike by its workforce results in a loss of 30% of the period's budgeted production labour hours.

Which of the following variances will occur as a result of the loss in production labour hours?

O   Adverse fixed overhead capacity variance
O   Adverse fixed overhead efficiency variance
O   Adverse direct labour efficiency variance
O   Adverse direct labour rate variance   **(2 marks)**

19.14 A firm with current assets of $40 million and current liabilities of $20 million buys $5 million of inventory on credit which increases its inventory level to $10 million.

What will the effect be on its current ratio and quick (acid test) ratio?

	Current ratio	Quick ratio
O	Increase by 25%	Unchanged
O	Reduce by 10%	Unchanged
O	Increase by 25%	Reduce by 20%
O	Reduce by 10%	Reduce by 20%

(2 marks)

19.15 A publishing company is researching the reading habits of the United Kingdom's population. It randomly selects a number of locations from around the UK and then interviews everyone who lives in these locations.

What is this approach to sampling known as?

O   Systematic sampling
O   Stratified sampling
O   Quota sampling
O   Cluster sampling   **(2 marks)**

19.16 A company has a single product with a selling price of $12 per unit, which is calculated as variable cost per unit, plus 20%. At an output level of 5,000 units it makes a loss of $8,000

What is the company's total fixed cost?

- ○ $2,000
- ○ $4,000
- ○ $18,000
- ○ $20,000   **(2 marks)**

The following information relates to questions 19.17 and 19.18.

The following data are available for product X

	Period budget	Period actual
Sales units	5,000	5,200
	$	$
Sales revenue	50,000	57,200
Manufacturing cost	30,000	31,200
Profit	20,000	26,000

19.17 What is the sales price variance?

- ○ $5,200 Adverse
- ○ $5,000 Favourable
- ○ $5,200 Favourable
- ○ $7,200 Favourable   **(2 marks)**

19.18 What is the sales volume profit variance?

- ○ $800 Favourable
- ○ $1,000 Favourable
- ○ $6,000 Favourable
- ○ $7,200 Adverse   **(2 marks)**

19.19 A firm has used linear regression analysis to establish the relationship between total cost and activity in units.

What does the slope of the regression line represent?

- ○ The variable cost per unit
- ○ The fixed cost per unit
- ○ The average cost per unit
- ○ Total variable costs   **(2 marks)**

19.20 A division has a capital employed of $2,000,000 and earns an operating profit of $600,000. It is considering a project that will increase operating profit by $20,000 but would increase its capital employed by $80,000. A rate of 15% is used to compute interest on capital employed.

What will be the effect on residual income and return on capital employed if the division accepts the project?

	Residual income	Return on investment
○	Increase	Increase
○	Increase	Decrease
○	Decrease	Increase
○	Decrease	Decrease

     (2 marks)

     (Total = 40 marks)

20 Mixed Bank 3   48 mins

20.1 A company wishes to carry out a national survey of adults' reading habits. To reduce travelling costs, the country was divided into constituencies. A sample of 50 constituencies was selected at random. With each of these constituencies, 5 polling districts were selected, again using random techniques. Interviewers will visit a random selection of 30 people on the electoral register of each district selected.

What sampling method is the company using?

○   Stratified
○   Systematic
○   Multi-stage
○   Simple random   **(2 marks)**

20.2 When opening inventories were 8,500 litres and closing inventories were 7,100 litres, William Co had a profit of $61,000 using marginal costing.

If the fixed overhead absorption rate was $4 per litre, what was the profit using absorption costing?

○ $61,000
○ $55,400
○ $56,500
○ $51,100   **(2 marks)**

20.3 A firm rents a photocopier with the following charges. A fixed rental amount is payable up to a certain number of copies each period. If the number of copies exceeds this amount, a constant charge per copy is made for all subsequent copies during that period.

Which of the following graphs depicts the total photocopier rental costs described?

○   Graph A

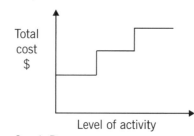

○   Graph B

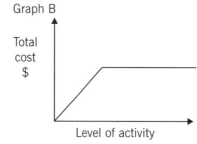

○   Graph C

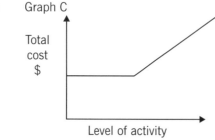

O   Graph D

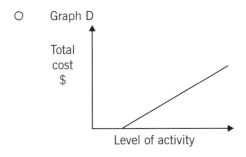

Total
cost
$

Level of activity

(2 marks)

20.4   The following data relate to the overhead expenditure of an organisation at two activity levels.

Square metres	12,750	15,100
Overheads	$73,950	$83,585

What is the estimated overhead expenditure if 16,200 square metres are to be cleaned?

O $25,626
O $44,745
O $88,095
O $192,645   **(2 marks)**

20.5   A management consultancy recovers overheads on the basis of chargeable consulting hours. Budgeted overheads were $615,000 and actual consulting hours were 32,150. Overheads were under-recovered by $35,000.

If actual overheads were $694,075, what was the budgeted overhead absorption rate per hour?

O $19.13
O $20.50
O $21.59
O $22.68   **(2 marks)**

20.6   A pet food company incurred the following costs last year for each of its three different markets.

	$
Dog food	1,345,000
Cat food	2,300,000
Food supplements	985,000

If a pie chart were used to represent the proportion of costs incurred by each area, what would be the angle of the section representing cat food?

O   179 degrees
O   77 degrees
O   120 degrees
O   106 degrees   **(2 marks)**

20.7 The following extract from a spreadsheet represents monthly regional sales figures for product A in the first quarter of the year.

	A	B	C	D	E
1	**Sales figures for Product A**				
2		January	February	March	Total
3	South	135,000	141,000	174,000	450,000
4	North	78,000	45,000	191,000	314,000
5	East	45,000	57,000	87,000	189,000
6	West	23,000	19,000	15,000	57,000
7	Total	281,000	262,000	467,000	1,010,000

Which formula would be used to calculate total sales in the West?

○ =SUM(B6:D6)
○ =(B6:D6)
○ SUM(B6:D6)
○ =TOTAL(B6:D6)   **(2 marks)**

20.8 Which TWO of the following statements relating to activity-based costing are true?

☐ Activity-based costs can be used to identify relevant costs for decision making.

☐ Activity-based costing cannot be used to cost services.

☐ Activity-based costing is a form of absorption costing.

☐ Activity-based costing is an alternative to traditional volume-based costing models.
    (2 marks)

20.9 Which of the following is a disadvantage of the payback method of investment appraisal?

○ It may lead to excessive investment in short-term projects
○ Its use will hinder liquidity
○ It is a fairly complex technique and not easily understood
○ It tends to maximise financial and business risk   **(2 marks)**

20.10 Which four of the following are aspects of value analysis?

(i)   Esteem value
(ii)   Exchange value
(iii) Net realisable value
(iv)   Use value
(v)   Cost value

○ (i), (ii), (iii), (iv)
○ (ii), (iii), (iv), (v)
○ (i), (iii), (iv), (v)
○ (i), (ii), (iv), (v)   **(2 marks)**

20.11 The direct materials involved in the manufacture of a Whoopie cost $2 per unit and the direct labour cost is $2.50 per unit. There are also direct expenses of $0.50 per Whoopie. Fixed costs apportioned to a Whoopie amount to $3.15.

What is the prime cost of a Whoopie?

- ○ $3.65
- ○ $4.50
- ○ $5.00
- ○ $8.15 **(2 marks)**

20.12 Absorption costing will result in the same profit as marginal costing in which THREE of the following situations?

- ☐ When inventory levels are constant
- ☐ When opening and closing inventory volumes are the same
- ☐ When no inventory is held as opening inventory and no inventory is held as closing inventory
- ☐ When opening inventory is greater than closing inventory
- ☐ When closing inventory is greater than opening inventory

(2 marks)

20.13 In process costing, what is an equivalent unit?

- ○ A unit of output in relation to which costs may be ascertained
- ○ The quantity of work achievable in one hour at standard levels of performance
- ○ Notional whole units which represent incomplete work
- ○ A unit of output which is identical to others previously manufactured in the same process

(2 marks)

20.14 A company has recorded the following costs over the last six months.

Month	Total cost	Units produced
	$	
1	74,000	3,000
2	72,750	1,750
3	73,250	2,000
4	75,000	2,500
5	69,500	1,500
6	72,750	2,000

Using the high low method, what is the total cost equation?

- ○ Total cost = $65,000 + ($3 × units produced)
- ○ Total cost = $71,000 + ($3 × units produced)
- ○ Total cost = $61,250 + ($1.25 × units produced)
- ○ Total cost = $70,250 + ($1.25 × units produced)

(2 marks)

20.15 Which of the following statements is/are correct?

- (i) Strategic planning is carried out by line managers.
- (ii) Non-financial information is relevant to management accounting.

- ○ (i) is true and (ii) is false
- ○ (ii) is true and (i) is false
- ○ Both are true
- ○ Both are false **(2 marks)**

20.16 Which of the following sampling methods require a sampling frame?

(i)   Random
(ii) Stratified
(iii) Quota
(iv) Systematic

O   (i) and (ii) only
O   (i), (ii) and (iii) only
O   (i), (ii) and (iv) only
O   (iii) only   **(2 marks)**

The following information is to be used for questions 20.17 and 20.18.

In a time series analysis, the multiplicative model is used to forecast sales and the following seasonal variations apply:

Quarter	1	2	3	4
Seasonal variation	1.2	1.3	0.4	?

The actual sales values for the first two quarters of 2006 were:

Quarter 1: $125,000
Quarter 2: $130,000

20.17 What is the seasonal variation for the fourth quarter?

O   −2.9
O   0.9
O   1.0
O   1.1   **(2 marks)**

20.18 Which of the following is true?

O   The trend line for sales decreased between quarter 1 and quarter 2.
O   The trend line for sales increased between quarter 1 and quarter 2.
O   The trend line for sales remained constant between quarter 1 and quarter 2.
O   The trend line for sales cannot be determined from the information given.   **(2 marks)**

20.19 A firm has used linear regression analysis to establish the relationship between total cost and activity in units.

What does the intercept of the regression line represent?

O   The variable cost per unit
O   The fixed cost per unit
O   The average cost per unit
O   Total fixed costs   **(2 marks)**

20.20 Which of the following statements are true?

(i)   Flexible budgets help managers to deal with uncertainty
(ii) Flexed budgets allow a more meaningful comparison to the made with actual results

O   (i) is true and (ii) is false
O   (ii) is true and (i) is false
O   (i) and (ii) are true
O   (i) and (ii) are false   **(2 marks)**

(Total = 40 marks)

21 Mixed Bank 4   36 mins

21.1 Most businesses assess the performance of management.

Which of the following is most likely to lead to short-termism?

- ○ Linking managers' rewards to share price
- ○ Setting quality based as well as financial targets for managers
- ○ Setting cost cutting targets
- ○ Making short-term targets realistic   **(2 marks)**

21.2 Which of the following best describes TQM?

- ○ Identifying the factors which cause the costs of an organisation's major activities

- ○ Applying a zero defect philosophy to the management of all resources and relationships within an organisation

- ○ Tracking and accumulating costs and revenues attributable to each product over its life

- ○ Estimating product costs by subtracting a desired profit margin from a selling price
                                                                       (2 marks)

21.3 Jay Co makes a product which passes through a single refining process. The following information is available for June.

Materials	15,000kg at $1.50 per kg
Labour	$2,100
Normal loss	10% of input
Scrap value of loss	56c per kg

The output for the period was 13,000 kg from the process. There was no opening or closing inventory during June.

What is the value credited to the process account for the normal loss and the abnormal loss for the period?

	Normal loss	Abnormal loss
○	$840	$880
○	$840	$911
○	$Nil	$280
○	$840	$Nil

(2 marks)

21.4 Gold Co makes and sells two products called the A and the U. The following information is available for May.

	Production	Sales
Product A	4,500 units	4,300 units
Product U	3,100 units	2,600 units

	Product A $	Product U $
Unit selling price	85	60
Unit variable costs		
Direct materials	20	10
Direct labour ($3/hr)	15	18
Variable production overheads	15	20

Fixed costs were $75,000 for May and are recovered on the basis of direct labour hours. There was no opening inventory for either product.

What is profit reported for May using marginal costing principles?

- ○ $72,700
- ○ $106,700
- ○ $153,700
- ○ $181,700 **(2 marks)**

21.5 Last month Zed Co purchased 750 kg of raw materials for $13,500. The material price variance was $1,125 favourable.

What was the standard price per kg of the raw materials?

- ○ $15.00
- ○ $16.50
- ○ $17.00
- ○ $19.50 **(2 marks)**

21.6 Under which sampling method is the population divided into categories?

- ○ Systematic
- ○ Quota
- ○ Random
- ○ Stratified **(2 marks)**

21.7 The price index for a commodity in the current year is 125 (base year = 100). The current price for the commodity is $31.50 per kg.

What was the price per kg in the base year?

- ○ $23.63
- ○ $25.20
- ○ $31.50
- ○ $39.38 **(2 marks)**

21.8 Two statements follow about data and information.

(i) Data is a scientific term for facts and figures.
(ii) Information is data which has been processed.

Which one of the following is correct with regard to the above two statements?

- ○ Both statements are false
- ○ Both statements are true
- ○ Statement (i) is true but statement (ii) is false
- ○ Statement (i) is false but statement (ii) is true **(2 marks)**

21.9 D Co forecasts costs using the model y = a + bx. The intercept is $20. When y = $270 then x = 50.

What is the value of the gradient?

- ○ −5
- ○ 5
- ○ 14.6
- ○ −14.6 **(2 marks)**

The following information relates to questions 21.10 and 21.11

A company produces and sells one type of product. The details for last year were as follows:

Production and Sales

	Budget	Actual
Production (units)	26,000	26,000
Sales (units)	28,000	25,000

There was no inventory at the start of the year.

Selling price and costs

	Budget	Actual
	$	$
Selling price per unit	80	80
Variable costs per unit	60	60
Fixed production overhead	143,000	113,000
Fixed selling costs	69,000	69,000

21.10 What would be the actual profit for the year using marginal costing?

- ○ $312,500
- ○ $318,000
- ○ $323,500
- ○ $682,000 **(2 marks)**

21.11 What would be the actual profit for the year using absorption costing?

- ○ $312,500
- ○ $318,000
- ○ $323,500
- ○ $682,000 **(2 marks)**

21.12 The costs of the factory maintenance department for Freer Co appear to have a variable element dependent upon the number of units produced. The fixed element of the costs steps up by $30,000 when 32,000 or more units are produced. The variable cost per unit is constant.

Volume of production
Units	$
28,000	160,000
34,000	208,000

What would be the total cost for 29,000 units and the total cost for 35,000 units?

	29,000 units	35,000 units
○	$163,000	$181,000
○	$163,000	$211,000
○	$296,000	$344,000
○	$296,000	$181,000

(2 marks)

The following information relates to questions 21.13 and 21.14.

A company operating a standard costing system has the following direct labour standards per unit for one of its products:

4 hours at $12.50 per hour.

Last month when 2,195 units of the product were manufactured, the actual direct labour cost for the 9,200 hours worked was $110,750.

21.13 What was the direct labour rate variance for last month?

    O $4,250 Favourable
    O $4,250 Adverse
    O $5,250 Favourable
    O $5,250 Adverse   **(2 marks)**

21.14 What was the direct labour efficiency variance for last month?

    O $4,250 Favourable
    O $4,250 Adverse
    O $5,250 Favourable
    O $5,250 Adverse   **(2 marks)**

21.15 The purchase price of an item of inventory is $110 per unit. In each six month period the usage of the item is 50,000 units. The annual holding costs associated with one unit equate to 3% of its purchase price. The cost of placing an order for the item is $15.

What is the Economic Order Quantity (EOQ) for the inventory item to the nearest whole unit?

    O   674
    O   953
    O   1,651
    O   10,000   **(2 marks)**

(Total = 30 marks)

22 Mixed Bank 5   24 mins

22.1 The costs of the factory maintenance department for C Co appear to have a variable element dependent upon the number of units produced. The fixed element of the costs steps up when 20,000 or more units are produced. At an activity level of 22,000 units, the fixed element of the cost is $25,000. The variable cost per unit is constant.

Volume of production

Units	$
18,000	200,000
22,000	245,000

What would be the total cost for 19,000 units and the total cost for 21,000 units?

	19,000 units	*21,000 units*	
O	$210,000	$235,000	
O	$215,000	$235,000	
O	$210,000	$230,000	
O	$231,660	$258,940	**(2 marks)**

22.2 A company has a capital employed of $300,000. It has a cost of capital of 10% per year. Its residual income is $30,000.

What is the company's return on investment?

O	1%	
O	10%	
O	18%	
O	20%	**(2 marks)**

22.3 Are the following statements, which refer to documents used in the material procurement procedures of a company, true or false?

(i) All purchase requisitions are prepared in the purchasing department and are then sent out to suppliers

(ii) All goods received notes are prepared in the goods inwards department

	Statement (i)	*Statement (ii)*	
O	False	False	
O	True	True	
O	True	False	
O	False	True	**(2 marks)**

22.4 A company uses standard marginal costing. Last month the standard contribution on actual sales was $40,000 and the following variances arose:

Sales price variance $1,000 Favourable
Sales volume contribution variance $3,500 Adverse
Fixed overhead expenditure variance $2,000 Adverse
There were no variable cost variances last month

What was the actual contribution for last month?

O	$35,500	
O	$37,500	
O	$39,000	
O	$41,000	**(2 marks)**

22.5   A company uses flexed budgets. The fixed budget for last month was based on 100% activity and showed direct costs of $100,000. Last month's actual direct costs were compared with the flexed budget to show the following:

	Actual	Variance
Direct costs	$93,600	$2,400 Adverse

What was the actual activity as a % of the fixed budget last month?

○   91.2%
○   93.6%
○   96.0%
○   97.5%   **(2 marks)**

22.6   A process operates with a normal loss of 5% of input. All losses have a realisable value of $38 per litre. Last month 10,000 litres were input to the process and good production was 9,200 litres. Process costs arising last month were $456,000. There was no work-in-progress.

What was the credit entry in the process account for abnormal loss last month?

○   11,400
○   13,440
○   13,800
○   14,400   **(2 marks)**

22.7   The price index for a commodity in the current year is 175 (base year = 100). The current price for the commodity is $92.70 per unit.

What was the price per unit in the base year?

○ $92.70
○ $25.20
○ $52.97
○ $188.78   **(2 marks)**

22.8   Dee Co uses a pie chart to show its sales for its various products. One of the segments on the pie chart is 120 degrees and this represents $200,000 worth of sales of the product D.

What is the total sales value for Dee Co?

○ $250,000
○ $500,000
○ $600,000
○ $900,000   **(2 marks)**

22.9   D Co forecasts costs using the model y = a + bx. The gradient is $40. When y = $1,100 then x = 20.

What is the value of the intercept?

○   300
○   1,100
○   1,500
○   1,900   **(2 marks)**

22.10 A company has under-absorbed fixed production overheads for the period by $9,000. The fixed production overhead absorption rate was $7 per unit and is based on the normal level of activity of 5,000 units. Actual production was 5,500 units.

What was the actual fixed production overheads incurred for the period?

○ $26,000
○ $29,500
○ $44,000
○ $47,500   **(2 marks)**

                                                                         (Total = 20 marks)

23 Budgeting   120 mins

23.1 J Co makes several products, including Component M.

The opening inventory of Component M at the start of January is expected to be 500 units.

Sales of Component M for January are budgeted at 4,000 units.

Sales are expected to increase by 10% until May when they stabilise.

Closing inventory at the end of each month is budgeted as 20% of next month's sales units.

Task 1

Complete the THREE extracts from the materials budget for next year:

(i) January closing inventory units
(ii) March sales units
(iii) May production units

	Jan	Feb	Mar	Apr	May	Jun
Sales of M (units)	4,000	4,400	(ii)	5,324		5,856
Opening inventory	500				1,171	
Closing inventory	(i)				1,171	
Production					(iii)	

(6 marks)

Task 2

J Co also makes Component F. Each unit of Component F uses 3 kgs of material G. Budgeted sales of Component F are forecast to be 20,000 during January. Opening inventory of material G is 3,000 kgs and closing inventory is going to be 3,500 kgs. Each kg of material G costs $2.50.

What is the material X purchases budget for April in $?

$ [   ]   **(2 marks)**

Task 3

Which of the following is NOT a reason why profit and cash flow might be different?

O   Purchase of non-current assets
O   Sale of non-current assets
O   Depreciation of non-current assets
O   Time delays with the issue of bank statements   **2 marks)**

(Total = 10 marks)

23.2 Given below is the forecast statement of profit or loss for a business for the three months ending 31 December together with forecast statements of financial position at that date and also at the previous 30 September.

FORECAST STATEMENT OF PROFIT OR LOSS
FOR THE THREE MONTHS ENDING 31 DECEMBER

	$'000
Revenue	860
Cost of sales	(600)
Gross profit	260
Depreciation	(20)
Overheads	(100)
Profit from operations	140

FORECAST STATEMENTS OF FINANCIAL POSITION

	31 December		30 September	
	$'000	$'000	$'000	$'000
Non-current assets		1,050		760
Current assets				
Inventory	100		100	
Receivables	85		45	
Cash	10		10	
	195		155	
Total assets		1,245		915
Equity and liabilities				
Equity share capital	600		600	
Retained earnings	500		200	
		1,100		800
Current liabilities				
Payables	100		75	
Accruals of overheads	45	145	40	115
Total equity and liabilities		1,245		915

Task 1

Calculate the actual cash receipts and cash payments for the quarter to 31 December.

	$'000
Sales receipts	
Purchase payments	
Overhead payments	

(6 marks)

Task 2

The business currently sells its product for $30 but it is anticipated that there will be a price increase of 4% from 1 February. The sales quantities are expected to be as follows:

January	21,000 units
February	22,000 units
March	22,800 units

All sales are on credit and 40% of cash is received in the month following the sale and the remainder, two months after the sale.

What are the receipts from January and February sales that are received in March?

	$
Receipts in March relating to January sales	
Receipts in March relating to February sales	

(2 marks)

Task 3

Which of the following statements applies to a flexible budget?

O   It is continuously updated by adding another accounting period when the earliest accounting period has come to an end

O   It is amended in response to changes in costs

O   It is produced before the control period and not subsequently changed in response to changes in activity, costs or revenues

O   It is amended in response to changes in the level of activity   **(2 marks)**

(Total = 10 marks)

23.3   HM Co commenced business on 1 October 20X2, to provide specialist contract cleaning services to industrial customers. All sales are on credit.

More favourable credit terms are offered to larger customers (class A) than to smaller customers (class B). All sales are invoiced at the end of the month in which the sale occurs. Class A customers will be given credit terms requiring payment within 60 days of invoicing, while class B customers will be required to pay within 30 days of invoicing.

Since it is recognised, however, that not all customers comply with the credit terms they are allowed, receipts from customers have prudently been estimated as follows:

Customer type	Within 30 days	31 to 60 days	61 to 90 days	91 to 120 days	Bad debts
Class A		50%	30%	15%	5%
Class B	60%	25%	10%		5%

The above table shows that customers are expected either to pay within 60 days of the end of the credit period, or not at all. Bad debts will therefore be written off 60 days after the end of the credit period.

Budgeted credit sales for each class of customer in the first 4 months of trading are as follows:

Customer type	October	November	December	January
	$'000	$'000	$'000	$'000
Class A	100	150	200	300
Class B	60	80	40	50

Assume all months are of 30 days.

Task 1

Complete the following budgeted cash inflows to be received by HM Co from customers in each of the three months of November 20X2, December 20X2 and January 20X3, based upon the prudently estimated receipts from customers.

	Nov	Dec	Jan
	$'000	$'000	$'000
Class A			
Class B			

(6 marks)

Task 2

Fixed operational overhead costs are estimated to be $25,000 per month, which includes $10,000 rent, $1,000 vehicle running costs, $3,000 vehicle depreciation and $11,000 wages.

What amount should be included in the cash budget for fixed operational overheads per month?

$ _____

(2 marks)

Task 3

HM Co is planning to purchase a new piece of cleaning equipment.

Which of the following would NOT be included in a cash budget in respect of the new equipment?

O   Annual overhead charge from Head Office based on the floor space occupied by the machine
O   Delivery cost of the new equipment
O   Purchase price of the new equipment
O   Disposal proceeds of the old equipment being replaced   **(2 marks)**

(Total = 10 marks)

23.4   RJM Co manufactures several product, one of which is Product M.

Product M uses four different types of materials. The materials used and their prices, in 20X6 and 20X7, are as follows.

	20X6		20X7	
	Kg	$ per kg	Kg	$ per kg
Material A	200	0.98	300	1.40
Material B	500	0.95	400	1.10
Material C	300	1.20	500	0.92
Material D	400	1.10	100	1.14

Task 1

Complete the table with the value of the price index for each material for 20X7 (with 20X6 as the base year) to the nearest whole number.

	Price index
Material A	
Material B	
Material C	
Material D	

(6 marks)

Task 2

RJM also manufactures Product J and has collected the following information about costs and volumes for the past six months:

Month	Volume	Total cost
		$
January	10,000	57,500
February	12,000	63,000
March	11,000	19,500
April	14,000	72,500
May	11,500	63,000
June	13,500	70,000

Using the high-low method, what is the fixed cost per month?

$ [   ]

(2 marks)

Task 3

In which of the following circumstances could RJM use the high-low equation to forecast future costs most accurately?

○ 15,000 units of Product J being manufactured in July
○ 11,000 units of Product J being manufactured in July
○ 11,000 units of Product R being manufactured in July
○ 11,000 units of Product J being manufactured in July in a new factory   **(2 marks)**

(Total = 10 marks)

23.5 A company, which manufactures a range of products, has decided to introduce a product costing system. As a first step it wishes to analyse the behaviour of its costs.

The following data is available for the previous four periods.

	A	B	C	D	E
1		Period 1	Period 2	Period 3	Period 4
2	Total costs ($)	214,559	239,970	243,183	259,541
3	Total output (units)	64,200	76,350	77,880	85,620

Task 1

Using the high-low method, select from the drop down list below, which of the following formulae will correctly calculate the cost of the variable element per unit.

Select...   ▼
=E2-B2/E3-B3
=(D2-B2)/(D3-B3)
=(E2-B2)/(E3-B3)
=D2-B2/D3-B3

(2 marks)

Task 2

Using the high-low method, complete the following linear equation for total costs:

y = [   ] + [   ] x

(4 marks)

Task 3

The following spreadsheet can be used to investigate the inter-relationship between advertising expenditure and sales.

	A	B	C	D	E
1	Monthly advertising				
2	Expenditure	Sales			
3	X	Y	X^2	Y^2	XY
4	1.2	132.5	1.44	17556.25	159
5	0.9	98.5	0.81	9702.25	88.65
6	1.6	154.3	2.56	23808.49	246.88
7	2.1	201.4	4.41	40561.96	422.94
8	1.6	161.0	2.56	25921.00	257.6
9	**7.4**	**747.7**	**11.78**	**117549.95**	**1175.07**

The cell E9 shows the total of the XY values.

Which of the following would be a correct entry for this cell?

○   =A9*B9
○   =SUM(E4:E8)
○   =SUM(A9:D9)
○   =C9*D9   (2 marks)

Task 4

For which of the following tasks would a spreadsheet be used?

(select all that apply)

	Tick box
Cash flow forecasting	
Monthly sales analysis by market	
Writing a memo	
Calculation of depreciation	

(2 marks)

(Total = 10 marks)

23.6   Great Southern Co manufactures hairdryers for the hotel industry, which it sells for $12 each. Variable costs of production are currently $6 per unit. New production technology is now available which would cost $250,000, but which could be used to make the hairdryers for a variable cost of only $4.50 per unit.

Fixed costs are expected to increase by $20,000 per year, 75% of which will be directly as a result of installing the new technology. Great Southern charges depreciation at 20% and seeks a return on its investments of at least 10%.

The new technology would have an expected life of 5 years and a resale value after that time of $60,000. Sales of hairdryers are estimated to be 50,000 units per year.

The management accountant has started preparing a spreadsheet to calculate the NPV of the project, and an extract is shown below:

A	B	C	D	E	F	G	H
1	Year	0	1	2	3	4	5
2	Investment $						
3	Sales proceeds $						
4	Contribution $						
5	Fixed costs $						
6	Depreciation $						
7	Net cash flow $						
8	Discount factor (to 3dp)						

Task 1

Which figures should be shown in the following cells ?

- C2 (1 mark) $ _____
- H3 (1 mark) $ _____
- D4 (2 marks) $ _____
- D5 (2 marks) $ _____
- D6 (1 mark) $ _____
- E8 (1 mark) $ _____

(8 marks)

Task 2

Which TWO of the following are advantages of the IRR method of investment appraisal?

☐ It takes into account the time value of money

☐ It is the superior investment appraisal technique

☐ It does not require the company's cost of capital

☐ It is quick and simple to calculate

☐ It is based on profits **(2 marks)**

(Total = 10 marks)

23.7 Fit Co owns and runs two local sports club. Last year the largest club made sales of $500,000 but as member numbers are declining they are thinking about refurbishing the gym and upgrading the equipment.

The expected costs and benefits of the refurbishment are as follows:

(i) New fitness equipment would cost $450,000 to buy and install. This includes a refurbishment of the gym space.

(ii) Sales are expected to rise to $550,000 in Year 1 if the changes are made, thereafter increasing by 5% per year. If the changes are not made sales are expected to fall by $40,000 per year.

(iii) Depreciation would be provided at $90,000 per year.

(iv) The manager of the gym has been to a conference to research the new equipment and receive training on the safe use of the equipment. The cost of the conference was $3,000. A further $20,000 would be spent on training the rest of the gym staff if the equipment was purchased.

(v) It is anticipated that electricity costs would rise by 5% of the total sales as a result of extra running costs of the new machines.

(vi) The manager of the other fitness centre would be required to cover the running of the gym when the new equipment is first introduced, while the current manager trains the remaining gym staff. It is anticipated he would stay for one month. He is paid an annual salary of $48,000. He would not be replaced at the other fitness centre during this month.

(vii) A 5 year maintenance contract would be entered into at a cost of $10,000 per year.

(viii) Interest on money borrowed to finance the refurbishment would be $6,000 per year.

(ix) Fit Co's cost of capital is 10% per year.

Required

Task 1

Indicate whether each of the following items are relevant or irrelevant cashflows for a net present value (NPV) evaluation of whether to refurbish the gym.

	Relevant	Irrelevant
Investment of $450,000 in the new equipment		
Depreciation of $90,000 over each of the five years		
Staff training costs of $20,000		
Temporary manager's salary of $4,000		
Conference and staff training costs of $3,000		
Interest costs of $6,000 per year		

(6 marks)

Task 2

Calculate the following values if the gym is refurbished:

Incremental sales in Year 1	$ _____
Present value of the maintenance costs over the life of the contract	$ _____
Additional electricity costs in Year 1	$ _____

(4 marks)

(Total = 10 marks)

23.8 The bookkeeper of House Co (a furniture retailer) has prepared a list of items of expenditure from last month, but cannot decide if they are capital or revenue and has asked for your help.

Task 1

Identify which of the following items are capital or revenue expenditure:

Expenditure	Capital	Revenue
Purchase of new delivery van		
Road tax for new delivery van		
Repairs to customer toilets		
Extension of customer car park		

(4 marks)

Task 2

House Co also manufactures furniture. It anticipates that they will sell 200 of their best selling beds in June 20X6. It is anticipated that sales will rise by 25% in July because of a planned sales promotion.

Inventory levels at the end of May are 15 units, and because of the sales promotion the sales manager has requested that inventory at the end of June is equal to 20% of July's forecast sales.

Using the drop down list, select the number of beds that should be manufactured in June to ensure that inventory levels are as required at the beginning of July.

Select...▼
200
215
235
250

(2 marks)

Task 3

House Co also plans to manufacture 90 sofas in June. Below are some extracts from the cost card for a sofa:

	$
Materials – 10m² of fabric @$50 per m²	500
Assembly labour - 8 hours @$15 per hour	120

How many metres of fabric should be purchased if 10% of material is wasted during the production process?

☐ metres

How much should be budgeted for labour for sofa production in June?

$ ☐

(4 marks)

(Total = 10 marks)

23.9 Gemma Co is preparing its budget for the coming year. Its production capacity is 10,000 units, but in the coming year it expects production and sales of its Product Q to be limited to 90% capacity. Cost estimates are made at Gemma Co using the high-low method and are based upon the following data.

Units of output/sales	Cost of sales $
9,800	44,400
7,700	38,100

The company's management is not certain that the estimate of sales is correct, and has asked for flexible budgets to be prepared at output and sales levels of 80% and 100% of its capacity. The sales price per unit has been fixed at $5.

Task 1

What is the variable cost per unit? $ ☐

What are Gemma Co's fixed costs? $ ☐

(4 marks)

Task 2
What is the budgeted profit for production and sales of 9,000 units?

O $4,224
O $3,000
O $600
O $1,000   (2 marks)

Task 3

Prepare the flexible budgets that Gemma Co's management has requested.

	Flexed budget 80% capacity $	Flexed budget 100% capacity $
Sales		
Variable costs		
Fixed costs		
Profit		

(4 marks)

(Total = 10 marks)

23.10 Tree Co has decided to use investment appraisal techniques when making decisions about future investment opportunities.

Task 1

Which TWO of the following techniques take no account of the time value of money?

- ☑ The payback period
- ☑ Net present value
- ☐ Discounted payback period
- ☐ Internal rate of return
- ☑ Return on capital employed

(2 marks)

Task 2

One of the projects Tree Co is considering is Project P. It has the following cash flows:

15%.

	$		
Capital investment	(60,000)	1	(60 00)
Profits before depreciation			
Year 1	20,000	0.870	17 400
Year 2	30,000	0.756	22 680
Year 3	40,000	0.658	26 320
Year 4	50,000	0.572	28 600

NPV. 35,000

What is Project P's payback period?

- ○ 2.75 years
- ○ 3 years
- ● 2 years
- ☑ 2.25 years

(2 marks)

Task 3

Tree Co has calculated its cost of capital to be 15%.

What are the NPV and discounted payback of Project P?

NPV $ 35,000 (to the nearest whole number)

Discounted payback ☐ years (to two decimal places) 2.

(4 marks)

Task 4

Is the following statement true or false?

By calculating the discounted payback period, we establish the time at which the NPV of an investment becomes positive.

- ☑ True
- ☐ False

(2 marks)

(Total = 10 marks)

24 Standard costing   120 mins

24.1 CT Co uses a standard absorption costing system and manufactures and sells a single product called the DG. The standard cost and selling price details for the DG are as follows.

	$ per unit
Variable cost	12
Fixed cost	4
	16
Standard profit	6
Standard selling price	22

The sales volume variance reported in June was $12,000 adverse.

CT Co is considering using standard marginal costing as the basis for variance reporting in the future.

Task 1

Calculate the sales volume variance that would be shown in a marginal costing operating statement for June.

Sales volume variance $ [   ] Adverse/Favourable

(2 marks)

Task 2

Which of the following would correctly calculate the fixed overhead volume variance?

O   The difference between budgeted hours of work and the actual hours of work multiplied by the standard absorption rate per unit.

O   The difference between the fixed overhead incurred and the fixed overhead absorbed

O   The difference between the budgeted fixed overhead expenditure and the actual fixed overhead expenditure.

O   The difference between actual and budgeted volume multiplied by the standard absorption rate per unit.

(2 marks)

CT Co has found that it has had an increasing adverse labour efficiency variance for the last 6 months. The company uses lots of temporary workers in a bid to meet sales demand for its main product.

Task 3

Which TWO of the following control actions could CT Co implement to try to eliminate this?

☐   Increase the hourly rate paid to temporary workers

☐   Offer overtime pay to the company's existing skilled employees on a piecework basis

☐   Implement training for the temporary employees

☐   Reduce the number of supervisors   **(2 marks)**

Task 4

A company has budgeted material costs of $125,000 for the production of 25,000 units per month. Each unit is budgeted to use 2 kg of material. The standard cost of material is $2.50 per kg. Actual materials in the month cost $136,000 for 27,000 units and 53,000 kg were purchased and used.

What was the adverse material price variance?

○ $1,000
○ $3,500
○ $7,500
○ $11,000   **(2 marks)**

(Total = 10 marks)

24.2   Connolly uses standard costing to control its costs and revenues. A standard cost card for its only product, the FY, is given below together with a standard cost operating statement for last month.

Standard cost card

	$ per unit
Selling price	100
Direct materials 3kg @ $10/kg	30
Direct labour 1 hours @$10 per hour	10
Fixed overhead 2 hours @ $5 per hour	10
Profit	50

Standard cost operating statement

	$	$	$
Budgeted profit	500,000		
Sales volume variance	50,000 (A)		
Standard profit on actual sales	**450,000**		
Sales price variance	10,000 (F)		
	460,000		

Production cost variances

	Adverse $	Favourable $	
Material price		10,000	
Material usage	8,000		
Labour rate	2,000		
Labour efficiency		1,000	
Fixed overhead expenditure	2,000		
Fixed overhead volume	1,000		
	13,000	**11,000**	**2,000(A)**
Actual profit			**458,000**

Task 1

Select the appropriate words, phrases or numbers to correctly complete the commentary on the last month's results.

Connolly uses standard Picklist 1 costing. In the last month actual selling price was Picklist 2 standard.

Actual units sold were Picklist 3 budgeted and actual sales revenue was $ Picklist 4.

Production was Picklist 5 than budgeted.

Materials caused the biggest cost variance, where a decision to pay Picklist 6 standard price resulted in the company using Picklist 7 budget.

Picklist 1 absorption, marginal

Picklist 2 higher than, lower than, equal to

Picklist 3 1,000 less than, 1,000 more than, 500 less than, 500 more than

Picklist 4 $890,000, $910,000, $460,000, $458,000

Picklist 5 100 units less than, 100 units more than, 200 units less than, 200 units more than

Picklist 6 less than, more than

Picklist 7 800kg more than flexed budget, 800kg more than original budget, 600kg more than flexed budget, 600kg more than original budget **(10 marks)**

(Total = 10 marks)

24.3 Ring Ring uses a standard cost operating statement to reconcile budgeted contribution with actual contribution. A standard cost operating system for January has been partly completed but some information is missing.

Standard cost card – Mobile phone		*$ per phone*
Selling price		100
Direct material		25
Direct labour		10
Production overhead		15
Standard contribution		50
Actual and budgeted activity levels in units	*Budget*	*Actual*
Sales	20,000	21,500
Production	20,000	22,000
Actual sales revenue and variable costs	$	
Sales	2,128,500	
Direct materials (purchased and used)	565,000	
Direct labour	210,000	
Variable production overhead	325,000	
Variances		
Total direct materials variances	15,000	Adverse
Total direct labour variances	10,000	Favourable
Total variable production overhead variances	5,000	Favourable

Task 1

Complete the missing figures to be included in reconciliation for the standard cost operating statement for January.

Sales volume variance $ [ ] Adverse/Favourable

Standard contribution on actual sales $ [ ]

Sales price variance $ [ ] Adverse/Favourable

Actual contribution $ [ ]

(8 marks)

Task 2

Which of the following would explain the sales volume variance achieved by Ring Ring?

O   Budgeted sales units were greater than budgeted production units
O   Actual sales units were greater than budgeted production units
O   Actual sales units were greater than budgeted sales units
O   Actual sales units were less than budgeted sales units

(2 marks)

(Total = 10 marks)

24.4 Kubrick uses a standard absorption costing system to control the cost of its only product. The flexed budget for production overhead for the company shows a budgeted total overhead cost of $200,000 per period when 5,000 tonnes are produced and $264,000 per period when 9,000 tonnes are produced.

In Period 9, when the actual output was 6,500 tonnes, total actual overhead cost was $245,000 ($125,000 fixed and $120,000 variable). The standard fixed overhead absorption rate is $24 per tonne.

Task 1

Using the high-low technique, calculate the following:

The budgeted variable overhead per tonne. $ [   ]

The budgeted fixed overhead per period. $ [   ]

(4 marks)

Task 2

Calculate the following:

The fixed overhead expenditure variance. $ [   ] Adverse/Favourable

The fixed overhead volume variance. $ [   ] Adverse/Favourable

(4 marks)

Task 3

Which of the following would result in an over absorption of overheads?

O   Absorbed overheads exceed actual overheads
O   Actual overheads exceed absorbed overheads
O   Budgeted overheads exceed absorbed overheads
O   Actual overheads exceed budgeted overheads

(2 marks)

(Total = 10 marks)

24.5 Mortensen manufactures wooden toys. It uses a standard costing system to control costs. The cutting department cuts the shapes which are sold as toy animals.

		$
Hardwood		16.00
Direct labour	30 minutes at $9 per hour	4.50
Fixed overhead	30 minutes at $4 per direct labour hour	2.00
		22.50

Fixed overhead absorption rates are based upon monthly fixed overheads of $26,000 and a budgeted monthly output of 13,000 sets of animals.

In the most recent month 14,000 sets of animals were made. 8,000 direct labour hours were worked and paid at $9.25 per hour. Actual fixed overheads were $23,000 for the month.

Task 1

Complete the following extract from the profit reconciliation for the most recent month:

Variance $ Favourable/Adverse
Fixed overhead expenditure
Fixed overhead efficiency
Fixed overhead capacity

(6 marks)

Task 2

Match the possible explanations of the cause of variances to the variance.

Volume variance
Efficiency variance
Expenditure variance
Capacity variance

Labour productivity was lower than expected
Labour productivity was higher than expected
Over-absorption of fixed overheads
Under-absorption of fixed overheads
Fixed overhead expenditure was higher than
expected
Fixed overhead expenditure was lower than expected
Labour worked more hours than expected
Labour worked fewer hours than expected

(4 marks)

(Total = 10 marks)

24.6 CC Co makes garden chairs, which have a standard direct material cost as follows:

6 kg of Material W at $15 per kg = $90 per chair

During October 20X5, 2,500 chairs were manufactured using 12,000 kg of Material W which cost $175,000.

Task 1

Calculate the following variances.

The direct material total variance $ [   ] Adverse/Favourable

The direct material price variance $ [   ] Adverse/Favourable

The direct material usage variance $ [   ] Adverse/Favourable

(6 marks)

Task 2

A company uses standard marginal costing. Its budgeted contribution for the last month was $30,000. The actual contribution for the month was $20,000, and the following variances have been calculated:

- Sales volume contribution variance $5,000 adverse
- Sales price variance $10,000 favourable
- Fixed overhead expenditure variance $3,000 favourable

Use the drop down box to select the total variable cost variance.

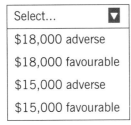

Select...   ▼
$18,000 adverse
$18,000 favourable
$15,000 adverse
$15,000 favourable

(2 marks)

Task 3

A company has calculated an adverse direct material variance by subtracting its flexed budgeted direct material cost from its actual direct material cost for the period.

Which TWO of the following could have caused the variance?

☐ An increase in direct material prices

☐ An increase in raw material usage per unit

☐ Units produced being greater than budgeted

☐ Units sold being greater than budgeted

(2 marks)

(Total = 10 marks)

24.7 Dream Co operates a standard costing system. It expects to produce 3,000 units of product X using 12,000 hours of labour. The standard cost of labour is $12.50 per hour.

In January the company actually made 2,195 units. The actual labour cost was $110,750 for the 9,200 hours worked.

Task 1

Calculate the following variances for Dream Co for January.

Total labour variance	$ ☐	Adverse/Favourable
Labour rate variance	$ ☐	Adverse/Favourable
Labour efficiency variance	$ ☐	Adverse/Favourable

(6 marks)

Task 2

Which of the following could give rise to an adverse labour efficiency variance?

○ The rate actually paid to workers was higher than the standard
○ Actual production took longer than expected
○ The rate actually paid to workers was lower than the standard
○ Actual production was quicker than expected

(2 marks)

Task 3

Dream Co's operating costs are 70% variable and 30% fixed.

Which of the following variances' values would change if the company switched from standard marginal costing to standard absorption costing?

○ Direct material efficiency variance
○ Variable overhead efficiency variance
○ Sales volume variance
○ Fixed overhead expenditure variance

(2 marks)

(Total = 10 marks)

24.8 Swindle Co makes widgets. Two types of labour are involved in the production of a widget, skilled and unskilled. Skilled labour is paid $15 per hour and unskilled $3 per hour. Twice as many unskilled labour hours as skilled labour hours are needed to produce a widget, six unskilled labour hours being needed.

A widget is made up of two different direct materials. Five kg of Material X and two metres of Material Z are needed. Material X costs $2 per kg and Material Z $5 per metre.

Variable production overheads are incurred at Swindle at the rate of $3.00 per direct skilled labour hour.

The basis of fixed cost absorption is direct skilled labour hours. For the coming year, budgeted fixed production overheads are $100,000 and budgeted production of widgets is 10,000 units.

Administration, selling and distribution overheads are added to products at the rate of $20 per widget, and a mark-up of 15% is made on each.

Task 1

Complete the standard cost card for a widget:

Standard cost card for a widget	$
Direct materials - X	
Direct materials - Z	
Direct labour - skilled	
Direct labour - unskilled	
Variable production overhead	
Fixed production overhead	
Admin selling and distribution overhead	
Standard cost of sale	
Standard profit	
Standard sales price	

(8 marks)

Task 2

How is a selling price variance calculated?

○   The difference between actual units sold and the budgeted quantity, valued at the standard selling price

○   The difference between the actual units sold and the budgeted quantity, valued at the standard profit per unit

○   The difference between budgeted and actual sales revenue

○   The difference between what the sales revenue should have been for the quantity sold, and what it was

(2 marks)

(Total = 10 marks)

24.9 The standard direct labour cost of product Fab is as follows:

3 hours of Grade B labour at $5 per hour = $15 per unit

During the last period, 3,000 units of product Fab were made, and the direct labour cost of the Grade B labour was $43,700 for 10,000 hours of work.

Task 1

Calculate the direct labour total variance, and analyse it into the direct labour rate variance and direct labour efficiency variance.

Direct labour total variance $ [   ] Adverse/Favourable

Direct labour rate variance $ [   ] Adverse/Favourable

Direct labour efficiency variance $ [   ] Adverse/Favourable

(6 marks)

Task 2

Complete the following sentence using the words listed. Not all of the words listed will be needed and some may be needed more than once.

The direct labour rate variance is the difference between the _____ cost and the _____ cost for the _____ number of _____ paid for.

standard
actual
units
hours

(2 marks)

Task 3

During the same period, 12,000 kgs of material Top was used to make the 3,000 units of product Fab, at a cost of $96,000. The direct material total variance was $3,000 (A).

What is the standard direct material cost per unit of Fab? (give your answer to the nearest whole $)

Standard direct material cost per unit $ [   ]

(2 marks)

(Total = 10 marks)

24.10 Diamond uses standard costing. The following data relates to labour Grade C.

Actual hours worked	12,600 hours
Standard allowance for actual production	10,800 hours
Standard rate per hour	$7.50
Rate variance (favourable)	$675

Task 1

What was the actual rate of pay per hour?

O $7.75
O $7.60
O $7.44
O $7.45

(2 marks)

Task 2

The standard material content of one unit of Ruby is 5 kg of material Sparkle, which should cost $20 per kg. In December 20X6, 6,000 units of Ruby were produced and there was an adverse material usage variance of $10,000.

Calculate the quantity of Sparkle used in December 20X6 (to the nearest whole kg)

Quantity of Sparkle used in December 20X6   [   ] kg

(2 marks)

Task 3

Crystal Co uses a standard absorption costing system. The following figures are available for the last accounting period, for which standard profit was $135,000.

	$
Sales volume variance	15,000 adverse
Sales price variance	10,500 favourable
Total variable cost variance	7,500 adverse
Fixed cost expenditure variance	5,500 favourable
Fixed cost volume variance	4,000 adverse

What was the actual profit for the period?

$ [   ]

(4 marks)

Task 4

Emerald uses standard marginal costing, instead of standard absorption costing.

Which TWO of the following are differences in the way that Emerald will calculate its variances, when compared with Crystal?

☐ The sales volume variance will be valued at standard contribution margin.

☐ The sales volume variance will be valued at standard profit margin.

☐ There will be no fixed cost volume variance.

☐ There will be no fixed cost expenditure variance.   **(2 marks)**

(Total = 10 marks)

25 Performance measurement   120 mins

25.1 Flyrite is a low cost airline. It was established 5 years ago and has grown rapidly. It operates flight routes to various countries. Customers book flights mainly using Flyrite's online booking system.

The company is keen to benchmark their performance against those of other low cost airlines and is considering installing a balanced score card approach. You have been asked to assist with gathering appropriate performance measures to use in the balanced scorecard. The following data is available:

Flyrite

Operating data for the year ended 31 December 20X1

Sales revenue	$250 million
Sales attributable to new routes	$13 million
Average capital employed	$110 million
Profit before interest and tax	$22 million
Number of customers	1,250,000
Number of customer complaints	37,500
Number of flights	2,500,000
Number of delayed flights	375,000

Task 1

Calculate the following ratios and other statistics for Flyrite for the year ended 31 December 20X1 (give your answer to one decimal place).

Return on capital employed   [   ] %

Operating profit margin   [   ] %

Asset turnover   [   ] times

Percentage of sales attributable to new routes   [   ] %

(6 marks)

Task 2

Calculate the following statistics for Flyrite (give you answer to the nearest whole percentage).

Percentage of customers who make a complaint   [   ] %

Percentage of flights delayed   [   ] %

(2 marks)

Task 3

Complete the following explanation of a balanced scorecard.

A balanced scorecard measures performance from four perspectives: financial success, process efficiency, growth and [   ]

Picklist
competitive advantage
customer satisfaction
increased market share
internal processes

Flyrite's performance measure of [   ] would be categorised under the growth perspective of the balanced scorecard.

Picklist
percentage of flights delayed
percentage of customer complaints
percentage of sales attributable to new routes   **(2 marks)**

(Total = 10 marks)

25.2   The directors of Nicol are reviewing the performance of its newest division, Division S. The division operates in the medical sales industry and manufactures and sells wound care products for hospitals.

The following information is available for the year ended 31 December 20X1 for Division S.

	Division S $
Sales	100,000
Operating profit	5,000
Capital employed	20,000
Imputed interest charge per annum	10%

Total wound care product sales in the industry for the year ended 31 December 20X1 were $1,000,000.

Task 1

Calculate the following performance measures for Division S (give your answer to the nearest whole number).

Return on sales	[ ] %
Asset turnover	[ ] times
Market share	[ ] %
Return on investment	[ ] %
Residual income	$ [ ]

(6 marks)

Task 2

Which TWO of the following are advantages of residual income as a measure of divisional performance over return on investment?

☐ It enables the performance of divisions of different sizes to be compared

☐ It relates the size of the division's income to the size of the investment

☐ It makes division managers aware of the cost of financing their divisions

☐ It gives an absolute measure of performance

(2 marks)

Task 3

Which TWO of the following are non-financial measures that could be used by Nicol?

☐ Profit per product

☐ Number of new products launched

☐ Sales revenue per product

☐ Number of customer complaints

(2 marks)

(Total = 10 marks)

25.3 Henderson manufactures and sells active wear. Below is a summary of the financial statements for the business for 20X1:

	20X1
	$'000
Sales	3,500
Cost of sales	1,750
Expenses	500
Interest	80
Share capital and reserves	3,200
Long term borrowings	800
Non-current assets	2,800
Receivables	400
Inventory	250
Payables	180

Task 1

Complete the table below to calculate the performance measures for 20X6 (please give your answer to two decimal places).

Performance measure	20X1
Return on capital employed	
Operating profit margin	
Asset turnover	
Interest cover	
Gearing (debt/debt + equity)	
Inventory days	
Receivables days	
Payables day	

(8 marks)

Task 2

Which of the following drop down options is NOT one of the four perspectives in a balanced scorecard?

Select...   ▼
Financial success
Non-financial success
Process efficiency
Customer satisfaction

(2 marks)

(Total = 10 marks)

25.4 Division K is a division of KW plc. The following information is relevant to Division K.

Capital employed	$40 million
Sales	$80 million
Operating profit	$10 million
Cost of capital	10% per annum

KW plc is considering two proposals.

Proposal 1

Invest a further $5m in non-current assets to earn additional annual operating profit of $1 million.

Proposal 2

Dispose of non-current assets at their net book value of $10m. This would lead to annual operating profits falling by $1.5m per annum. Proceeds from the disposal of these non-current assets would not be credited to Division K (but to the Holding Company of KW plc instead).

Task 1

Calculate the following performance measures for Division K BEFORE considering the two new proposals.

Return on investment (ROI)   [   ] %

Residual income (RI) $[   ] million

(4 marks)

Task 2

Are each of the following statement true or false in relation to the two proposals KW plc is considering?

	True	False
Proposal 1 will increase ROI	☐	☐
Proposal 1 will increase RI	☐	☐
Proposal 2 will decreased ROI	☐	☐
Proposal 2 will decrease RI	☐	☐

(4 marks)

Task 3

Which TWO of the following are advantages of return on investment as a measure of divisional performance compared to residual income residual income?

☐ It gives an absolute measure of performance.

☐ It makes manages aware of the cost of financing their division.

☐ It is more easily understood by divisional managers.

☐ It helps in comparing the performance of the managers of divisions of different sizes.

(2 marks)

(Total = 10 marks)

25.5 Pyllon training has two divisions which its treats as separate investment centres, JC and GC.

The following information is available for each division for the year ended 31 March 20X1:

	JC $	GC $
Sales	50,000	60,000
Operating profit	700	675
Capital employed	3,500	4,500

Total sales in the industry in which Pyllon operates were $2,500,000 for the year ended 31 March 20X1.

Pyllon uses an imputed interest charge of 10%

Task 1

Calculate the following performance measures for Pyllon(give your answer to the nearest whole number).

Return on investment for division JC ☐ %

Return on investment for division GC ☐ %

Residual income for division JC $ ☐

Residual income for division GC $ ☐

Market share for division JC ☐ %

Asset turnover for division GC ☐ times

(6 marks)

Task 2

Which TWO of the following are disadvantages of using residual income as a performance measure?

☐ Comparisons between divisions of different sizes is difficult

☐ It does not relate the size of the centres income to the size of the investment

☐ It does not make divisional managers aware of the cost of financing their divisions

☐ It is not directly related to net present value (NPV). **(2 marks)**

Task 3

Pyllon wishes to introduce the use of some non-financial performance measures to the divisions.

Which TWO of the following would be examples of non-financial performance indicators?

☐ Number of new customers

☐ % increase in market share

☐ Return on sales

☐ Sales to each new customer   **(2 marks)**

(Total = 10 marks)

25.6 JB Co manufactures and sells car radios. Below is a summary of the financial statements for the business for 20X6:

	20X6 $'000
Sales	2,540
Cost of sales	1,425
Expenses	600
Interest	11
Share capital and reserves	2400
Long term loan	250
Non-current assets	1650
Receivables	347
Inventory	180
Payables	318
Bank balance	36

Task 1

Complete the table below to calculate the performance measures for 20X6. (Give your answers to two decimal places.)

		20X6
(i)	Gross profit margin	
(ii)	Return on capital employed	
(iii)	Asset turnover	
(iv)	Current ratio	
(v)	Quick ratio	
(vi)	Inventory holding period in days	
(vii)	Payables payment period in days	
(viii)	Receivables period in days	

(8 marks)

Task 2

Product quality is associated with which perspective of performance in a balanced scorecard?

○ Customer perspective

○ Financial perspective

○ Innovation and learning

○ Internal business processes   **(2 marks)**

(Total = 10 marks)

25.7 Cycle Co, a mail order company operating in a very competitive market, has undergone a strategic review and has identified the retention of existing customers as one if its critical success factors. To achieve this, it wants to install a new call centre to enable customers to place orders over the phone. It has been estimated that the sales value of orders that will be placed using the new system will average $1,000 per hour.

The system that Cycle has chosen will require a regular annual software update, during which time customers will not be able to call, and orders will be lost. The system may be updated at one of four levels: W, X, Y or Z. The costs of the updates, and the estimates of hours lost, are as follows.

Level	Update cost $	Hours lost
W	10,000	15
X	8,000	21
Y	9,750	19
Z	7,500	27

Task 1

Using the data provided, recommend which level of maintenance should be chosen.

○ W
○ X
○ Y
○ Z   **(3 marks)**

Task 2

Determine whether each of the following measures represents a CSF or a KPI:

Measure	CSF	KPI
95% customer complaint resolution		
Successful relationships with key suppliers		
Negotiation of favourable terms for new project finance		
Gain in market share by 2% each month		
Lower the cost of capital by 1.5%		

(5 marks)

Task 3

Which of the following is a definition of a 'critical success factor' for an organisation?

○ A statement of what the organisation intends to achieve over a period of time
○ A measurable indicator of organisational performance
○ A performance requirement that is fundamental to competitive success
○ A basic belief of the people who work in the organisation   **(2 marks)**

(Total = 10 marks)

25.8 The following information is available for the year ended 31 December 20X6 for Diva Co.

	$
Revenue	220,000,000
Cost of sales	110,130,000
Other costs	85,670,000
Operating profit	24,200,000
Total non-current assets	100,970,000
Inventory	2,100,000
Trade receivables	3,200,000
Cash	15,956,463
Total assets	**122,226,463**
Trade payables	15,200,000
Other current liabilities	9,500,000
Long term borrowings	28,000,000
Share capital	10,000,000
Reserves	59,526,463
Equity and liabilities	**122,226,463**

Task 1

Calculate the following performance measures for Diva Co for 20X6 (to two decimal places):

Asset turnover		times
Inventory days		days
Payables days		days
Current ratio		
Quick ratio		
Return on capital employed		%

(6 marks)

Task 2

For the year end 31 December 20X5, Diva's inventory days were lower than in 20X6.

Which TWO of the following could explain this?

- [ ] A slowdown in trading
- [ ] A lengthening of the time taken by customers to pay for their goods
- [ ] A build-up in inventory levels
- [ ] A reduction of inventory levels
- [ ] A lengthening of the average time taken to pay suppliers

(2 marks)

Task 3

Non-financial performance indicators are sometimes referred to as 'leading indicators'.

What does this mean?

○   They are more important than financial indicators
○   They tell the firm that something has gone wrong after it has gone wrong
○   They give early warning signs of problems
○   They are more understandable for non-financial staff

(2 marks)

(Total = 10 marks)

25.9   Task 1

Identify whether the following measures are financial or non-financial indicators

Indicator	Financial	Non-financial
Number of customer complaints		
Market share		
Earnings per share		
Machine down time		
Employee attitudes		
Residual income		

(4 marks)

Task 2

Jungle sells cages and tanks for exotic pets. It reported net income of $150,000 during the year, before preference dividends of $25,000. Jungle had 100,000 $5.00 ordinary shares in issue during the year.

Calculate Jungle's return on equity.

[　　　　　] %

(2 marks)

Task 3

In the last year Jungle's tank production division reported a return on investment of 20%, and its controllable profit was $60,000. Its cost of finance was 15% per year.

What was the division's residual income?

○ $3,000
○ $57,000
○ $58,200
○ $15,000

(2 marks)

Task 4

State whether these measures are absolute or relative.

Residual income   absolute / relative
Return on equity   absolute / relative

(2 marks)

(Total = 10 marks)

25.10 3E Co has decided to improve its performance measurement processes. The following information relates to quarter 2:

Budgeted hours   1,000 standard hours
Standard hours for work produced   1,225 standard hours
Actual hours worked   1,300

Task 1

Calculate the following ratios for 3E Co for quarter 2 (to the nearest whole percent).

Capacity ratio   [   ] %

Activity ratio   [   ] %

Efficiency ratio   [   ] %

(6 marks)

Task 2

In quarter 3 the ratios were calculated as follows:

Capacity ratio: 120%

Efficiency ratio: 110%

Indicate, by ticking the correct boxes in the table below, which explanations relate to each ratio.

	More labour hours were worked than budgeted	Labour hours produced fewer units per hour than budgeted	Labour hours produced more units per hour than budgeted	Fewer labour hours were worked than budgeted
Capacity ratio				
Efficiency ratio				

(2 marks)

Task 3

Which TWO of the following statements about benchmarking are true?

☐ The ultimate aim of benchmarking is to improve performance
☐ Competitive benchmarking can be used to compare internal departments
☐ Benchmarking is suitable for non-profit seeking entities
☐ Benchmarking is quick and straightforward   **(2 marks)**

(Total = 10 marks)

Answers

1 Accounting for management

1.1   The correct answers are: It should be relevant for its purposes and it should be communicated to the right person.

Complete accuracy is not necessarily an **essential** quality of good information. It needs to be **sufficiently accurate** for its purpose, and often there is no need to go into unnecessary detail for pointless accuracy. The costs of providing good information should not outweigh the benefits therefore 'It should be provided whatever the cost' is incorrect.

1.2   The correct answer is: Tactical planning. Tactical planning is used by middle management to decide how the resources of the business should be employed to achieve specific objectives in the most efficient and effective way.

1.3   The correct answers are: They are used to aid planning and they may include non-financial information.

Management accounts are prepared for internal use within an organisation and there is no law that states that they must be prepared. Their purpose is to help with planning, control and decision making and therefore they may use non-financial information as well as financial information..

1.4   The correct answer is: (iii) only.

Statement (i) is a description of a management information system, not a management control system.

Statement (ii) is the 'wrong way round'. The strategy is the course of action that a business might pursue in order to achieve its objectives.

Statement (iii) is correct. Data is the 'raw material' which is processed into useful information.

1.5   The correct answers are: Complete and Accurate.

Good information is not necessarily extensive. Too much information may tend to obscure the important points. Neither is good information true and fair, this is an accounting concept, but management accounting information should be correct.

1.6   The correct answer is: Tactical.

Monthly variance reports are an example of tactical management information.

1.7   The correct answer is: Both are true.

Statement (i) is true and this is why cost accounting is, in general, unsuitable for decision-making. Statement (ii) is true. However, the way the data is analysed is different.

1.8   The correct answer is: Establishing objectives.

The planning stage involves establishing objectives and selecting appropriate strategies to achieve those objectives.

1.9   The correct answer is: Management accounting systems provide information for the use of decision-makers within an organisation.

Financial accounting systems provide information for legal requirements, shareholders and tax authorities. Management accounting systems provide information specifically for the use of decision-makers (managers) within the organisation.

1.10   The correct answers are: Total sales value per product and total material usage

The other two items have been processed in some way to provide meaningful information whereas total sales value per product and total material usage are the basic data for further processing.

2a Sources of data

2a.1   The correct answers are: Data collected by a bank in a telephone survey to monitor the effectiveness of the bank's customer services and Focus group feedback about potential flavours of a new biscuit.

Data collected by a survey or focus group for a particular project are primary data sources.

Historical records of transport costs were not collected specifically for the preparation of forecasts, therefore these are secondary data.

The *Annual Abstract of Statistics* is a source of secondary external data.

2a.2   The correct answers are: Qualitative data are data that cannot be measured and Population data are data arising as a result of investigating a group of people or objects.

It is primary data that is collected for a specific purpose not secondary data. Continuous data (rather than discrete data) can take on any value. Quantitative data can be measured, whereas qualitative data cannot be measured because it is subjective.

2a.3   The correct answer is: Population data.

Foreign exchange rates and interest rates are likely to be obtained from financial newspapers. Details of industry costs are more likely to be found in trade journals.

2a.4   The correct answer is: Big Data analytics relies on digital information.

Information may be written, verbal or confidential, but if it is not digitised it cannot be analysed by Big Data analytics.

2a.5   The correct answer is: 1 and 3 only

Big data is collected from diverse sources and much of the resulting data is unstructured; for example, one significant source of big data can be the opinions and preferences that people express via social media. So Option 2 is incorrect.

Big data analytics is a recent development and enhances an organisation's ability to analyse and reveal insights in data which had previously been too difficult or costly to analyse – due to the volume and variability of the data involved. Option 1 correctly identifies this point. One of the key features of big data is the speed with which data flows into an organisation (with much data being available in real time, or almost in real time). If an organisation can then also process this data quickly, this can improve its ability to respond effectively to customer requirements or market conditions. Option 3 identifies this point.

2a.6   The correct answer is: 1 and 2 only

Statements 1 and 2 are true.

The McKinsey Global Institute said that 'retailers exploiting data analytics at scale across their organisations could increase their operating margins by more than 60 percent' and that 'the US healthcare sector could reduce costs by 8 percent through data-analytics efficiency and quality improvements'

David McCourt, 'Getting Big Impact with Big Data,' McKinsey Quarterly, January 2015, www.mckinsey.com/insights/business_technology/getting_big_impact_from_big_data

Statement 3 is false. One of the criticisms of big data is that the focus is often on finding correlations between data sets with less of an emphasis on causation. It is easier to identify correlations between two variables than to determine what is actually causing the correlation.

2b Presenting information

2b.1   The correct answer is: 144 degrees

Material	Cost $	Percentage %	Degrees
W	2,250	25	90
X	3,000	33.3	120
Y	3,600	40	144
Z	150	1.7	6
	9,000	100	360

3,600/9,000 × 360° = 144°

2b.2   The correct answer is: Multiple bar chart.

2b.3   The correct answer is: In June, the gap between the sales of strawberry and the sales of chocolate reduced.

2b.4   The correct answer is: Line graph

A line graph would be most suitable here. A percentage component bar chart would not show how the total sales values have fluctuated. A scatter diagram would show fluctuations but it would not be as clear as a line graph. A pie chart would not show the fluctuations.

2b.5   The correct answer is: 3 only

> **ACCA examining team comments**
>
> This question covers syllabus area Presenting information using tables charts and graphs. Previous questions in this area have focussed on the construction of charts and graphs and have been well answered. However, this one was quite poorly done. This suggests that candidates are focussing on the mechanics of constructing tables, charts and graphs and are not considering the best way of presenting information to an audience. Pie charts are best used to show the relative size of the component elements of a total (eg a company's total sales analysed by geographic markets). Bar charts are used to display and compare the number, frequency or other measure (eg mean) for different discrete categories of data. For example, a company's sales in different years. Scatter diagrams are best used to exhibit data in order to compare how two variables vary with each other. In this case the relationship between demand and advertising expenditure would be best shown by a scatter diagram.

3a Cost classification

3a.1   The correct answer is: Direct expense

The royalty cost can be traced in full to the product, ie it has been incurred as a direct consequence of making the product. It is therefore a direct expense. Selling expense, production overhead and administrative overhead are all overheads or indirect costs which cannot be traced directly and in full to the product.

3a.2   The correct answers are: A stores assistant in factory store and factory cleaning staff

The wages paid to the stores assistant and cleaning staff in the factory cannot be traced in full to a product or service, therefore these are indirect labour costs.

3a.3   The correct answer is: Factory overheads

Overtime premium is always classed as factory overheads unless it is:

- Worked at the specific request of a customer to get the order completed.

- Worked regularly by a production department in the normal course of operations, in which case it is usually incorporated into the direct labour hourly rate.

3a.4   The correct answers are: Staple to attach fire retardant labels to chairs and The salary of the sales director

Rather than each staple being allocated to a particular product, a box of staples would be treated as a general production overhead. The salary of the sales director is a selling overhead.

3a.5   The correct answers are: Selling prices and Controllable costs

The manager of a profit centre usually has control over how revenue is raised, ie selling prices and over the controllable costs incurred in the centre.

Apportioned head office costs are uncontrollable from the point of view of the profit centre manager. A responsibility centre manager does not have control over the capital investment in the centre unless the centre is designated an investment centre.

3a.6   The correct answer is: A cost which can be influenced by its budget holder.

Controllable costs are items of expenditure which can be directly influenced by a given manager within a given time span.

3a.7   The correct answers are: Customer account and Cheque received and processed

It would be appropriate to use the cost per customer account and the cost per cheque received and processed for control purposes.

Stationery costs and the telephone bill are expenses of the department, therefore they are not suitable cost units.

3a.8   The correct answer is: A cost that relates to a time period which is deducted as expenses for the period and is not included in the inventory valuation.

A period cost is charged against the sales for the period. It is not carried forward in inventory to a future period.

3a.9   The correct answer is: As a production overhead

The supervisors are engaged in the production activity, therefore as an administration overhead can be eliminated. They supervise the production of all products, therefore their salaries are indirect costs because they cannot be specifically identified with a cost unit. This eliminates 'as a direct labour cost' and 'as a direct production expense'. The salaries are indirect production overhead costs, therefore as a production overhead is correct.

3a.10   The correct answers are: Rental of the finished goods warehouse and Depreciation of its own fleet of delivery vehicles

Remember you are only looking for costs that are **directly related** to getting the finished goods from the production line to your customers. Before they can be distributed, finished goods may have to be temporarily **stored** in a warehouse therefore the **rental** of the warehouse will be regarded as a **distribution cost**. In addition, you will need **delivery vehicles** for distribution purposes – any costs related to these vehicles will be classed as distribution costs. Commission paid to sales staff and the marketing campaign costs are **selling costs**.

3a.11   The correct answer is: A function or location for which costs are ascertained.

A cost centre acts as a 'collecting place' for costs before they are analysed further.

3a.12   The correct answer is: 10410

For (10) machining department use of (410) indirect materials the code is 10410.

10440 has an incorrect expense type.

13410 and 13440 have the incorrect cost centre code. The code indicates the cost centre *incurring* the cost, ie receiving the materials.

3b Cost behaviour

3b.1   The correct answer is: Constant in total when production volume changes

Within the relevant range, fixed costs are not affected by the level of activity, therefore 'Constant in total when production volume changes' is correct.

3b.2   The correct answer is: $110,305

$$\text{Variable overhead} = \frac{97,850 - 84,865}{15,950 - 13,500} = \frac{12,985}{2,450}$$

$$= \$5.30 \text{ per square metre}$$

Fixed overhead   = $84, 865 – ($5.30 × 13,500)
= $84,865 – $71,550 = $13,315

Overheads on 18,300 square metres   = $13,315 + ($5.30 × 18,300)
= $13,315 + $96,990
= $110,305

3b.3   The correct answer is: Graph 2 shows that costs increase in line with activity levels.

3b.4   The correct answer is: Graph 1 shows that fixed costs remain the same whatever the level of activity.

3b.5   The correct answer is: Graph 1 shows that cost per unit remains the same at different levels of activity.

3b.6   The correct answer is: Graph 4 shows that semi-variable costs have a fixed element and a variable element.

3b.7   The correct answer is: Graph 3 shows that the step fixed costs go up in 'steps' as the level of activity increases.

3b.8   The correct answer is: $5,100

	Units	*$*
High output	1,100	18,300
Low output	700	13,500
Variable cost of	400	4,800

Variable cost per unit $4,800/400 = $12 per unit

Fixed costs = $18,300 – ($12 × 1,100) = $5,100

3b.9   The correct answer is: A semi-variable cost.

The salary is part fixed ($650 per month) and part variable (5 cents per unit). Therefore it is a semi-variable cost.

3b.10   The correct answer is: A step cost.

The cost described will increase in **steps**, remaining fixed at each step until another supervisor is required. Such a cost is known as a **step cost**.

3b.11   The correct answer is: Sales revenue = 62,500 + (25 × advertising expenditure)

Independent variable x = advertising expenditure

Dependent variable y = sales revenue

Highest x = month 6 = $6,500
Highest y = month 6 = $225,000

Lowest x = month 2 = $2,500
Lowest y = month 2 = $125,000
Using the high-low method:

	Advertising expenditure	Sales revenue
	$	$
Highest	6,500	225,000
Lowest	2,500	125,000
	4,000	100,000

Sales revenue generated for every $1 spent on advertising $= \dfrac{\$100,000}{\$4,000} = \$25$ per $1 spent.

∴ If $6,500 is spent on advertising, expected sales revenue = $6,500 × $25 = $162,500

∴ Sales revenue expected without any expenditure on advertising = $225,000 − $162,500 = $62,500

∴ Sales revenue = 62,500 = (25 × advertising expenditure)

3b.12 The correct answer is: The cost described is a stepped fixed cost.

A stepped fixed cost is fixed in nature but only within certain levels of activity.

3b.13 The correct answer is: $30

	Activity level	Cost
	Units	$
Highest	10,000	400,000
Lowest	5,000	250,000
	5,000	150,000

Variable cost per unit $= \dfrac{\$150,000}{5,000\,\text{units}} = \$30$

3b.14 The correct answer is: The diagram shown depicts annual factory power cost where the electricity supplier sets a tariff based on a fixed charge plus a constant unit cost for consumption but subject to maximising arrival charge.

3b.15 The correct answer is: $1.25

Using the high-low method:

Units	Cost
	$
20,000	40,000
4,000	20,000
16,000	20,000

Variable cost per unit $= \dfrac{\$20,000}{16,000\,\text{units}}$

$= \$1.25$

3b.16 The correct answer is: Graph A

Graph A shows that up to 30,000 units, each unit costs a constant price per unit. After 30,000 units, the gradient of the new variable cost line is more gentle which indicates that the cost per unit is lower than the cost when 0 – 30,000 units are purchased.

3b.17 The correct answer is: $3,000

	Production	Total cost
	Units	$
Level 2	5,000	9,250
Level 1	3,000	6,750
	2,000	2,500

Variable cost per unit $= \dfrac{\$2,500}{2,000\,\text{units}}$

$= \$1.25$ per unit

Fixed overhead = $9,250 − ($1.25 × 5,000) = $3,000

3b.18   The correct answer is: $1.67 per unit

> **ACCA examining team comments**
>
> This question relates to study guide reference A3(h).
>
> The high-low technique estimates variable cost per unit by looking at the change in costs between the highest and lowest levels of output. The correct answer is A. This can be calculated by finding the change in cost between the highest and lowest output levels not explained by the step in fixed costs ($9,500 – $4,000 – $500 = $5,000) , and dividing by the change in output between the highest and lowest output levels. ($5,000 / (4,000 units – 1,000 units) = $1.67 per unit.
>
> Many candidates incorrectly based their calculations on the change in costs between the highest and lowest levels of cost, and hence selected option D (($10,000 – $4,000)/ (3,000 units – 1,000 units) or C (($10,000 – $4,000 – $500)/ (3,000 units – 1,000 units). This mistake suggests some confusion between the independent variable, output, and the dependent variable, cost.

3b.19   The correct answer is: Fixed Variable Semi-variable

> **ACCA examining team comments**
>
> The key to the question is to understand that for variable costs the cost per unit is constant, whilst for fixed costs the total cost is constant. Cost X can quickly be identified as a fixed cost as the total cost between the two output levels is unchanged (10,000 units x $3 = 15,000 units x $2). Cost Y is a variable cost because the cost per unit is constant. Cost Z meets neither of these criteria because it contains elements of both fixed and variable cost, and therefore is a semi variable cost.

3b.20   The correct answer is: $1.80

> **ACCA examining team comments**
>
> Since the variable cost is $1 lower per unit after 15,000 units, the total cost for 20,000 units must be adjusted first before using the high low method. Therefore, the total cost for 20,000 would be $68,000 + (20,000 – 15,000)units × $1=$73,000
>
> Variable cost per unit can then be calculated as (assuming that there is no change in variable cost) = ($73,000 – $39,400) / (20,000 units – 8,000 units) = $2.80
>
> Variable cost per unit after 15,000 units would then need to adjusted for the $1 lower as = $2.80 – $1.00 = $1.80.
>
> The syllabus clearly indicates that candidates need to be able to calculate semi-variable costs, stepped fixed costs and changes in variable cost per unit when using the high low technique. Candidates need to practise the calculations required in this area

4a Forecasting

4a.1 The correct answer is: 0.98

From the data given, it is clear that the correlation is **positive** and **strong**. The correlation coefficient describing a positive strong relationship is 0.98.

4a.2 The correct answer is: 17%

$$Y = 20 - 0.25X$$
$$X = 12$$
$$\therefore Y = 20 - 0.25(12) = 17\%$$

4a.3 The correct answers are: A correlation coefficient numerically close to 1 and A large sample is used to calculate the regression equation

A correlation coefficient numerically close to 1 and a large sample is used to calculate the regression equation and increase the reliability of forecasting.

A correlation coefficient close to +1 or –1 indicates a strong linear relationship between X and Y. The regression equation is therefore more reliable for forecasting.

Working to a high number of decimal places gives spurious accuracy unless both the data itself is accurate to the same degree and the methods used lend themselves to such precision.

Forecasting for values of X outside the range of the original data leads to unreliable estimates, because there is no evidence that the same regression relationships hold for such values.

The regression equation is worthless unless a sufficiently large sample was used to calculate it. In practice, samples of about ten or more are acceptable.

4a.4 The correct answer is: 0.98

The formula for the correlation coefficient is provided in your exam. There are no excuses for getting this question wrong.

$$\text{Correlation coefficient, } r = \frac{n\Sigma XY - \Sigma X\Sigma Y}{\sqrt{[n\Sigma X^2 - (\Sigma X)^2][n\Sigma Y^2 - (\Sigma Y)^2]}}$$

$$= \frac{(4 \times 157) - (12 \times 42)}{\sqrt{[4 \times 46 - 12^2][4 \times 542 - 42^2]}}$$

$$= \frac{628 - 504}{\sqrt{(184 - 144) \times (2,168 - 1,764)}}$$

$$= \frac{124}{\sqrt{40 \times 404}}$$

$$= \frac{124}{127.12}$$

$$= 0.98 \text{ (to 2 decimal places)}$$

4a.5 The correct answers are: There is a strong relationship between the level of car ownership and the number of road deaths and 53% of the variation in the level of road deaths from one country to the next can be explained by the corresponding variation in the level of car ownership

High levels of correlation do not prove that there is cause and effect.

A correlation coefficient of 0.73 would generally be regarded as indicating a strong linear relationship between the variables.

The coefficient of determination provides this information and is given by squaring the correlation coefficient, resulting in 53% in this case.

The coefficient of determination provides this information and not the correlation coefficient. Remember that you must square the correlation coefficient in order to obtain the coefficient of determination.

4a.6   The correct answers are: The estimate is not reliable because X is outside the range of the data and The estimate is not reliable because the sample is small

When X = 20, we don't know anything about the relationship between X and Y since the sample data only goes up to X = 10. 'The estimate is not reliable because X is outside the range of the data' is therefore true.

Since a correlation coefficient of 0.8 would be regarded as strong (it is a high value) the estimate would be reliable. 'The estimate is not reliable because the correlation is low' is therefore not true.

With such a small sample and the extrapolation required, the estimate is unlikely to be reliable. 'The estimate is reliable' is therefore not true.

The sample of only six pairs of values is very small and is therefore likely to reduce the reliability of the estimate. 'The estimate is not reliable because the sample is small' is therefore true.

4a.7   The correct answer is: Y must be the dependent variable

The independent variable is denoted by X and the dependent one by Y.

4a.8   The correct answer is: 25.36

$$a = \frac{\sum y}{n} - b\frac{\sum x}{n}$$

where b = 17.14

$\sum x = 5.75$

$\sum y = 200$

n = 4

$$a = \frac{200}{4} - 17.14 \times \frac{5.75}{4}$$

$$= 50 - (17.14 \times 1.4375)$$
$$= 50 - 24.64$$
$$= 25.36 \text{ (to 2 decimal places)}$$

4a.9   The correct answer is: 2.33

$$a = \frac{\sum y}{n} - b\frac{\sum x}{n}$$

$$= \frac{330}{11} - b\frac{x440}{11}$$

$$b = \frac{n\sum xy - \sum x\sum y}{n\sum x^2 - (\sum x)^2}$$

$$= \frac{(11 \times 13,467) - (440 \times 330)}{(11 \times 17,986) - 440^2}$$

$$= \frac{148,137 - 145,200}{197,846 - 193,600}$$

$$= \frac{2,937}{4,246}$$

$$= 0.6917$$

$$\therefore a = \frac{330}{11} - (0.6917 \times \frac{440}{11}$$

$$= 30 - 27.668$$

$$= 2.332$$

$$= 2.33 \text{ (to 2 decimal places)}$$

4a.10   The correct answer is: 0

The correlation coefficient can take on any value from –1 to +1.

4a.11   The correct answer is: 92

y = 7.112 + 3.949x

If x = 19, trend in sales for month 19 = 7.112 + (3.949 × 19) = 82.143

Seasonally-adjusted trend value = 82.143 × 1.12 = 92

If you failed to select the correct option, rework the calculation carefully. You shouldn't have too much trouble with this question since it is just a matter of plugging in a value for x into the equation given in the question.

4a.12   The correct answer is: 300

If x = 16, y = 345.12 – (1.35 × 16) = 323.52

Forecast = trend + seasonal component = 323.52 – 23.62 = 299.9 = 300 (to nearest unit)

4a.13   The correct answer is: 5,109

$$\frac{4,700}{0.92} = 5,109 \text{ (to the nearest whole number)}$$

4a.14   The correct answer is: 123

y   = 9.82 + (4.372 × 24)

y   = 114.748

∴ forecast = 114.748 + 8.5
= 123.248
= 123

4a.15   The correct answer is: There must be no unforeseen events and The model used must fit the past data

Forecasts are made on the assumption that everything continues as in the past.

If the model being used is inappropriate, for example, if an additive model is used when the trend is changing sharply, forecasts will not be very reliable.

Provided a multiplicative model is used, the fact that the trend is increasing need not have any adverse effect on the reliability of forecasts.

Provided the seasonal variation remains the same in the future as in the past, it will not make forecasts unreliable.

4a.16   The correct answer is: To obtain an instant estimate of the trend

Seasonally adjusting the values in a time series removes the seasonal element from the data thereby giving an instant estimate of the trend.

4a.17   The correct answer is: (38, 40)

X = 38 and Y = 40

$$\frac{X + 36 + Y}{3} = 38$$

$$\frac{36 + Y + 41}{3} = 39$$

Y = (3 × 39) – 36 – 41 = 40

$$\frac{X + 36 + 40}{3} = 38$$

X = (38 × 3) – 36 – 40 = 38

4a.18   The correct answer is: 91

If   t = 1 in the first quarter of 20X5
     t = 8 in the fourth quarter of 20X6

Trend (Y)   = 65 + (7 × 8)
            = 121

Forecast   = trend + seasonal component
            = 121 + (–30)
            = 121 – 30
            = 91

4a.19   The correct answer is: $1,344

In the first month of 20X9, t = 13

∴ Y   = $1,500 – $(3 × 13)
      = $1,461

Forecast   = trend × seasonal component
            = $1,461 × 0.92
            = $1,344

4a.20   The correct answers are: The trend must continue as in the past and The same pattern of seasonal variation must continue as in the past

Provided the multiplicative model is used, it does not matter if the trend is increasing or decreasing.

Forecasts are made on the assumption that the previous trend will continue.

In general, extrapolation does not produce reliable estimates but in forecasting the future using time series analysis we have no option but to extrapolate.

Forecasts are made on the assumption that previous seasonal variations will continue.

4a.21   The correct answer is: When the trend is increasing or decreasing

When the trend is increasing or decreasing, additive seasonal components change in their importance relative to the trend whereas multiplicative components remain in the same proportion to the trend. Option B is therefore a circumstance in which the multiplicative model would be preferred to the additive model.

4a.22   The correct answer is: $140,000

In 20X9, t = 9
y = 20t – 10
y = (20 × 9) – 10
y = 180 – 10 = 170
∴ Forecast profits for 20X9 = 170 – 30 = 140
                                        = $140,000

4a.23   The correct answer is: 477,700

The additive model

Y = T + S

where   Y = actual series
        T = trend
        S = seasonal

The seasonally-adjusted value is an estimate of the trend.

∴ Y = T + S
   T = Y – S
   T = 567,800 – (+90,100)
   T = 477,700

4a.24   The correct answer is: (i) is true and (ii) is false

A Paasche index requires quantities to be ascertained each year and so constructing a Paasche index may therefore be costly. A Laspeyre index only requires them for the base year so (i) is true. The denominator of a Laspeyre index is fixed and therefore the Laspeyre index numbers for several different years can be directly compared. (ii) is therefore false.

4a.25   The correct answer is: 144

$$\text{Fisher's ideal index} = \sqrt{(\text{Laspeyre index} \times \text{Paasche index})}$$

$$= \sqrt{(150.00 \times 138.24)}$$

$$= \sqrt{20{,}736}$$

$$= 144$$

4a.26   The correct answer is: $0.93

$$\frac{106}{91} \times \$0.80 = \$0.93$$

4a.27   The correct answer is: $14.33

$(\$5 \times 430 \div 150) = \$14.33$

4a.28   The correct answer is: $39.23

$\$10 \times 510 \div 130 = \$39.23$

4a.29   The correct answer is: (i) and (ii) only

Spreadsheets are commonly used by management accountants (which include variance analysis, cash flow budgeting and forecasting) to produce management accounts, not financial accounts.

4a.30   The correct answer is: Writing a memo

A spreadsheet is unlikely to be used for writing a memo.

4a.31   The correct answer is: $4.13

ACCA examining team comments

The question relates to study guide references A3h and C2n.

The correct answer is B. This is calculated by firstly adjusting the overhead cost from 2 years ago to current price levels by multiplying by 155/121, to obtain a cost of $4,740. This figure is then used in a high low calculation (change in cost divided by change in activity) to obtain the variable cost per unit (($13,000 - $4,740) / (3,000 units − 1,000 units) = $4.13).

The most popular choice was alternative C, which was selected by majority of candidates. This indicates that although competent in the high low technique they failed to adjust costs to current price levels. In analysing cost data it is important that inflation is allowed for. Those who chose option D indicated that either they guessed badly, or that they could competently perform the high low calculation and that they realised a need to adjust the figures for inflation but failed to do so correctly and multiplied by 121/155). Finally a minority chose alternative A, again possibly suggesting a bad guess or alternatively that they indexed costs to price levels from two years ago.

4a.32   The correct answer is: 4,053

> **ACCA examining team comments**
>
> The question relates to study guide reference C2k.
>
> The correct answer is D. This is calculated by firstly computing the trend for fourth quarter of 2015 (Y = 4,000 + 6 × 8 = 4,048) and then adding a seasonal adjustment of 5, to give forecast sales of 4,053.
>
> The most popular choice was alternative C. This indicates that many candidates were able to calculate the trend but failed to apply the seasonal adjustment. Distracters (the incorrect answers to objective test questions) are often based upon partially complete calculations. Candidates are advised not to stop thinking as soon as they generate a number that corresponds with one of the options offered. A good way of avoiding this trap is not to look at the answers until you are satisfied that you have fully completed your calculation.
>
> Answer A used a value of 4 for period 4 of 2015 and generated the wrong trend figure, but then correctly processed the seasonal adjustment. Finally a minority of candidates selected answer B, indicating that they could correctly calculate trend but subtracted rather than added the seasonal adjustment.

4a.33   The correct answer is: 2,500

> **ACCA examining team comments**
>
> Spreadsheet based questions are commonly some of the worst answered questions in the exam and this one proved no exception. The correct answer is 2,500. This is arrived at by averaging the four quarter moving totals that straddle quarter 4, 2014.((9,000 + 11,000) ÷ 2 = 10,000). This gives a centred moving total, which when averaged over the four quarters (10,000 ÷ 4) gives 2,500. The most popular choice was 10,000. Candidates here failed to complete the final step and chose the centred moving total rather than a centred moving average. It is common practice by the examining team, when writing multiple choice questions, to offer distracters (wrong answers) based on a figure that occurs part way through the calculation of the right answer. With this in mind candidates should make sure their calculations are complete before looking at the 4 alternative answers on offer.

4a.34   The correct answer is: $5.38

> **ACCA examining team comments**
>
> The correct answer is $5.38, chosen by only a small minority of candidates. To arrive at this answer candidates needed to firstly use the price index data to express the 2012 overhead cost in 2013 prices ($12,000 x 140/130 = $12,923). Then they needed to use the high low method to calculate variable cost per unit. (($14,000 - $12,923)/(1,200 units − 1,000 units) = $5.38).

4b Summarising and analysing data

4b.1   The correct answer is: $24

Total of invoices   =   average × 10 = 20 × 10

15 + 22 + 14 + 21 + 15 + 20 + 18 + 27   =   152

$$2X + 152 = 200$$
$$2X = 200 - 152 = 48$$
$$X = \$24$$

$19 is incorrect because it represents the arithmetic mean of the values (excluding the Xs), ie 152 ÷ 8 = 19. It also represents the median of the values shown.

If you selected $48 then this indicates that you only accounted for one $X instead of two.

$15 represents the mode and is therefore incorrect.

4b.2   The correct answer is: $65

To calculate a mean factory wage we need to determine total wages and total number of employees.

Department	Mean wage $	Number of employees	Total wage $
W	50	× 20	= 1,000
X	100	× 5	= 500
Y	70	× 10	= 700
Z	80	× 5	= 400
		40	2,600

Mean factory wage = $2,600/40 = $65

$50 represents the most frequently occurring wage ($50) or the mode and is therefore incorrect.

$70 represents the second most frequently occurring wage and is also incorrect.

$75 is simply the average of the mean wages (an unweighted average), ie 50 + 100 + 70 + 80 = 300 ÷ 4 = 75. This option is also incorrect.

4b.3   The correct answer is: 36

To calculate a mean speed we need to know the distance and the time of the journey.

Time = 20/30 hr + 10/60 hr = 5/6 hr
∴ Mean speed = 30 miles ÷ 5/6 hr = 36 mph

40 is incorrectly calculated as follows.

(20 miles × 30 mph) + (10 miles × 60 mph) = 600 + 600 = 1,200

Total distance travelled = 30 miles
∴ Mean speed = 1,200 ÷ 30 = 40 mph (incorrect)

Remember that you need to know the length of time that it took to travel the 30 mile distance.

45 mph represents an average of 30 mph and 60 mph (30 + 60 = 90 ÷ 2 = 45). This is also incorrect.

4b.4   The correct answer is: 14.50

In order of magnitude scores are

8   9   11   12   14   15   17   21   24   34

Position of median is $\frac{10+1}{2}$ = 5½ and therefore the median is the average of 5th and 6th items, that is of 14 and 15. The median is therefore 14.5.

4b.5   The correct answer is: 31

The median is the middle value in order of magnitude.

9   12   23   24   28   34   43   56   78   87

In this case there are two middle values, 28 and 34, and so the median is their average = (28 + 34)/2 = 31.

28 and 34 represent the two middle values and are therefore incorrect. The average of the two middle values must be calculated when establishing the median of a set of scores.

26 is incorrect since it represents the average between the 4th and 5th items (24 and 28).

4b.6   The correct answer is: Process X

The coefficient of variation $= \dfrac{\text{Standard deviation}}{\text{Mean}}$

The coefficients of variation are calculated as follows:

W: $\dfrac{10}{100} \times 100 \; = 10\%$

X: $\dfrac{5}{40} \times 100 \; = 12\frac{1}{2}\%$

Y: $\dfrac{8}{80} \times 100 \; = 10\%$

Z: $\dfrac{12}{150} \times 100 \; = 8\%$

4b.7   The correct answer is: Data A

	A	B	C	D
Mean	150	175	200	250
Standard deviation	25	20	25	30
Coefficient of variation*	0.167	0.114	0.125	0.120

*Coefficient of variation $= \dfrac{\text{Standard deviation}}{\text{Mean}}$

The bigger the coefficient of variation, the wider the spread. The largest coefficient of variation is for that of data set A. The correct answer is therefore Data A.

4b.8

4

The mode is the most frequently occurring number of loaves required by a shopper, ie 4 loaves.

Remember, the mode is the most frequently occurring item.

4b.9   The correct answer is: 2 and 3 only

☑ The standard deviation will increase by 14%

☑ The coefficient of variation will be unaltered

If everybody's salary rises by 14%, the mean salary will also rise by 14%. In computing the standard deviation, we work out $(x - \bar{x})^2$ for each employee, add up the results, divide by n and then take the square root. If each employee's salary and the mean salary are all increased by 14%, each $(x - \bar{x})$ will rise by 14%. Because the squaring is followed by square rooting, the overall effect will be to increase the standard deviation by 14%.

Since both the standard deviation and the mean increase by 14%, the coefficient of variation, which is the one divided by the other, will be unchanged.

4b.10   The correct answer is: Relative dispersion

The spreads of two distributions can be compared by using the coefficient of variation (or the coefficient of relative dispersion).

4b.11   The correct answer is: Project B $4,760

The expected value for each project is as follows.

Project A   (0.45 × $4,000) + (0.55 × $2,000)   = $1,800 + $1,100
                                                    = $2,900

Project B   (0.64 × $8,000) + (0.36 × ($1,000)) = $5,120 − $360
                                                    = $4,760

Project B has a higher expected value of profit which means that it could offer a better return than A, so Project B should be chosen (with an expected profit of $4,760).

The first two options are incorrect because project A does not have the highest expected value.

If you selected the last option, you forgot to take account of the expected loss of $1,000 and treated it as a profit instead.

4b.12   The correct answer is: $710,000

Expected value = probability × profit

Contract	Probability	Estimated profits $	Expected value $
A	1/2	500,000	250,000
B	1/5	800,000	160,000
C	1/3	900,000	300,000
		2,200,000	710,000

$300,000 is incorrect because it is just the highest expected value (from Contract C).

$733,000 is the arithmetic mean of the estimated profits ($2,200,000 ÷ 3 = $733,000).

$900,000 is the maximum expected profit from any one contract, ie $900,000 from Contract C.

4b.13   The correct answer is: 3,900

The expected value = (1,000 × 0.3) + (4,000 × 0.5) + (8,000 × 0.2) = 3,900

4,000 represents the most likely sales level, you forgot to calculate the expected value.

4,333 represents the arithmetic mean, you forgot to calculate the expected value.

13,000 is the total of estimated sales at different levels of probability, you forgot to calculate the expected level of sales.

4b.14   The correct answer is: EV of demand = ⟨ 6,500 ⟩ units

Workings

Demand Units	Probability	Expected value Units
5,000	0.1	500
6,000	0.6	3,600
8,000	0.3	2,400
		6,500

4b.15   The correct answer is: EV of unit variable costs = $ ⟨ 3.70 ⟩ (to 2 decimal places)

Workings

Variable costs $	Probability	Expected value $
3.00	0.1	0.30
3.50	0.5	1.75
4.00	0.3	1.20
4.50	0.1	0.45
		3.70

4b.16   The correct answer is: EV of profit = $ | 10,950 |

Workings

	$
Sales 6,500 × $10	65,000
Less variable costs 6,500 × $3.70	24,050
Contribution	40,950
Less fixed costs	30,000
	10,950

4b.17   The correct answer is:0.15

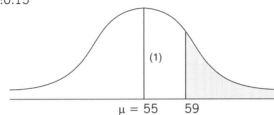

Standard deviation (σ) = $\sqrt{\text{variance}}$

= $\sqrt{14.44}$

= 3.8

We are therefore looking for the probability corresponding to the shaded area on the graph above. Using normal distribution tables we can calculate the area (1) above.

$$z = \frac{x - \mu}{\sigma}$$

$$= \frac{59 - 55}{3.8}$$

$$= 1.05$$

A z value of 1.05 corresponds to a probability of 0.3531.

∴ Area (1) = 0.3531 and therefore the shaded area that we are interested in = 0.5 – 0.3531 = 0.1469 = 0.15.

If you incorrectly selected 0.35, you forgot to deduct the probability of area (1) from 0.5.

You could have eliminated 0.5 immediately. The probability of a score of 55 or more (not 59) is exactly 0.5.

0.85 is also incorrect and represents the probability of a score of 59 or **less**, ie 0.5 + 0.3531 = 0.8531 or 0.85.

4b.18   The correct answer is: 78.35

25% of normal frequencies will occur between the mean and the upper quartile. From normal distribution tables, 25% of frequencies lie between the mean and a point 0.67 standard deviations above the mean.

The standard deviation is the square root of the variance and is $\sqrt{25}$ = 5 in this case.

The upper quartile is therefore 0.67 × 5 = 3.35 above the mean

∴ The upper quartile = 3.35 + 75 = 78.35

You should have been able to eliminate the first two options straightaway since 58.25 and 71.65 are **below** the mean. The upper quartile of any distribution will be **above** the mean. 71.65 represents the **lower quartile** (75 – 3.35).

If you had forgotten to take the square root of the variance in order to obtain the standard deviation, you would have calculated the upper quartile as being 0.67 × 25 = 16.75 above the mean, ie 75 + 16.75 = 91.75. 91.75 is therefore also incorrect for this reason.

4b.19   The correct answer is: 167

It is always best to sketch a rough diagram first when tackling a normal distribution question such as this.

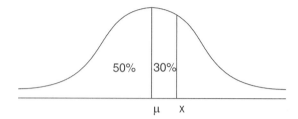

$\mu = 150$
$\sigma = 20$

We need to find the point X such that 30% of the distribution falls between the mean and x.

From normal distribution tables, we can see that 30% of the distribution lies between the mean and 0.84 standard deviations above the mean.

If $z = \dfrac{x - \alpha}{\sigma}$

$0.84 = \dfrac{x - 150}{20}$

$x - 150 = 0.84 \times 20$
$x - 150 = 16.8$
$x = 16.8 + 150$
$= 166.8$

Therefore 80% of the distribution lies below the point 167 (approximately).

You must make sure that you are confident with reading normal distribution tables in OT questions – you are unlikely to gain any marks at all in such questions if you read them incorrectly.

4b.20   The correct answer is: 0.675099

Total area under normal curve = 1

Therefore each of four areas = 0.25

The table shows the area between 0 and the specified value of Z so we must find the value 0.25 in the table and the Z value that corresponds most closely to it.

Z = 0.67

Sketch a normal distribution curve and divide it into four areas if you are not convinced about the answer to this question!

4b.21   The correct answer is: 8%

$\mu = 50$ cm
$\sigma = 5$ cm

57 cm is 7 cm above the mean = 1.4 standard deviations above the mean.

Using normal distribution tables, the proportion between the mean and 1.4 standard deviations above the mean = 0.4192

∴ The percentage of tubes at least 57 cm long is (0.5 – 0.4192) = 0.0808 = 8.08%

The percentage is closest to 8%.

42% represents the proportion of tubes between 50 and 57 cm long.

58% represents the proportion of tubes below the mean and above 57cm.

92% represents the proportion of tubes below 57 cm.

4b.22   The correct answer is: 0.0082

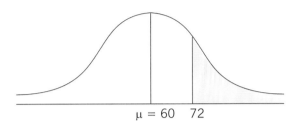

μ = 60   72

We are interested in the shaded area shown in the graph above. We can calculate z score using the following formula.

$$z = \frac{X - \mu}{\sigma}$$

$$= \frac{72 - 60}{\sqrt{25}}$$

$$= \frac{12}{5}$$

$$= 2.4$$

Using normal distribution tables, we can calculate that the probability of a score between 60 and 72 is 0.4918 (where z = 2.4). The probability of a score greater than 72 is 0.5 – 0.4918 = 0.0082.

4b.23   The correct answer is: 76.42%

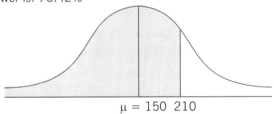

μ = 150 210

We are interested in the shaded area shown in the graph above. We can calculate the z score using the following formula.

$$z = \frac{X - \mu}{\sigma}$$

$$= \frac{210 - 150}{\sqrt{6,944}}$$

$$= \frac{60}{83.33} = 0.72$$

From normal distribution tables, the probability of a value between 150 and 210 is 0.2642. Therefore the probability of a value less than 210 = 0.5 + 0.2642 = 0.7642 or 76.42%.

If you selected 23.58%, you incorrectly subtracted 0.2642 from 0.5 instead of adding it.

If you selected 26.42%, you forgot to add your answer to 0.5.

If you selected 72.00%, you forgot to convert your z score into a probability using normal distribution tables.

4b.24   The correct answer is: 656.7

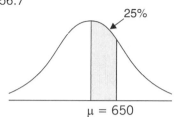

25% of normal frequencies will occur between the mean and the upper quartile. From normal distribution tables, 25% of frequencies lie between the mean and a point 0.67 standard deviations above the mean (ie our z score is 0.67).

Let x = upper quartile

If $z = \dfrac{x - \mu}{\sigma}$

and $\sigma = \sqrt{100} = 10$

$$0.67 = \frac{x - 650}{10}$$
$$(0.67 \times 10) = x - 650$$
$$6.7 = x - 650$$
$$x = 650 + 6.7$$
$$= 656.7$$

Therefore the upper quartile = 656.7 and the correct answer is therefore 656.7.

If you selected 643.3, you calculated the lower quartile of the distribution (the question required you to calculate the upper quartile).

If you chose 717.0, you forgot to calculate the standard deviation (and used the value given for the variance, ie 100).

If you chose 812.5, you simply took 25% of the mean (650 × 25% = 162.5) and added it to the mean (162.5 + 650 = 812.5) which is not the correct way to calculate the upper quartile.

4b.25   The correct answer is: 0.32

Total area under normal curve = 1.

Therefore each of eight areas = 0.125 (0.125 × 8 = 1).

Normal distribution tables show the area between 0 and the specified value of z so we must find the value of 0.125 in the tables and the z value that corresponds most closely to it.

z = 0.32

Sketch a normal distribution curve and divide it into eight areas if you are not convinced about the answer to this question!

4b.26   The correct answer is: 0.0314

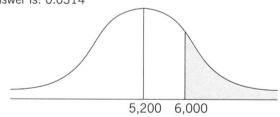

We are interested in calculating the area of the shaded part of the graph above.

We can find the area of the graph that lies between 5,200kg and 6,000kg as follows.

BPP
LEARNING MEDIA

Using $z = \dfrac{x - \mu}{\sigma}$

$z = \dfrac{6,000 - 5,200}{430}$

$z = 1.86$

$z = 1.86$ corresponds to an area of 0.4686. However, we are interested in the shaded area = 0.5 – 0.4686 = 0.0314.

If you selected 0.2343, you divided the probability obtained (0.4686) by 2 instead of subtracting it from 0.5.

If you selected 0.4686, you forgot to subtract 0.4686 from 0.5.

If you selected 0.9686, you added 0.4686 to 0.5 instead of subtracting it.

4b.27 The correct answers are: If a sample is selected using random sampling, it will be free from bias and In quota sampling, investigators are told to interview all the people they meet up to a certain quota.

A **sampling frame** is a numbered list of all items in a **population** (not a **sample**).

Cluster sampling involves selecting one definable subsection of the population which therefore makes the potential for bias considerable.

4b.28 The correct answer is: None of the above

In quota sampling, investigators are told to interview all of the people they meet up to a certain quota.

5 Accounting for materials

5.1 The correct answer is: (i) and (ii) only

Among other things, the GRN is used to update the inventory records and to check that the quantity invoiced by the supplier was actually received. The GRN does not usually contain price information. Therefore the correct answer is (i) and (ii) only.

5.2 The correct answer is: 1,750

Free inventory balance	=	units in inventory + units on order from suppliers – units outstanding on customers' orders
13,000	=	units in inventory + 27,500 – 16,250
∴ Units in inventory	=	13,000 – 27,500 + 16,250 = 1,750

5.3 The correct answer is: 1,710 units

Reorder level = maximum usage × maximum lead time
= 95 × 18
= 1,710 units

5.4 The correct answer is: 2,860 units

Maximum level = reorder level + reorder quantity – (minimum usage × minimum lead time)
= 1,710 + 1,750 – (50 × 12) = 2,860 units

5.5 The correct answer is: 163

$$EOQ = \sqrt{\dfrac{2CoD}{C_h}} = \dfrac{2 \times \$80 \times 2,500}{\$15} = 163$$

5.6   The correct answer is: (i), (ii) and (iii)

Stock-outs arise when too little inventory is held (i); safety inventories are the level of units maintained in case there is unexpected demand (ii); and a reorder level can be established by looking at the maximum usage and the maximum lead-time (iii). Therefore, they are all correct statements with regards to inventories.

5.7   The correct answer is: order quantity

The economic batch quantity is used to establish the optimal order quantity.

5.8   The correct answer is: 1,155

$$EOQ = \sqrt{\frac{2C_oD}{C_H}}$$

Where $C_o = 20$
$D = 12,500 \times 4 = 50,000$
$C_H = 10\% \times \$15 = 1.50$

$$EOQ = \sqrt{\frac{2 \times 20 \times 50,000}{1.50}}$$

$$= \sqrt{1,333,333}$$

$$= 1,155 \text{ units}$$

5.9   The correct answer is: EOQ Lower Total annual holding cost Lower

If there is a decrease in the cost of ordering a batch of raw material, then the EOQ will also be lower (as the numerator in the EOQ equation will be lower). If the EOQ is lower, than average inventory held (EOQ/2) with also be lower and therefore the total annual holding costs will also be lower.

5.10   The correct answer is: 7,800 units

Reorder level = maximum usage × maximum lead time
          = 520 × 15
          = 7,800 units

5.11   The correct answer is: (ii), (iii) and (iv) only

Statement (i) is not correct. A debit to stores with a corresponding credit to work in progress (WIP) indicates that **direct materials returned** from production were $18,000.

Statement (ii) is correct. **Direct costs of production** are 'collected' in the WIP account.

Statement (iii) is correct. **Indirect costs of production or overhead** are 'collected' in the overhead control account.

Statement (iv) is correct. The purchases of materials on credit are credited to the creditors account and debited to the material stores control account.

Therefore the correct answer is (ii), (iii) and (iv) only.

5.12   The correct answer is: $3,000

Annual holding cost

= [buffer (safety) inventory + reorder level/2)] × holding cost per unit

= [500 + (2,000/2)] × $2

= $3,000

5.13   The correct answer is: 300 units

The economic order quantity is 300 units.

The formula for the economic order quantity (EOQ) is

$$EOQ = \sqrt{\frac{2C_oD}{C_h}}$$

With C_o = $10

D   = 5,400 ÷ 12 = 450 per month

C_h = $0.10

$$EOQ = \sqrt{\frac{2 \times \$10 \times 450}{\$0.10}}$$

$$= \sqrt{90,000}$$

$$= 300 \text{ units}$$

5.14   The correct answer is: 400

The level of safety inventory is 400 units (to the nearest whole unit).

Let x = safety inventory

$$\text{Average inventory} = \text{safety inventory (x)} + \frac{\text{reorder quantity}}{2}$$

3,400   = $x + \dfrac{6,000}{2}$

3,400   = x + 3,000

x   = 3,400 – 3,000

∴x   = $\underline{400}$ units

5.15   The correct answer is: 175 units

The economic order quantity is 175 units (to the nearest whole unit).

$$EOQ = \sqrt{\frac{2C_oD}{C_h}}$$

$$= \sqrt{\frac{2 \times \$100 \times 1,225}{\$8}}$$

$$= \sqrt{30,625}$$

$$= 175 \text{ units}$$

5.16   The correct answer is: 6,180 units

Reorder level = maximum usage × maximum lead time

= 130 × 26 = 3,380 units

Maximum level   = reorder level + reorder quantity – (minimum usage × minimum lead time)

= 3,380 + 4,000 – (60 × 20)

= 6,180 units

5.17 The correct answer is: 31,623 units

$$EBQ = \sqrt{\frac{2C_0D}{C_h(1-D/R)}}$$

$$Q = \sqrt{\frac{2 \times 125 \times 5,000}{0.0025(1-5,000/10,000)}}$$

$$= \sqrt{\frac{1,250,000}{0.00125}}$$

= 31,623 units

5.18 The correct answer is: At point C

The EOQ is found where the holding costs equal the ordering costs. You need to read the value of units on the x axis of the graph at point C.

5.19 The correct answer is: $44,953.50

The company could order the EOQ amount of 160 or it could order 300 units and take a discount of 2%. We need to work out which is the cheapest option.

		$
Purchases (no discount)	1,800 × $25	45,000
Holding costs (W1)		360
Ordering costs (W2)		360
Total annual costs		45,720

Workings

1   Holding costs   = average inventory × holding cost for one unit of inventory for one year

    Average inventory   = order quantity ÷ 2

                           = 160 ÷ 2 = 80 units

    Holding cost for one unit of inventory for one year = $4.50

    ∴ holding costs   = 80 units × $4.50 = $360

2   Ordering costs   = number of orders × ordering costs per order ($32)

    Number of orders   = Annual demand ÷ order quantity

                           = 1,800 ÷ 160

                           = 11.25 orders

    ∴ ordering cost   = 11.25 orders × $32

                           = $360

With a discount of 2% and an order quantity of 300 units, unit costs are as follows.

		$
Purchases	$45,000 × 98%	44,100.00
Holding costs (W1)		661.50
Ordering costs (W2)		192.00
Total annual costs		44,953.50

Workings

1   Holding costs   = average inventory × holding cost for one unit of inventory for one year

    Average inventory   = order quantity ÷ 2

                            = 300 ÷ 2 = 150 units

    Holding cost for one unit of inventory for one year = $4.50 × 98% = $4.41

    ∴ holding costs   = 150 units × $4.41 = $661.50

2   Ordering costs   = number of orders × ordering costs per order ($32)

    Number of orders   = Annual demand ÷ order quantity

        = 1,800 ÷ 300

        = 6 orders

    ∴ ordering cost   = 6 orders × $32

        = $192

The cheapest option is to order 300 at a time and accept the discount.

Workings for both questions 5.20 and 5.21.

| | | | FIFO | | | LIFO | |
		Units	$/unit	Value $	Units	$/Unit	Value $
Purchase	1/1	4,000	2.50	10,000	4,000	2.50	10,000
	31/1	1,000	2.00	2,000	1,000	2.00	2,000
		5,000		12,000	5,000		12,000
Sales	15/2	(3,000)	2.50	(7,500)	(1,000)	2.00	(2,000)
					(2,000)	2.50	(5,000)
		2,000		4,500	2,000		5,000
Purchase	28/2	1,500	2.50	3,750	1,500	2.50	3,750
		3,500		8,250	3,500		8,750
Sales	14/3	(500)	2.50	(1,250)	(500)	2.50	(1,250)
		3,000		7,000	3,000		7,500

5.20   The correct answer is: $7,000

    See workings above. If you selected the wrong option then check your workings carefully against the above table.

5.21   The correct answer is: $7,500

    See workings above. If you selected the wrong option then check your workings carefully against the above table.

5.22   The correct answer is: $4,492

		Units	$
Opening inventory	300 × $25	300	7,500
Issue on 2 Jan	256 × $25	(250)	(6,250)
		50	1,250
Receipt on 12 Jan		400	10,300
		450	11,550
Issues on 21 Jan and 29 Jan (11,550/450) × (200 + 75)		(275)	(7,058)
		175	4,492

6 Accounting for labour

6.1   The correct answer is: 107.4%

    Budgeted hours = 3,000 + 8,000 + 7,000 + 9,000 = 27,000

$$\text{Capacity ratio} = \frac{\text{actual hours worked}}{\text{budgeted hours}} = \frac{29,000}{27,000} \times 100\% = 107.4\%$$

6.2   The correct answer is: 96.2%

Product	Units	Standard hours	
W	12,000	(× 0.2)	2,400
X	25,000	(× 0.4)	10,000
Y	16,000	(× 0.5)	8,000
Z	5,000	(× 1.5)	7,500
			27,900

$$\text{Efficiency ratio} = \frac{\text{Standard hours produced}}{\text{Actual hours worked}} = \frac{27,900}{29,000} \times 100\% = 96.2\%$$

6.3   The correct answer is: A piece rate scheme with a minimum guaranteed wage

The graph shows a constant wage up to a certain level of output, which is payable even at zero output. This is the minimum guaranteed wage. Above a certain output the wage cost rises at a constant rate. This is the piece rate payable in addition to the minimum wage.

Graphs for the other options would look like this:

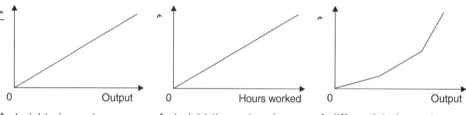

A straight piece rate scheme   A straight time rate scheme   A differential piece rate scheme

6.4   The correct answer is: $50

	Hours
Standard time for 180 units (× 4/60)	12
Actual time taken	7
Time saved	5

	$
Basic pay 7 hours × $5	35
Bonus: 60% × 5 hours saved × $5 per hour	15
	50

6.5   The correct answer is: $47.90

Number of units qualifying for payment   = 210 − 17
                                         = 193

Piecework payment to be made:

	$
First 100 units @ $0.20	20.00
Last 93 units @ $0.30	27.90
	47.90

6.6   The correct answer is: $140.40

The overtime premium paid at the specific request of a customer would be treated as a direct cost because it can be traced to a specific cost unit.

The four hours of machine breakdown is idle time. It cannot be traced to a specific cost unit therefore it is an indirect cost.

The direct wages cost is as follows.

	$
Basic pay for active hours (38 hours × $3.60)	136.80
Overtime premium re: customer request (2 hours × $1.80)	3.60
	140.40

6.7   The correct answers are: Group bonus schemes are appropriate when increased output depends on a number of people all making extra effort and Non-production employees can be rewarded as part of a group incentive scheme

Group bonus schemes are useful to reward performance when production is integrated so that all members of the group must work harder to increase output, for example in production line manufacture. 'Group bonus schemes are appropriate when increased output depends on a number of people all making extra effort' is therefore true.

Group bonus schemes are not effective in linking the reward to a particular individual's performance. Even if one individual makes a supreme effort, this can be negated by poor performance from other members of the group. Therefore 'With a group bonus scheme, it is easier to award each individual's performance' is not true.

Non-production employees can be included in a group incentive scheme, for example when all employees in a management accounting department must work harder to produce prompt budgetary control reports. 'Non-production employees can be rewarded as part of a group incentive scheme' is therefore true.

Group bonus schemes are easier to administer because they reduce clerical effort required to measure output and calculate individual bonuses. 'Compared with individual schemes, group bonus schemes are difficult to administer' is therefore false.

6.8   The correct answer is:

	Debit	Credit
Work in progress account	70,800	
Overhead control account	2,500	
Wages control account		73,300

The overtime was not worked for any specific job and is therefore an **indirect wages cost** to be 'collected' in the overhead control account. Similarly, the holiday pay is an **indirect cost**, therefore the total **debit to the overhead control account** is $2,500. The **direct wages** of $70,800 is **debited to the work in progress account** and the total wages cost is **credited to the wages control account**.

6.9   The correct answer is: 20%

Reduction in number of employees = 30 – 20 = 10
Number of employees leaving   = 15
∴ Number of employees replaced   = 15 – 10 = 5

$$\text{Labour turnover rate} = \frac{\text{replacements}}{\text{average no. of employees in period}} \times 100\%$$

$$= \frac{5}{(30 + 20) \div 2} \times 100\%$$

$$= 20\%$$

6.10   The correct answer is: $5.04

	Hours
Standard time for 80 units (× 9/60)	12
Actual time taken	8
Time saved	4

Group bonus : 70% × 4 hours saved × $6 per hour = $16.80

Jane's share of bonus = 50% × ($16.80 × 60%)
                       = $5.04

6.11   The correct answer is:

DR   Overhead control   CR   Wages control

Indirect wages are 'collected' in the overhead control account, for subsequent absorption into work in progress.

6.12   The correct answer is: 0.26%

$$\text{Labour turnover rate} = \frac{\text{Replacements}}{\text{Average number of employees in period}} \times 100\%$$

$$= \frac{10}{(4,000 + 3,800) \div 2} \times 100$$

$$= 0.26\%$$

7a Accounting for overheads

7a.1   The correct answer is: $10,160

Number of employees in packing department = 2 direct + 1 indirect = 3

Number of employees in all production departments = 15 direct + 6 indirect = 21

Packing department overhead

Canteen cost apportioned to packing department	=	$\frac{\$8,400}{21} \times 3$
	=	$1,200
Original overhead allocated and apportioned	=	$8,960
Total overhead after apportionment of canteen costs	=	$10,160

7a.2   The correct answer is: $0.60 per machine hour

Department 1 appears to undertake primarily machine-based work, therefore a machine-hour rate would be most appropriate.

$$\frac{\$27,000}{45,000} = \$0.60 \text{ per machine hour}$$

7a.3   The correct answer is: $0.72 per direct labour hour

Department 2 appears to be labour-intensive therefore a direct labour-hour rate would be most appropriate.

$$\frac{\$18,000}{25,000} = \$0.72 \text{ per direct labour hour}$$

7a.4   The correct answers are: Using a predetermined absorption rate avoids fluctuations in unit costs caused by abnormally high or low overhead expenditure or activity levels and Using a predetermined absorption rate offers the administrative convenience of being able to record full production costs sooner

'Using a predetermined absorption rate avoids fluctuations in unit costs caused by abnormally high or low overhead expenditure or activity levels' is correct because a constant unit absorption rate is used throughout the period. 'Using a predetermined absorption rate offers the administrative convenience of being able to record full production costs sooner' is correct because 'actual' overhead costs, based on actual overhead expenditure and actual activity for the period, cannot be determined until after the end of the period. 'Using a predetermined absorption rate avoids problems of under/over absorption of overheads because a constant overhead rate is available' is incorrect because under/over absorption of overheads is caused by the use of predetermined overhead absorption rates.

Using a predetermined absorption rate still requires the use of an appropriate base and so ' Using a predetermined absorption rate avoids the problems associated with choosing an appropriate absorption base' is false.

7a.5   The correct answer is: Absorbed overheads exceed actual overheads

'Absorbed overheads exceed budgeted overheads' could lead to under-absorbed overheads if actual overheads far exceeded both budgeted overheads and the overhead absorbed. 'Actual overheads exceed absorbed overheads' could lead to under-absorbed overheads if overhead absorbed does not increase in line with actual overhead incurred.

7a.6   The correct answer is: $405,000

Budgeted absorption rate for fixed overhead   = $360,000/8,000
                                              = $45 per unit

Fixed overhead absorbed   = 9,000 units × $45
                          = $405,000

7a.7   The correct answer is: Under absorbed by $27,000

Actual fixed overhead incurred $432,000
Fixed overhead absorbed $405,000 (from question 6)
Fixed overhead under absorbed $27,000

7a.8   The correct answer is: The value of the machinery in each cost centre

The insurance cost is likely to be linked to the cost of replacing the machines, therefore the most appropriate basis for apportionment is the value of machinery.

7a.9   The correct answer is: (i), (ii), (iii) and (iv)

All of the overhead absorption methods are suitable, depending on the circumstances.

Method 1, direct labour hours, is suitable in a labour-intensive environment.

Method 2, machine hours, is suitable in a machine-intensive environment.

Method 3, a percentage of prime costs, can be used if it is difficult to obtain the necessary information to use a time-based method. **Method 4**, a rate per unit, is suitable if all cost units are identical.

7a.10   The correct answer is: Indirect material issued from inventory was $22,800 and Indirect wages costs incurred were $180,400

'Indirect material issued from inventory was $22,800' is correct. The cost of indirect material issued is 'collected' in the overhead control account **pending absorption into work in progress**.

'Overhead absorbed during the period was $210,000' is incorrect. The overhead cost **incurred** was $210,000. The overhead **absorbed into work in progress** during the period was $404,800.

'Overhead for the period was over absorbed by $8,400' is incorrect. The $8,400 is **debited to the statement of profit or loss**, indicating an extra charge to compensate for the overhead **under absorbed**.

'Indirect wages costs incurred were $180,400' is correct. The indirect wage cost is 'collected' in the overhead control account **pending absorption into work in progress**.

7a.11   The correct answer is: Only production related costs should be considered

Only production related costs should be considered when considering the allocation, apportionment and reapportionment of overhead in an absorption costing situation.

7a.12   The correct answer is: $30,000

	$
Actual fixed production overheads	X
Absorbed fixed production overheads (4,500 × $8)	36,000
Over-absorbed fixed production overheads	6,000

Actual fixed production overheads   = $36,000 – $6,000
                                    = $30,000

7a.13   The correct answer is: $15

	Production cost centre	
	Primary	*Finishing*
Allocated and apportioned	$96,000	$82,500
Total direct labour hours	9,600 hours	6,875 hours
Fixed overhead absorption rate	$10 per hour	$12 per hour

Workings

(1)   Total direct labour hours – Primary = (6,000 × 36/60) hours + (7,500 × 48/60) hours
= (3,600 + 6,000) hours
= 9,600 hours

(2)   Total direct labour hours – Finishing = (6,000 × 25/60) hours + (7,500 × 35/60) hours
= (2,500 + 4,375) hours
= 6,875 hours

Budgeted fixed overhead cost per unit for Product Y

Primary   = 48 minutes/60 minutes × $10 per hour
= $8 per unit

Finishing   = 35 minutes/60 minutes × $12 per hour
= $7 per unit

Total   = $8 + $7
= $15 per unit of Product Y

7a.14   The correct answer is: Under absorbed by $3,875

	$
Absorbed overhead (30,000 hours × $3.50)	105,000
Actual overhead	108,875
Under-absorbed overhead	3,875

7a.15   The correct answer is: $127,000
Using simultaneous equations:

Let P   = overheads for department P after reapportionment
X   = overheads for department X after reapportionment
Y   = overheads for department Y after reapportionment

P   = 95,000 + 0.4X + 0.3Y
X   = 46,000 + 0.1Y
Y   = 30,000 + 0.2X

X   = 46,000 + 0.1 (30,000 + 0.2X)
X   = 46,000 + 3,000 + 0.02X
X   = 49,000 + 0.02X
X   – 0.02X = 49,000
0.98X = 49,000
X   = 49,000/0.98
= 50,000

If X   = 50,000
Y   = 30,000 + (0.2 × 50,000)
Y   = 30,000 + 10,000
Y   = 40,000
∴ X   = 50,000 and Y = 40,000

∴ P   = 95,000 + 0.4X + 0.3Y
= 95,000 + (0.4 × 50,000 + (0.3 × 40,000)
= 95,000 + 20,000 + 12,000
= 127,000

7a.16   The correct answer is: Overhead was $12,500 under absorbed

Production overhead absorption rate = $150,000/60,000
= $2.50 per machine hour

Production overhead absorbed   = $2.50 × 55,000 hours
= $137,500

Production overhead incurred   = $150,000

Production overhead under absorbed = $ 12,500

7a.17   The correct answer is: 14,850

$$\text{Budgeted hours} = \frac{\text{Budgeted overheads}}{\text{Budgeted overhead absorption rate}}$$

$$= \frac{\$475,200}{\$32}$$

$$= 14,850$$

7a.18   The correct answer is: 45 per machine hour

The machine hour absorption rate is (to the nearest $) $45 per machine hour.

$$\text{Machine hour absorption rate} = \frac{\text{Budgeted overheads}}{\text{Budgeted machine hours}}$$

$$= \frac{\$690,480}{15,344}$$

$$= \$45 \text{ per machine hour}$$

7a.19   The correct answer is: $25

The budgeted overhead absorption rate was $25 per machine hour (to the nearest $).

	$
Actual overheads incurred	496,500
Over-absorbed overhead	64,375
Actual overheads absorbed	560,875

$$\frac{\text{Actual overheads absorbed}}{\text{Actual machine hours}} = \text{Amount absorbed per machine hour}$$

$$\frac{\$560,875}{22,435} = \$25 \text{ per machine hour}$$

7a.20   The correct answer is: Under absorbed by $25,000

Fixed production overhead was under absorbed by $25,000

	$
Overhead absorbed (110,000 std hours × $2.50)	275,000
Overhead incurred	300,000
Overhead under absorbed	25,000

The overhead is under absorbed because the overhead absorbed was less than the overhead incurred.

7a.21   The correct answers are: If the direct method is used, the order in which the service cost centre overheads are reapportioned is irrelevant and The step down method results in costs being reapportioned between service cost centres

The direct method results in costs being re-apportioned between production centres (not between service centres) so 'The direct method results in costs being reapportioned between service cost centres' is false. When using the direct method, it doesn't matter in which order the service overheads are re-apportioned so 'If the direct method is used, the order in which the service cost centre overheads are reapportioned is irrelevant' is true. 'The step down method results in costs being reapportioned between service cost centres' is true but 'If the step down method is used, the order in which the service cost centre overheads are reapportioned is irrelevant' is false because the order does matter when using the step-down approach.

7a.22   The correct answer is: $354,888

Direct method

	Production departments		Service centres	
	Mixing	Stirring	Stores	Canteen
Overheads	216,400	78,800	181,600	47,200
Reapportion stores (50:30)	(5/8) 113,500	(3/8) 68,100	(181,600)	–
Reapportion canteen (45:40)	24,988	22,212	–	(47,200)
	354,888	169,112		

7a.23   The correct answer is: $351,416

Step down method

	Production departments		Service centres	
	Mixing	Stirring	Stores	Canteen
Overheads	216,400	78,800	181,600	47,200
Reapportion stores (50:30:20)	90,800	54,480	(181,600)	36,320
			–	83,520
Reapportion canteen (45:40)	44,216	39,304		(83,520)
	351,416	172,584		–

7a.24   The correct answer is: $368,000

ACCA examining team comments

The question relates to study guide reference B2d. The correct answer is $368,000. Standard absorption costing will include $96,000 of the period's overhead (2,000 units × 4 labour hours × $12 per hour) in the valuation of closing inventory. Under standard marginal costing the $96,000 would be charged against the period's profit resulting in a profit $96,000 lower than $464,000. This type of question is included in virtually every costing textbook and it is disappointing that only a minority of candidates selected the correct alternative. The most common answer was $440,000, ($464,000 – 2000 units × $12 per labour hour) suggesting some misunderstanding of overhead absorption rates or careless reading of the question. $344,000 was also a popular answer ($464,000 – 2,000 units ÷ 20,000 units × 100,000 hours × $12 per labour hour) indicating that many candidates believed that inventories should be valued on the basis of actual labour hours in a standard absorption costing system. On the bright side, only a small proportion of candidates selected $560,000, which indicates that most candidates understand that in periods of rising finished goods inventories, absorption costing will show higher profits than marginal costing.

7a.25   The correct answer is: Actual direct labour hours were 800 less than budgeted

ACCA examining team comments

The debit to the profit or loss account implies that overheads were under absorbed. We are told that actual overhead expenditure was in line with budget, so the only cause of the under absorption has to be actual activity being less than budgeted. A shortfall of 800 direct labour hours would lead to an under absorption of 800 direct labour hours x $5 per hour = $4,000. Overall candidates need to make sure they understand the causes of under or over absorption of overhead and the bookkeeping entries involved.

7a.26   The correct answer is: $75,467

> **ACCA examining team comments**
>
> By examining the second row of figures in the table it is clear that service department X's costs are reapportioned on a 40% , 50% , 10%. On the final reapportionment no overhead is reapportioned to service department Y, so the balance of overhead should be reapportioned 40/90 and 50/90. This results in the following total production overhead for production department 1. ($60,000 + $8,000 + $7,200) + 40/90 x $600 = $75,467.

7b Absorption and marginal costing

7b.1   The correct answer is: Impossible to calculate without more information

We know that the profit using marginal costing would be higher than the absorption costing profit, because inventories are decreasing. However, we cannot calculate the value of the difference without the fixed overhead absorption rate per unit.

Difference in profit = 2,000 units inventory reduction × fixed overhead absorption rate per unit

7b.2   The correct answer is: $3,600 higher

Difference in profit = change in inventory level × fixed overhead per unit
                      = (2,400 – 2,700) × ($4 × 3)
                      = $3,600

The absorption profit will be higher because inventories have increased, and fixed overheads have been carried forward in inventories.

7b.3   The correct answer is: $90,000

Difference in profit = change in inventory level × fixed overhead per unit
                      = (15,000 – 20,000) × $8
                      = $40,000

The inventory level increased during the period therefore the absorption costing profit is higher than the marginal costing profit.

Marginal costing profit = $130,000 – $40,000 = $90,000

7b.4   The correct answer is: $45,400

Contribution per unit   = $30 – $(6.00 + 7.50 + 2.50)
                           = $14
Contribution for month   = $14 × 5,200 units
                           = $72,800
Less fixed costs incurred = $27,400
Marginal costing profit   = $45,400

7b.5   The correct answer is: $48,400

	$	$
Sales (5,200 at $30)		156,000
Materials (5,200 at $6)	31,200	
Labour (5,200 at $7.50)	39,000	
Variable overhead (5,200 at $2.50)	13,000	
Total variable cost		(83,200)
Fixed overhead ($5 × 5,200)		(26,000)
Over-absorbed overhead (W)		1,600
Absorption costing profit		48,400

Working

	$
Overhead absorbed (5,800 × $5)	29,000
Overhead incurred	27,400
Over-absorbed overhead	1,600

7b.6 The correct answer is: 52,500

Inventory levels increased by 3,000 units and absorption costing profit is $105,000 higher ($955,500 – $850,500).

∴ Fixed production cost included in inventory increase:

$$= \frac{\$105,000}{3,000} = \$35 \text{ per unit of inventory}$$

$$\frac{\text{Budgeted fixed costs}}{\text{Fixed cost per unit}} = \frac{\$1,837,500}{\$35} = 52,500 \text{ units}$$

7b.7 The correct answer is: $9.00

Decrease in inventory levels	= 48,500 – 45,500 = 3,000 units
Difference in profits	= $315,250 – $288,250 = $27,000

$$\text{Fixed overhead per unit} = \frac{\$27,000}{3,000} = \$9 \text{ per unit}$$

If you selected one of the other options you attempted various divisions of all the data available in the question!

7b.8 The correct answer is: Methods (i), (ii), (iii) and (iv)

All of the methods are acceptable bases for absorbing production overheads. However, the **percentage of prime cost has serious limitations** and the rate per unit can only be used if all cost units are identical.

7b.9 The correct answer is: All direct and indirect costs

Under absorption costing all associated costs are included in the total cost of a product.

7b.10 The correct answer is: $74,550

If inventory levels increase in a period, absorption costing will show a higher profit than marginal costing.

Difference in profit = change in inventory levels × overhead absorption rate per unit

= (750 units – 300 units) × $5 per unit

= 450 units × $5

= $2,250

	$
Marginal costing profit	72,300
Increase in profit	2,250
Absorption costing profit	74,550

7b.11 The correct answer is: $600,000

Contribution per unit	= selling price – variable cost
	= $10 – $6
	= $4 per unit

Total contribution	= 250,000 units × $4 per unit = $1,000,000
Total fixed costs	= 200,000 units × $2 per unit
	= $400,000

Marginal costing profit	= total contribution – total fixed costs
	= $1,000,000 – $400,000
	= $600,000

7b.12   The correct answer is: $38,500

If inventory levels increase in a period, absorption costing will show a higher profit than marginal costing.

Difference in profit = change in inventory levels × overhead absorption rate per unit

= (350 – 100) units × $4 per unit
= 250 units × $4
= $1,000

	$
Marginal costing profit	37,500
Increase in profit	1,000
Absorption costing profit	38,500

7b.13   The correct answer is: $1,120 lower

Fixed production overhead absorption rate $= \dfrac{\$48,000}{12,000\,\text{units}}$

$= \$4$ per unit

Increase in inventory levels = (12,000 – 11,720) units
= 280 units

∴ Difference in profit   = 280 units × $4 per unit
= $1,120

Marginal costing profits are lower than absorption costing profits when inventory levels increase in a period, therefore marginal costing profit will be $1,120 lower than absorption costing profits for the same period.

7b.14   The correct answer is: $396,000

If budgeted fixed overhead expenditure	= 100%
Actual fixed overhead expenditure	= 110%
∴ Variance	= 10%

If variance = $36,000 = 10% × budgeted fixed overhead expenditure

Budgeted fixed overhead expenditure	= $36,000/0.1
	= $360,000
∴ Actual fixed overhead expenditure	= 110% × $360,000
	= $396,000

7b.15   The correct answer is: $25,000

Increase in inventory = (18,000 – 16,500) units
= 1,500 units

∴ Difference in profit   = 1,500 units × $10
= $15,000

Profits under marginal costing will be $15,000 less than profits under absorption costing ie $40,000 – $15,000 = $25,000.

7b.16   The correct answer is: 12,500

Any difference between marginal and absorption costing profit is due to changes in inventory.

	$
Absorption costing profit	2,000
Marginal costing loss	(3,000)
Difference	5,000

Change in inventory = Difference in profit/fixed product cost per unit

= $5,000/$2 = 2,500 units

Marginal costing loss is lower than absorption costing profit therefore inventory has gone up – that is, production was greater than sales by 2,500 units.

Production = 10,000 units (sales) + 2,500 units = 12,500 units

7b.17   The correct answer is: $120,000 lower

	Units
Opening inv	900
Closing inv	300
Decrease	600

$$600 \times \left(\frac{\$500,000}{2,500}\right) = 120,000 \text{ lower}$$

7b.18   The correct answer is: 10,000

> **ACCA examining team comments**
>
> The correct answer is 10,000. This can be calculated by multiplying the increase in finished goods inventory of 1,000 units (2,000 units produced less 1,000 units sold) by the fixed production cost per unit that will be included in absorption costing closing inventory valuation.
>
> The distracters were all based around the $4,000 over-absorption of fixed production cost. The first distracter of 4,000 suggests that the difference in profits will be equal to the over-absorption of fixed production cost, whereas 6,000 and 14,000 suggest that it is due to a difference in inventory valuation and over-absorption of fixed production cost. Incorrect answers were roughly evenly spread around the 3 distracters, suggesting a misunderstanding of under- or over-absorption (or possibly a high level of guessing).
>
> Under- or over-absorption adjustments to profit do not cause a difference between marginal and absorption costing profits. They simply ensure that absorption costing charges the same amount of fixed overhead as marginal costing.
>
> If we look in more detail at the situation it is apparent that the over-absorption of $4,000 was caused by the production of 400 units more than budgeted ($4,000 ÷ $10 per unit). Budgeted production would therefore be 1,600 units (2,000 units actually produced less the 400 units above).
>
> It follows that budgeted fixed production cost was therefore 1,600 units × $10 per unit = $16,000. As actual fixed production cost was equal to budgeted, marginal cost fixed production costing would have recorded an actual fixed production cost of $16,000.
>
> Absorption costing would have charged $20,000 of fixed production cost to product (2,000 units produced × $10 per unit), however the adjustment for over-absorption would have corrected this overcharge and reduced this cost by $4,000, resulting in the same fixed production cost as marginal costing.
>
> *The important point is that it is not under- or over-absorption that causes the difference between profits under absorption and marginal costing principles. The difference in profits is caused by the difference in finished goods inventory valuations.*

7b.19   The correct answer is: 2 and 3

> **ACCA examining team comments**
>
> The most popular answer was '3 only'. This suggests that these candidates correctly understood two things: (i) over a period of time in which total production levels are equal to total sales levels, the profit calculated under marginal and absorption costing principles will be the same. Over the three years involved total sales are 15,000 units and total production is 15,000 units And (ii) in a period when production is greater than sales the profits calculated under absorption costing principles would show a higher profit than under marginal costing principles, rather than a lower profit as suggested in the question However these candidates failed to appreciate that marginal costing inventory valuations (marginal production cost) are lower than those under absorption costing (full production cost). The correct answer is '2 and 3', selected by very few candidates, suggesting that most candidates have very little understanding of the area.

BPP LEARNING MEDIA

7b.20 The correct answer is: Total contribution will double between the two output levels

---

ACCA examining team comments

This was a badly answered question with only 20% of candidates choosing the correct answer. It covers syllabus area B 2 a and A 3g. Candidates often appear to find questions that ask for the effect of a change in input data on performance indicators difficult. It may help them to "invent" simple figures to test the validity of the statements on offer. For example if we assume a sales price of $10 per unit ,a variable cost of $2 per unit and a fixed cost of $4,000 per period, then the following figures can be quickly produced.

Sales units	1,000	2,000
	$	$
Sales revenue	10,000	20,000
Variable cost	2,000	4,000
Total contribution	8,000	16,000
Fixed cost	2,000	2,000
Operating profit	6,000	14,000

It is soon apparent that 'Total contribution will double between the two output levels' is correct, and that the rest are incorrect.

8a Process costing

8a.1   The correct answer is: 2,175 kgs

Good production   = input – normal loss – abnormal loss
= (2,500 – (2,500 × 10%) – 75)kg
= 2,500 – 250 – 75
= 2,175 kg

8a.2   The correct answer is: Material 50 litres Conversion costs 25 litres

Work in progress   = 300 litres input – 250 litres to finished goods
= 50 litres
Equivalent litres for each cost element are as follows.

	Material		Conversion costs	
	%	Equiv. litres	%	Equiv. litres
50 litres in progress	100	50	50	25

8a.3   The correct answer is: Nil

There is no scrap value available for any losses therefore the normal loss would have a zero value. The normal loss does not carry any of the process costs therefore the other options are all incorrect.

8a.4   The correct answer is: (ii) and (iii) only

Expected output = 2,000 units **less** normal loss (5%) 100 units = 1,900 units

In situation (i) there is an **abnormal loss** of 1,900 – 1,800 = 100 units
In situation (ii) there is an **abnormal gain** of 1,950 – 1,900 = 50 units
In situation (iii) there is an **abnormal gain** of 2,000 – 1,900 = 100 units

Therefore the correct answer is (ii) and (iii) only.

8a.5   The correct answer is: The same as good production

Abnormal losses are valued at the same unit rate as good production, so that their occurrence does not affect the cost of good production.

8a.6   The correct answer is: 400 litres

The total loss was 15% of the material input. The 340 litres of good output therefore represents 85% of the total material input.

Therefore, material input = $\dfrac{340}{0.85}$ = 400 litres

8a.7   The correct answer is: $16,800

Step 1.   Determine output and losses

Input Units	Output	Total Units	Materials Units	%	Labour and overhead Units	%
	Finished units (balance)	400	400	100	400	100
500	Closing inventory	100	100	100	80	80
500		500	500		480	

Equivalent units

Step 2.   Calculate the cost per equivalent unit

Input	Cost $	Equivalent production in units	Cost per unit $
Materials	9,000	500	18
Labour and overhead	11,520	480	24
			42

Step 3.   Calculate total cost of output

Cost of completed units = $42 × 400 units = $16,800

8a.8   The correct answer is: $3,720

Using the data from answer 7 above, extend **step 3** to calculate the value of the work in progress.

	Cost element	Number of equivalent units	Cost per equivalent unit $	Total $
Work in progress:	Materials	100	18	1,800
	Labour & overhead	80	24	1,920
				3,720

8a.9   The correct answer is: 630

STATEMENT OF EQUIVALENT UNITS

	Total Units	Materials		Labour		Overheads
Output to process 2*	600	600		600		600
Closing WIP	100 (100%)	100	(50%)	50	(30%)	30
	700	700		650		630

Equivalent units

*500 units input + opening WIP 200 units – closing WIP 100 units.

8a.10   The correct answer is: $13,200

STATEMENT OF COSTS PER EQUIVALENT UNIT

	Materials $	Labour $	Overheads $	Total
Opening stock	2,400	1,200	400	
Added during period	6,000	3,350	1,490	
Total cost	8,400	4,550	1,890	
Equivalent units	700	650	630	
Cost per equivalent unit	$12	$7	$3	$22

Value of units transferred to process 2 = 600 units × $22 = $13,200

8a.11   The correct answer is: 9,985 units

	Equivalent units				
	Total Units		Materials Units		Conversion costs Units
Output to finished goods	9,850		9,850		9,850
Closing inventory	450	(100%)	450	(30%)	135
	10,300		10,300		9,985

8a.12   The correct answer is: $11.6

Input costs = 2,000 units × $4.50 = $9,000

Conversation costs   = $13,340

Normal loss   = 5% × 2,000 units × $3 = $300

Expected output   = 2,000 units – 100 units = 1,900 units

$$\text{Cost per unit of output} = \frac{\text{Input costs}}{\text{Expected output}}$$

$$= \frac{\$9,000 + \$13,340 - \$300}{1,900\,\text{units}}$$

$$= \frac{\$22,040}{1,900\,\text{units}} = \$11.6 \text{ (to one decimal place)}$$

8a.13   The correct answer is: $22,040

	$
Material	9,000
Conversion costs	11,970
Less scrap value of normal loss (300 × $1.50)	(450)
Cost of process	20,520

Expected output   = 3,000 – (10% × 3,000)
                   = 3,000 – 300 = 2,700 units

$$\text{Costs per unit} = \frac{\text{Input costs} - \text{scrap value of normal loss}}{\text{Expected output}} = \frac{\$20,520}{2,700} = \$7.60$$

Value of output   = 2,900 × $7.60 = $22,040

8a.14   The correct answer is: $29,532

Abnormal gain = 276 units – 112 units = 164 units

Cost per unit of good production = $29,744/5,408 = $5.50

∴ Value of abnormal gain = 164 units × $5.50 = $902

The value of the input can be found as the balancing figure in the value columns of the process account.

Polishing process account

	$		$
Input (balancing figure)	29,532	Output	29,744
Abnormal gain	902	Normal loss (276 × $2.50)	690
	30,434		30,434

8a.15   The correct answer is: Neither of them

Statement (i) is incorrect. Units of normal loss are valued at their scrap value (which may be nil).

Statement (ii) is incorrect. Units of abnormal loss are valued at the same rate as good units.

Therefore the correct answer is neither of them.

8a.16   The correct answer is: (Total input cost ÷ expected output units) – scrap value per unit

> **ACCA examining team comments**
>
> The principle here is that whilst it is reasonable to build the net cost of normal (expected) losses into production cost (because they are a normal feature of the process) , it is not reasonable to do the same with abnormal losses, because, as their name suggests, they are not a normal feature of the process. The production cost of abnormally lost units is the same as the cost of good production (Total input cost less the revenue from the sale of normal losses ÷ expected output). In this case no losses are expected, so this is equal to total input cost ÷ expected output. Because the abnormal losses can be sold for scrap, their net cost is the cost per unit of making them, less the revenue derived from their sale that is (Total input cost ÷ expected output) – scrap value per unit.

8a.17   The correct answer is: $4,545

> **ACCA examining team comments**
>
> This is arrived at as follows: First calculate the expected output from the input of 10,000 kg= (100%-12% of Normal loss)= 8,800 kg
>
> Since the actual output was 9,200kg and expected output is 8,800kg, then the abnormal• gain is 400kg
>
> The cost per kg of output must be calculated next:
>
> | | |
> |---|---|
> | Material input (10,000 kg) = | $100,000 |
> | Conversion = | $50,000 |
> | Total cost | $150,000 |
> | Less Normal loss | |
> | (12%*10,000*$5) | ($6,000) |
> | Net total cost of output | $144,000 |
>
> The cost per kg of output =(($ 144,000/10,000 kg x 88%(expected output)) = $16.36
>
> The net value of the abnormal gain after the amount for the normal loss is deducted from• the cost per kg output = ($16.36 – $5.00) × 400 kg = $4,545.

8b Process costing, joint products and by-products

8b.1   The correct answer is: $2.50

Total production inventory

	$
Opening inventory	1,000
Direct materials added	10,000
Conversion costs	12,000
	23,000
Less closing inventory	3,000
Total production cost	20,000

	Production Units		Sales value $		Apportioned cost $
P	4,000	(× $5)	20,000	($20,000 × 20/80)	5,000
R	6,000	(× $10)	60,000	($20,000 × 60/80)	15,000
			80,000		20,000

Product R cost per unit = $15,000/6,000 = $2.50 per unit.

8b.2   The correct answer is: $8,000

From the previous answer, total production cost to be apportioned = $20,000.

	Production Units		Apportioned cost $
P	4,000	($20,000 × 4/10)	8,000
R	6,000	($20,000 × 6/10)	12,000
	10,000		20,000

8b.3   The correct answer is: (iii) only

Statement (i) is incorrect because the value of the product described could be relatively high even though the output volume is relatively low. This product would then be classified as a joint product.

Statement (ii) is incorrect. Since a by-product is not important as a saleable item, it is not separately costed and does not absorb any process costs.

Statement (iii) is correct. These common or joint costs are allocated or apportioned to the joint products.

8b.4   The correct answer is: $103,273

Net process costs

	$
Raw material input	216,000
Conversion costs	72,000
Less by-product revenue	(4,000)
Net process cost	284,000

	Production Units		Sales value $		Apportioned cost $
E	21,000	(× $15)	315,000	($284,000 × 315/495)	180,727
Q	18,000	(× $10)	180,000	($284,000 × 180/495)	103,273
			495,000		284,000

8b.5   The correct answer is: $58,193

No costs are apportioned to the by-product. The by-product revenue is credited to the sales account, and so does not affect the process costs.

	Units		Sales value $		Apportioned cost $
L	3,000	(× $32)	96,000	($230,000 × 96/332)	66,506
M	2,000	(× $42)	84,000	($230,000 × 84/332)	58,193
N	4,000	(× $38)	152,000	($230,000 × 152/332)	105,301
			332,000		230,000

8b.6   The correct answer is: $36,400

Total production units = 412,000 + 228,000

= 640,000 units

Joint costs apportioned to Product H $= \dfrac{228,000}{640,000} \times \$384,000 = \$136,800$

Further processing costs = $159,600

∴ Total product cost of Product H = $(136,800 + 159,600) = $296,400

∴ Closing inventory value of Product H $= \dfrac{28,000}{228,000} \times \$296,400 = \$36,400$

8b.7   The correct answer is: $77,616

Sales value of production

W   (12,000 units × $10) $120,000
X   (10,000 units × $12) $120,000

Joint production costs will be apportioned equally between the two products as the sales value of production is the same for each product.

Joint production costs allocated to X = $776,160/2 = $388,080

$$\text{Value of closing inventory} = \frac{2,000}{10,000} \times \$388,080 = \$77,616$$

8b.8   The correct answer is: $3,840

> **ACCA examining team comments**
>
> This question covers syllabus heading B3 bxii To get the correct answer candidates had to negotiate three steps: (i) calculate the amount of cost apportioned to product A ($12,000 × 600/(600 + 400) = $7,200) (ii) then calculate how much of this cost is to be charged against A's sales in the period ($7,200 x 480/600 = $5,760) (iii) then calculate the gross profit earned using the gross profit margin given ($5,760×40/60 = $3,840).
>
> The most popular answer was $2,880. These candidates appear to have correctly calculated step (i) ($12,000 x 600/(600 + 400) = $7,200) but then incorrectly applied the gross profit margin of 40% to this figure.($7,200 × 40% = $2,880) This approach fails to match production costs against sales and secondly applies the gross profit margin to cost rather than sales revenue.

8b.9   The correct answer is: Both products will have the same return on sales ratio (operating margin)

> **ACCA examining team comments**
>
> This question covers syllabus area B3b (xi) and required knowledge of the different methods of apportioning joint costs. If joint costs are apportioned on a relative sales value basis and there are no further costs after split off point then all joint products will have the same amount of profits per $ of sales. This is arguably the major benefit of this method. Because one product cannot be produced without the other, it makes sense to make them appear equally profitable.
>
> This means that the first statement is correct.

8b.10   The correct answer is: Pre-separation costs are apportioned to the by-product to calculate its profit

> **ACCA examining team comments**
>
> Joint products and by-products arise where the manufacture of one product makes inevitable the manufacture of other products. Whilst joint products have significant sales value, by –product sales value is relatively insignificant. There are two basic approaches to accounting for by products. Either their net realisable value can be netted off against pre-separation point costs (effectively the same as the treatment of a normal loss). The first two options are examples of this approach, and were chosen majority of candidates. Alternatively their income can be added to the revenue of the main product. 'By-product income less post-separation costs is added to the sales of the main product' is an example of this approach. 'Pre-separation costs are apportioned to the by-product to calculate its profit' involves apportioning pre separation costs to the by-product. This treats the by-product in the same way as a joint product and is clearly inappropriate. No knowledge of the other approaches is required to appreciate that this approach is incorrect.

8b.11   The correct answer is: $13,860

> **ACCA examining team comments**
>
> The correct answer is $13,860, which was the second most popular selection by candidates. To calculate this candidates need firstly to calculate a unit cost ($5,000 – 400 kg × $1)/2000 units= $2.30 per unit). This can then be used to calculate a profit on the 1,800 units sold (1,800 units × ($10 - $2.30) = $13,860). $13,400 was the most popular selection. Candidates who chose this alternative ignored closing inventory and charged all costs to units sold (instead of units produced). Hence their unit cost was ($5,000 – 400 kg × $1)/1800 units= $2.55 per unit. Profit under this unit cost becomes (1,800 units × ($10 - $2.555) = $13,400). Candidates who selected this answer appear to have a problem in distinguishing between cost of production and cost of sales.

9a Job, batch and service costing

9a.1   The correct answer is: Process costing

Process costing is a costing method used where it is not possible to identify separate units of production, or jobs, usually because of the continuous nature of the production process. The manufacture of liquid soap is a **continuous production process.**

9a.2   The correct answer is: $606

	$
Selling price of job	1,690
Less profit margin (30/130)	390
Total cost of job	1,300
Less overhead	694
Prime cost	606

9a.3   The correct answer is: $404

	$
Direct materials (5 × $20)	100
Direct labour (14 × $8)	112
Variable overhead (14 × $3)	42
Fixed overhead (14 × $5*)	70
Other overhead	80
Total cost of job 173	404

*Fixed production overhead absorption rate $= \dfrac{\$200,000}{40,000}$

$= \$5$ per direct labour hour

9a.4   The correct answer is: $72,761

The most logical basis for absorbing the overhead job costs is to use a percentage of direct labour cost.

$$\text{Overhead} = \frac{\$24,600}{\$(14,500 + 3,500 + 24,600)} \times \$126,000$$

$$= \frac{\$24,600}{\$42,600} \times \$126,000$$

$$= \$72,761$$

9a.5 The correct answer is: $217,323

Job number	WIP $
AA10 (26,800 + 17,275 + 14,500) + ($\frac{14,500}{42,600}$ × 126,000)	101,462
CC20 (18,500 + 24,600 + 72,761)	115,861
	217,323

9a.6 The correct answer is: (i), (iii) and (iv) only

The actual material and labour costs for a batch (**i and iv**) can be determined from the material and labour recording system. Actual manufacturing overheads cannot be determined for a specific batch because of the need for allocation and apportionment of each item of overhead expenditure, and the subsequent calculation of a predetermined overhead absorption rate. Therefore **item (ii)** is incorrect and **item (iii)** is correct.

9a.7 The correct answer is: (i) and (ii) only

The vehicle cost per passenger-kilometre (i) is appropriate for cost control purposes because it **combines** the distance travelled and the number of passengers carried, **both of which affect cost**.

The fuel cost for each vehicle per kilometre (ii) can be useful for control purposes because it **focuses on a particular aspect** of the cost of operating each vehicle.

The fixed cost per kilometre (iii) is not particularly useful for control purposes because it **varies with the number of kilometres travelled**.

9a.8 The correct answer is: $5.00

Number of occupied room-nights = 40 rooms × 30 nights × 65%
= 780

Room servicing cost per occupied room-night = $\frac{\$3,900}{780}$ = $5

9a.9 The correct answer is: $41.67

Weeks during year	= 52 – 4 = 48
Hours worked per year	= 48 × 35 hours
	= 1,680 hours
Hours chargeable to clients	= 1,680 × 90% = 1,512
Hourly charge rate	= $\frac{\$3,000 + \$18,000}{1,512} = \frac{\$21,000}{1,512}$
	= $13.89 per hour
Price for 3-hour 'colour and cut'	= $13.89 × 3 = $41.67

9a.10 The correct answer is: (i) and (ii)

A college and a hotel are likely to use service costing. A plumber works on separately identifiable jobs and is therefore more likely to use job costing.

9a.11 The correct answer is: (i), (ii) and (iii)

An airline company, a railway company and a firm of accountants are **all** considered to be service industries.

9a.12 The correct answer is: $11,466

Assignment 789

	$
Senior consultant – 54 hours × $40	2,160
Junior consultant – 110 hours × $25	2,750
Overhead absorption – 164 hours × $20	3,280
Total cost	8,190
40% × total cost = 40% × $8,190	3,276
Final fee	11,466

9a.13   The correct answer is: $170

Total cost – job number 1012

	$
Direct materials	45
Direct labour	30
Prime cost	75
Production overheads (30/7.5 × $12.50)	50
Total production cost	125
Non-production overheads (0.6 × $75)	45
Total cost – job number 1012	170

9a.14   The correct answer is: $0.002 per kg-km

First we calculate the total number of kg-km.
Kg × km taken   = 250,000 kg × 7,500 km
                  = 1,875,000,000 kg-km
∴ cost per kg-km = $3,750,000/1,875,000,000 = $0.002 per kg-km

9a.15   The correct answer is: $0.010

ACCA examining team comments

The question relates to study guide reference B3c(ii).

The correct answer is $0.010. The cost per kilogram/kilometre of sand delivered is the cost of carrying one kilogram of sand for one kilometre. Kilogram kilometres can be calculated by multiplying the weight of goods delivered to each customer by the distance covered. (500 kg × 200km + 180 kg × 1200km = 316,000 kilogram kilometres.) If truck costs are divided by this figure a cost of $0.010 is obtained. $2.186 represents the cost per kilometre travelled (($3,060 / 1,400 km). $0.003 can be obtained by dividing truck cost by 680 kg × 1,400 kilometres = 952,000. This is a meaningless figure as it does not allow for different weights travelling different distances. Finally $4.500 represents the average cost per kilogram delivered ($3,060 / 680 kg = $4.50).

9b   Alternative costing principles

9b.1   The correct answer is: Maturity.

During this period, prices tend to fall but profits remain high due to good sales volume.

9b.2   The correct answer is: Growth.

During the growth phase the product begins to make a profit. This is due to economies of scale being received as increased demand for the product occurs.

9b.3   The correct answer is: Market price – desired profit margin

Target cost means a product cost estimate derived by subtracting a desired profit margin from a competitive market price.

9b.4   The correct answer is: Growth.

The product life cycle stages can be summarised as follows:

Introduction: Basic quality, few competitors, high promotion costs

Growth: As stated in question

Maturity: Most competitive stage, product extension strategies, for example, new markets

Decline: Exit strategy needs to be identified.

9b.5   The correct answer is: Statement 1 is true and statement 2 is false

Statement 1 is true. More accurate feedback can be obtained since the costs of research and development are also taken into account. Statement 2 is false. Individual profitability for products is more accurate.

BPP
LEARNING MEDIA

9b.6   The correct answer is: An external failure cost

This is a cost arising from inadequate quality discovered after the transfer of ownership, an external failure cost.

9b.7   The correct answer is: Target costing

Target costing involves setting a target cost by subtracting a desired profit margin from a competitive market price.

10a Budgeting

10a.1   The correct answer is: (i), (ii) and (iv)

Coordination (i) is an objective of budgeting. Budgets help to ensure that the **activities of all parts of the organisation are coordinated towards a single plan.**

Communication (ii) is an objective of budgeting. The budgetary planning process **communicates targets** to the managers responsible for achieving them, and it should also provide a **mechanism for junior managers to communicate to more senior staff** their estimates of what may be achievable in their part of the business.

Expansion (iii) is not in itself an objective of budgeting. Although a budget may be set **within a framework of expansion plans**, it is perfectly possible for an organisation to **plan for a reduction in activity.**

Resource allocation (iv) is an objective of budgeting. Most organisations face a situation of **limited resources** and an objective of the budgeting process is to ensure that these resources are allocated among budget centres in the most efficient way.

10a.2   The correct answer is: The company's activities are limited by the level of sales it can achieve

The **principal budget factor** is the factor which limits the activities of an organisation.

Although cash and profit are affected by the level of sales, sales is not the only factor which determines the level of cash and profit.

10a.3   The correct answer is: $8,688

The total production cost allowance in a budget flexed at the 83% level of activity would be $8,688 (to the nearest $)
Direct material cost per 1% = $30

Labour and production overhead:

			$
At	90%	activity	6,240
At	80%	activity	6,180
Change	10%		60

Variable cost per 1% activity = $60/10% = $6

Substituting in 80% activity:

Fixed cost of labour and production overhead	= $6,180 – (80 × $6)
	= $5,700

Flexed budget cost allowance:

		$
Direct material $30 × 83		2,490
Labour and production overhead:		
variable $6 × 83		498
fixed		5,700
		8,688

10a.4   The correct answer is: Spreadsheets are very useful for word-processing

          Spreadsheets are not useful for word processing

10a.5   The correct answer is: C4

10a.6   The correct answer is: =D4-D5

10a.7   The correct answer is: =G6/G2*100

10a.8   The correct answer is: =[(0.9*F3) + (0.1*F4)]

          Budgeted production = budgeted sales + closing inventory – opening inventory. In March, 10% of March's sales (found in cell F3) will still be inventory at the beginning of the month and 10% of April's sales (cell F4) will be in inventory at the end of the month. Production for March will therefore be

          March's sales (F3) + 10% of April's sales (F4) – 10% of March's sales (F3)

          Or

          =[(0.9*F3) + (0.1*F4)]

10a.9   The correct answer is: $4,755 (A)

          The volume variance for last month was $4,755 Adverse

          The volume variance is the increase in cost resulting from a change in the volume of activity, ie the difference between the original budget and the flexed budget.

          Volume variance   = $126,100 – $130,855
                               = $4,755 (A)

10a.10   The correct answer is: $2,725 (A)

          The expenditure variance for last month was $2,725 Adverse

          The expenditure variance is the difference between the flexed budget and the actual results.

          Expenditure variance   = $130,855 – $133,580
                                        = $2,725 (A)

10a.11   The correct answer is: $62,000

          ACCA examining team comments

          Majority of candidates incorrectly selected $72,000 (profit per unit × actual sales). This suggests that these candidates knew that the budget should be flexed to the actual output level of 6,000 units but that they failed to appreciate that total fixed costs (in this case fixed production overhead) do not vary with output. The fixed production overhead cost per unit contained in the standard cost is an average fixed cost per unit based on the budgeted output level of 8,000 units. This implies a total fixed production overhead of $40,000 ($5 per unit × 8,000 units). This total budgeted fixed production overhead will not change with volume. The correct answer of $62,000 can be calculated by multiplying the standard contribution per unit by the actual output level and the subtracting the budgeted fixed production overhead. (($118 - $80 – $21) × 6,000 units - $40,000 = $62,000). Only a minority of candidates selected this alternative.

10a.12   The correct answer is: $55,000

> **ACCA examining team comments**
>
> This question covers syllabus area C4d budget flexing. The correct answer is 55,000. To arrive at this answer a candidate needs to understand that contribution varies in linear proportion to volume, but that fixed costs do not. Accordingly they need to calculate that the contribution at 6,000 units will be $72,000 (6,000 × ($30 -$18)), and that fixed costs will be made up of the budgeted fixed costs at 4,000 units (4,000 × $4 = $16,000) plus the step up fixed costs of $1,000, making $17,000 in total. Profit at an output level of 6,000 units is therefore $72,000 - $17,000 = $55,000. In short 6,000 units × ($30 -$18) – 4,000 units × $4 - $1,000 = $55,000. $56,000, chosen by a minority of candidates, was nearly correct, candidates simply did not deduct the step in fixed costs. Note that distracters (incorrect answers) in objective testing questions sometimes are based on figures arrived at by incomplete calculations. Candidates should try to avoid choosing answers until they are sure that their calculations are complete.

10a.13   The correct answer is: B8 + B7 + B4

> **ACCA examining team comments**
>
> Contribution is equal to sales revenue less variable cost. B8 + B7 + B4 represents sales revenue less variable production costs and variable selling costs and is correct. It is worrying that only a minority of candidates can correctly define contribution.

10a.14   The correct answer is: 3,000

> **ACCA examining team comments**
>
> Direct material is always a variable cost. This is confirmed in this case by its deduction from sales to calculate contribution. The most sensible way to calculate a total variable cost variance is against a flexed budget figure. (It can be seen that the direct labour variance has been calculated against flexed budget cost in the spreadsheet.)
>
> The flexed budget direct material cost (cell C5) has a value of $27,000 ($21,600/1,200 units x 1,500 units). The direct material variance becomes $27,000 - $24,000 = $3,000 favourable.

10b The budgetary process

10b.1   The correct answer is: The budgeted cash flow, budgeted statement of profit or loss and budgeted statement of financial position

The **master budget** is the summary budget into which all subsidiary budgets are consolidated. It usually comprises the **budgeted statement of profit or loss**, **budgeted statement of financial position** and **budgeted cash flow statement**.

The master budget is used **in conjunction with the supporting subsidiary budgets**, to plan and control activities. The subsidiary budgets are not in themselves a part of the master budget.

10b.2   The correct answer is: (ii), (iv), (v), (i), (vi), (iii)

Since there are no production resource limitations, sales would be the principal budget factor and the sales budget (ii) would be prepared first. Budgeted inventory changes included in the finished goods inventory budget (iv) would then indicate the required production for the production budget (v). This would lead to the calculation of the material usage (i) which would then be adjusted for the budgeted change in material inventory (vi) to determine the required level of budgeted material purchases (iii).Therefore the correct answer is (ii), (iv), (v), (i), (vi), (iii).

10b.3   The correct answers are: Sales volume from the sales budget and Budgeted change in finished goods inventory

Since there are no production resource limitations, sales would be the principal budget factor therefore the sales budget must be prepared before the production budget . The budgeted change in finished goods inventory would then indicate the required volume for the production budget.

The material purchases, would be information derived **from** the production budget after adjusting for material inventory changes, and the standard direct labour cost per unit, would be required for the **production cost budget**, but not for the production budget, which is **expressed in volume terms.**

10b.4   The correct answer is: Sales quantity – opening inventory of finished goods + closing inventory of finished goods

Any opening inventory available at the beginning of a period will **reduce** the additional quantity required from production in order to satisfy a given sales volume. Any closing inventory required at the end of a period will **increase** the quantity required from production in order to satisfy sales and leave a sufficient volume in inventory. Therefore we need to **deduct** the opening inventory and **add** the required closing inventory.

10b.5   The correct answer is: Raw materials inventories are budgeted to increase

Once the material usage budget has been prepared, based on the budgeted production volume, the usage is adjusted for the budgeted change in materials inventories in order to determine the required budgeted purchases. If purchases exceed production requirements this means that raw material inventories are being increased, and the correct answer is C.

10b.6   The correct answer is: 24,500 units

	Units
Required for sales	24,000
Required to increase inventory (2,000 × 0.25)	500
	24,500

10b.7   The correct answer is: 175,000 kgs

	Units
Required increase in finished goods inventory	1,000
Budgeted sales of Alpha	60,000
Required production	61,000

	kg
Raw materials usage budget (× 3 kg)	183,000
Budgeted decrease in raw materials inventory	(8,000)
Raw materials purchase budget	175,000

10b.8   The correct answer is: 16,000 units

	Units
Budgeted sales	18,000
Budgeted reduction in finished goods	(3,600)
Budgeted production of completed units	14,400
Allowance for defective units (10% of output = 1/9 of input)	1,600
Production budget	16,000

10b.9   The correct answer is: $10,500

	Hours
Active hours required for production = 200 × 6 hours =	1,200
Allowance for idle time (20% of total time = 25% of active time)	300
Total hours to be paid for	1,500
× $7 per hour	
Direct labour cost budget	$10,500

10b.10 The correct answer is: 225,000 hours

	Units
Planned increase in inventories of finished goods	4,600
Budgeted sales	36,800
Budgeted production (to pass quality control check)	41,400

This is 92% of total production, allowing for an 8% rejection rate.

$$\text{Budgeted production} = \frac{100}{92} \times 41,400 = 45,000 \text{ units}$$

Budgeted direct labour hours = (× 5 hours per unit) 225,000 hours

10b.11 The correct answer is: $300,000

Before you can work out the total cost, you have to determine how many labour hours are required. You can calculate the number of hours required for the units quite easily: 4,800 × 5 = 24,000 hours. However 20% of labour time is idle, which means that 24,000 hours is only 80% of the total hours required to produce 4,800 units. Total hours = 24,000 × (100/80) = 30,000 hours.

Total cost = 30,000 hours × $10 per hour = $300,000

10b.12 The correct answer is: (i), (ii) and (iii)

Statement (i) is true because certain factors are often out of the manager's control. The level of sales (or production) will be out of the manager's control and a flexed budget will account for this. Statement (ii) is true. The major purpose of a fixed budget is at the planning stage when it seeks to define the broad objectives of the organisation. Statement (iii) is true because forecast volumes are very unlikely to be equal to actual volumes and so the variances will contain large volume differences.

10b.13 The correct answer is: $49,480

		Received in September $
August sales	$60,000 × 60% × 98%*	35,280
July sales	$40,000 × 25%	10,000
June sales	$35,000 × 12%	4,200
		49,480

*This reduction allows for the 2% settlement discount.

If you selected $46,260 you misinterpreted 'month **after** sale' to be the month the sale was made. The invoices are issued on the last day of each month, therefore cash receipts in respect of each month's sales will begin in the following month.

$50,200 makes no allowance for the settlement discount and $50,530 includes the receipt of bad debts; those amounts will never be received cash.

10b.14 The correct answer is: $60,532

	$
40% of May sales for cash (40% × $55,000)	22,000
70% of April credit sales less 2% discount (70% × 60% × $70,000 × 98%)	28,812
27% of March credit sales (27% × 60% × $60,000)	9,720
	60,532

If you selected $61,120 you forgot to allow for the two per cent discount. $66,532 works on the assumption that receipts from cash sales occur in the month after sale; by definition, **cash sales receipts occur as soon as the sale is made**. If you selected $86,620 you calculated the credit receipts on the basis that all sales were made on credit; **only 60 per cent of sales were on a credit basis**.

10b.15   The correct answer is: $50,200

Payments in June will be in respect of May purchases.

	May
Production requirements (8,400 units × 3 kg)	25,200 kg
Closing inventory	4,100 kg
	29,300 kg
Less opening inventory	4,200 kg
Purchase budget	25,100 kg
× $2 per kg = payment for purchases in June	$50,200

$25,100 is the figure for the quantity of material to be paid for, not its value. $48,800 is the value of June purchases, which will be paid for in July. If you selected $50,600 your adjustments for opening and closing material inventories were the wrong way round.

10b.16   The correct answer is: $231,000

	$
75% × May wages cost = 75% × 8,400 × $7 × 4 hours	176,400
25% × April wages cost = 25% × 7,800 × $7 × 4 hours	54,600
Wage payments for May	231,000

10b.17   The correct answer is: $285,567

	$
Cash sales in December ($402,000 × 10%)	40,200
Receipts from November credit sales ($390,000 × 90%× 30% × 99%)	104,247
Receipts from October credit sales ($224,000 × 90% × 70%)	141,120
Total sales receipts in December	285,567

10b.18   The correct answer is: $45,310

	$
Variable production overhead payment:	
for August production (12,600 × $5 × 30%)	18,900
for September production (5,500 × $5 × 70%)	19,250
Total variable production overhead payment	38,150
Fixed overhead cash payment ($9,440 – $2,280)	7,160
Total cash payment	45,310

10b.19   The correct answer is: $14,700

	Units	$
High activity	3,000	12,900
Low activity	2,000	11,100
Increase	1,000	1,800

$$\text{Variable cost per unit} = \frac{\$1,800}{1,000} = \$1.80 \text{ per unit}$$

Fixed cost, substituting in high activity = $12,900 – (3,000 × $1.80)
                                          = $7,500

	$
Budget cost allowance for 4,000 units:	
Variable cost (4,000 × $1.80)	7,200
Fixed cost	7,500
	14,700

$7,200 is the variable cost allowance only and $7,500 is the fixed cost allowance only. If you selected $13,460 your variable cost per unit calculation was upside down ($1,000/1,800 instead of $1,800/1,000).

10b.20 The correct answer is: $289,000

Workings

Purchases	July $	August $	Paid in Month September $	October $	November $
July $250,000	59,375[1]	175,000[2]	12,500[3]		
August $300,000		71,250[4]	210,000[5]	15,000[6]	
September $280,000			66,500[7]	196,000[8]	14,000[9]
			289,000		

1	$250,000 × 25% × 0.95	= $59,375
2	$250,000 × 70%	= $175,000
3	$250,000 × 5%	= $12,500
4	$300,000 × 25% × 0.95	= $71,250
5	$300,000 × 70%	= $210,000
6	$300,000 × 5%	= $15,000
7	$280,000 × 25% × 0.95	= $66,500
8	$280,000 × 70%	= $196,000
9	$280,000 × 5%	= $14,000

10b.21 The correct answer is: (i) and (ii) only

An adverse labour efficiency variance means that employees are taking too long to produce the products. Employing more highly skilled labour should help to speed up the process so statement (i) is applicable. Supervision of employees may help to improve efficiency standards by ensuring less time is wasted by employees. So statement (ii) is applicable. Asking employees to work paid overtime will not help to improve the efficiency because it is unlikely to reduce the number of hours worked. Employees may even slow down further and become more inefficient if they think that they can work overtime and be paid extra wages. So statement (iii) is not applicable.

10b.22 The correct answer is: (iii) only

The direct material price variance is too small to be material and is therefore not worth investigating.

The labour rate variance can be explained by the company wide increase of 2% and so it is not worthy of investigation.

The sales volume variance is large and should be investigated, even though it is favourable. Managers need to plan for the future and need to know whether the increase in sales is a one off or likely to continue into the next quarter.

10b.23 The correct answer is: To facilitate control by establishing a budget relevant to actual activity levels

A flexible budget facilitates control by establishing a budget relevant to actual activity levels.

10b.24 The correct answer is: (i) and (ii) only

Statement (iii) is false. If output levels are stable, a fixed budget is appropriate as the additional time and effort required to produce a flexible budget would not be justified.

10b.25 The correct answer is: =B3+C4-B4

> **ACCA examining team comments**
>
> To arrive at this answer candidates had to understand that production units = sales units + closing inventory of finished goods − opening inventory of finished goods, and that the opening inventory for August was the closing inventory for July. =B3-B4 was the most popular answer presumably on the basis that it totalled the column.

11 Making budgets work

11.1 The correct answer is: Staff suggestions may be ignored leading to de-motivation

Staff suggestions may be ignored leading to de-motivation. Psuedo-participation occurs when managers pretend to involve staff but actually ignore their input. This may lead to a less realistic budget and will certainly be de-motivating if the staff involved find out what is going on.

11.2 The correct answer is: (i) and (ii) only

It is generally agreed that the existence of some form of target or expected outcome is a greater motivation than no target at all. Therefore (i) is true. The establishment of a target, however, raises the question of the degree of difficulty or challenge of the target. Therefore (ii) is true. If the performance standard is set too high or too low sub-optimal performance could be the result. The degree of budget difficulty is not easy to establish. It is influenced by the nature of the task, the organisational culture and personality factors. Some people respond positively to a difficult target. Others, if challenged, tend to withdraw their commitment. So (iii) is not true.

11.3 The correct answer is: A budget which is set without permitting the ultimate budget holder to participate in the budgeting process

A budget which is set without permitting the ultimate budget holder to participate in the budgeting process.

11.4 The correct answer is: All of (i), (ii) and (iii)

Participative budgeting should be used in all three circumstances.

11.5 The correct answer is: A cost which can be influenced by its budget holder.

12a Capital expenditure budgeting

12a.1 The correct answer is: An opportunity cost

An opportunity cost is the value of the benefit sacrificed when one course of action is chosen, in preference to another.

12a.2 The correct answer is: (i), (iii) and (iv) only

A decision is about the future, therefore relevant costs are future costs (i). If a cost is unavoidable then any decision taken about the future will not affect the cost, therefore unavoidable costs are not relevant costs (ii). Incremental costs are extra costs which will be incurred in the future therefore relevant costs are incremental costs (iii). Differential costs are the difference in total costs between alternatives and they are therefore affected by a decision taken now and they are associated with relevant costs (iv).

12a.3 The correct answer is: $2,000

	$
Opportunity cost (net realisable value)	1,200
Cost of disposal in one year's time	800
Total relevant cost of machine	2,000

12a.4 The correct answer is: (i), (ii) and (iii) only

Purchases of raw materials would be classed as revenue expenditure, not capital expenditure. The others are capital expenditure.

BPP
LEARNING MEDIA

12b Methods of project appraisal

12b.1   The correct answer is: $30.38

Current rate is 6% pa payable monthly

∴ Effective rate is 6/12% = ½% compound every month

∴ In the six months from January to June, interest earned =

($1,000 × [1.005]^6) – $1,000 = $30.38

12b.2   The correct answer is: $270

$2,070 = 115% of the original investment

∴ Original investment $= \dfrac{100}{115} \times \$2{,}070$

                          = $1,800

∴ Interest   = $2,070 – $1,800

                          = $270

$310.50 is calculated (incorrectly) as follows.

$\dfrac{x}{\$2{,}070} = 15\%$

∴ x = 0.15 × $2,070
      = $310.50

Make sure that you always tackle this type of question by establishing what the original investment was first.

12b.3   The correct answer is: $15,219

We need to calculate the effective rate of interest.

8% per year (nominal) is 2% per quarter. The effective annual rate of interest is [1.02^4 – 1] = 0.08243 = 8.243%.

Now we can use S = X(1 + r)^n
                S = 12,000 (1.08243)^3
                S = $15,218.81

∴ The principal will have grown to approximately $15,219.

12b.4   The correct answer is: $1,800 in exactly four years from now

		$
PV of $1,200 in one year	= $1,200 × 0.926 =	1,111.20
PV of $1,400 in two years	= $1,400 × 0.857 =	1,199.80
PV of $1,600 in three years	= $1,600 × 0.794 =	1,270.40
PV of $1,800 in four years	= $1,800 × 0.735 =	1,323.00

12b.5   The correct answer is: 4.06%

Effective quarterly rate	= 1% (4% ÷ 4)
Effective annual rate	= [(1.01)^4 – 1]
	= 0.0406 = 4.06% pa

You should have been able to eliminate options A and B immediately. 1% is simply 4% ÷ 4 = 1%. 4% is the nominal rate and is therefore not the effective annual rate of interest.

12b.6   The correct answer is: 9.85%

The formula to calculate the IRR is $a\% + \left[\dfrac{A}{A-B} \times (b-a)\right]\%$

where   a = one interest rate
        b = other interest rate
        A = NPV at rate a
        B = NPV at rate b

IRR $= 9\% + \left[\dfrac{22}{22+4} \times 1\right]\%$

$= 9 + 0.85 = 9.85\%$

12b.7   The correct answer is: $1,017

The discount factor for 10 years at 7% is 0.508.

∴ Original amount invested   = $2,000 × 0.508
                             = $1,016

But $1,016 × 1.07^{10} is just under $2,000 so $1,017 is the correct answer.

12b.8   The correct answer is: 26.8%

If house prices rise at 2% per calendar month, this is equivalent to $(1.02)^{12} = 1.268$ or 26.8% per year.

12b.9   The correct answer is: $5,073

Annuity   = $700

Annuity factor = 1 + 6.247 (cumulative factor for 9 years, first payment is **now**)
                = 7.247

Annuity $= \dfrac{\text{PV of annuity}}{\text{Annuity factor}}$

$700 $= \dfrac{\text{PV of annuity}}{7.247}$

$700 × 7.247   = PV of annuity

PV of annuity = $5,073 (to the nearest $)

12b.10   The correct answer is: 9%

Annuity $= \dfrac{\text{Present value of annuity}}{\text{Annuity factor}}$

Annuity factor $= \dfrac{86,400}{19,260}$ = 4.486

From tables, this annuity factor corresponds to an interest rate of 9% over six years.

12b.11   The correct answer is: $480,000

The present value of a perpetuity is:

$PV = \dfrac{a}{r}$

where   a = annuity = $24,000
        r = cost of capital as a proportion   = 5%   = 0.05

∴ PV $= \dfrac{24,000}{0.05}$

= $480,000

12b.12   The correct answer is: 18%

The internal rate of return (IRR) of the investment can be calculated using the following formula.

$$IRR = a\% + \left(\frac{A}{A-B} \times (b-a) \right)\%$$

where   a = first interest rate = 12%
        b = second interest rate = 20%
        A = first NPV = $24,000
        B = second NPV = $(8,000)

$$IRR \quad = 12\% + \left(\frac{24,000}{24,000+8,000} \times (20-12) \right)\%$$

$$= 12\% + 6\%$$
$$= 18\%$$

12b.13   The correct answer is: 2 years and 6 months

Workings

Project Beta

Year	Cash inflow $	Cumulative cash inflow $
1	250,000	250,000
2	350,000	600,000
3	400,000	1,000,000
4	200,000	1,200,000
5	150,000	1,350,000
6	150,000	1,500,000

Project Beta has a payback period of between 2 and 3 years.

$$\text{Payback period} = 2\text{ years} + \left[\frac{\$200,000}{\$400,000} \times 12\text{ months} \right]$$

$$= 2\text{ years} + 6\text{ months}$$

12b.14   The correct answer is: Between 3 and 4 years.

Workings

Project Alpha

Year	Cash flow $	Discount factor 10%	PV $	Cum. PV $
0	(800,000)	1.000	(800,000)	(800,000)
1	250,000	0.909	227,250	(572,750)
2	250,000	0.826	206,500	(366,250)
3	400,000	0.751	300,400	(65,850)
4	300,000	0.683	204,900	139,050
5	200,000	0.621	124,200	263,250
6	50,000	0.564	28,200	291,450

The discounted payback period is therefore between three and four years.

12b.15   The correct answer is: Initial investment ÷ annual net cash inflow

The payback period is the time that is required for the total of the cash inflows of a capital investment project to equal the total of the cash outflows, ie initial investment ÷ annual net cash inflow.

12b.16   The correct answer is: Between 10% and 15%

	$
Investment	(60,000)
PV of cash inflow	64,600
NPV @ 10%	4,600

	$
Investment	(60,000)
PV of cash inflow	58,200
NPV @ 15%	(1,800)

The IRR of the machine investment is therefore between 10% and 15% because the NPV falls from $4,600 at 10% to –$1,800 at 15%. Therefore at some point between 10% and 15% the NPV = 0. When the NPV = 0, the internal rate of return is reached.

12b.17   The correct answer is: $61,016

Let x = investment at start of project.

Year	Cash flow $	Discount factor 10%	Present value $
0	x	1.000	(x)
1 – 5	18,000	3.791	68,238
			7,222

∴ –x + $68,238 = $7,222

x = $68,238 – $7,222

x = $61,016

12b.18   The correct answer is: The discount rate (%) at which the net present value of the cash flows from an investment is zero

IRR is the discount rate at which the net present value of the cash flows from an investment is zero.

12b.19   The correct answer is: Between 3.0 years and 4.0 years

At the end of year 3, $74,600 has been 'paid back'. The remaining $15,400 for payback will be received during year 4.

12b.20   The correct answer is: 8.67%

$(1.021)^4 - 1 = 0.0867 = 8.67\%$

12b.21   The correct answer is: $18,750

$1,500/0.08 = 18,750$

12b.22   The correct answer is: Investment Exe 4.04% Investment Wye 4.66%

ACCA examining team comments

The question relates to study guide reference C5d. The answer can be arrived at by calculation (Investment Exe annual effective return = $1.02^2 - 1 = 0.0404$ or 4.04% and investment Wye annual effective return = $1.20^{0.25} - 1 = 0.0466$ or 4.66%). Alternatively the answer can be 'reasoned' out: investment Exe's semi annual compounding must result in a higher effective annual rate than 4% (2 × 2%) and a 20% return over a 4 year period must have an effective annual rate of less than 5% (20% ÷ 4 years) when the compounding effect is allowed for.

12b.23   The correct answer is: $333

> **ACCA examining team comments**
>
> The question relates to study guide reference C5j.
>
> The correct answer is $333.
>
> A four year payback period implies an (equal) annual cash flow of $12,000 ÷ 4 years = $3,000 per year. As these cash flows run for 6 years the NPV is equal to $333 (–$12,000 + annuity factor for 6 years @ 12% × $3,000 = –$12,000 + 4.111 × $3,000 = $333). The –$3,778 distracter is based upon an incorrect calculation of annual cash flow ($12,000 ÷ 6 years = $2,000 per year), suggesting a misunderstanding of the payback method.
>
> In the –$2,899 distracter the NPV was based on a project life of 4 years rather than 6 suggesting a failure to read the question carefully.
>
> Finally –$5,926's NPV was based upon a combination of the other two distracters, that is, an annual cash flow of $2,000 for 4 years.

13   Standard costing

13.1   The correct answer is: $90

		$ per unit	$ per unit
Material P	7 kg × $4	28	
Material S	3 kg × $9	27	
			55
Direct labour	5hr × $7		35
Standard prime cost of product J			90

13.2   The correct answer is: A standard which includes some allowance for losses, waste and inefficiencies. It represents the level of performance which is attainable under efficient operating conditions

An attainable standard assumes efficient levels of operation, but includes **allowances** for normal loss, waste and machine downtime.

13.3   The correct answer is: The operating standards set for production should be the attainable level

It is generally accepted that the use of **attainable standards** has the optimum motivational impact on employees. Some allowance is made for unavoidable wastage and inefficiencies, but the attainable level can be reached if production is carried out efficiently.

13.4   The correct answer is: 1.25 litres

Required liquid input = 1 litre × $\frac{100}{80}$ = 1.25 litres

13.5   The correct answer is: Focusing management reports on areas which require attention and ignoring those which appear to be performing within acceptable limits

When management by exception is operated within a standard costing system, only the variances which exceed acceptable tolerance limits need to be investigated by management with a view to control action. Adverse and favourable variances alike may be subject to investigation, therefore 'Using management reports to highlight exceptionally good performance, so that favourable results can be built upon to improve future outcomes' is incorrect.

Any efficient information system would ensure that only managers who are able to act on the information receive management reports, even if they are not prepared on the basis of management by exception. Therefore 'Sending management reports only to those managers who are able to act on the information contained within the reports' is incorrect.

13.6   The correct answer is: (i), (ii) and (iii) only

Standard costing provides targets for achievement, and yardsticks against which actual performance can be monitored (**item (i)**). It also provides the unit cost information for evaluating the volume figures contained in a budget (**item (ii)**). Inventory control systems are simplified with standard costing. Once the variances have been eliminated, all inventory units are valued at standard price (**item (ii)**).

Item (iv) is incorrect because standard costs are an **estimate** of what will happen in the future, and a unit cost target that the organisation is aiming to achieve.

13.7   The correct answer is: $90.00

Standard labour cost per unit = 9 hours $\times \dfrac{100}{90} \times$ \$9 = \$90

14a   Cost variances

14a.1   The correct answer is: Price $2,400 (F)   Usage $900 (A)

Since inventories are valued at standard cost, the material price variance is based on the materials purchased.

	$
12,000 kg material purchased should cost (×$3)	36,000
but did cost	33,600
Material price variance	2,400 (F)
800 units manufactured should use (× 14 kg)	11,200 kg
but did use	11,500 kg
Usage variance in kg	300 kg (A)
× standard price per kg	× $3
Usage variance in $	$900 (A)

14a.2   The correct answer is: $2,500 (A)

	$
2,300 hours should have cost (× $7)	16,100
but did cost	18,600
Rate variance	2,500 (A)

14a.3   The correct answer is: $2,800 (F)

260 units should have taken (× 10 hrs)	2,600 hrs
but took (active hours)	2,200 hrs
Efficiency variance in hours	400 hrs (F)
× standard rate per hour	× $7
Efficiency variance in $	$2,800 (F)

14a.4   The correct answer is: Expenditure $1,656 (F) Efficiency $4,140 (A)

Standard variable production overhead cost per hour = $11,550 ÷ 5,775 = $2

	$
8,280 hours of variable production overhead should cost (× $2)	16,560
but did cost	14,904
Variable production overhead expenditure variance	1,656 (F)

Standard time allowed for one unit = 5,775 hours ÷ 1,925 units = 3 hours

2,070 units should take (× 3 hours)	6,210 hours
but did take	8,280 hours
Efficiency variance in hours	2,070 hours (A)
× standard variable production overhead cost per hour	× $2
Variable production overhead efficiency variance	$4,140 (A)

14a.5   The correct answer is: Expenditure $700 (A) Volume $3,200 (F)

Fixed overhead expenditure variance

	$
Budgeted fixed overhead expenditure (4,200 units × $4 per unit)	16,800
Actual fixed overhead expenditure	17,500
Fixed overhead expenditure variance	700 (A)

The variance is adverse because the actual expenditure was higher than the amount budgeted.
Fixed overhead volume variance

	$
Actual production at standard rate (5,000 × $4 per unit)	20,000
Budgeted production at standard rate (4,200 × $4 per unit)	16,800
Fixed overhead volume variance	3,200 (F)

The variance is favourable because the actual volume of output was greater than the budgeted volume of output.

If you selected an incorrect option you misinterpreted the direction of one or both of the variances.

14a.6   The correct answer is: Capacity $1,600 (F) Efficiency $400 (F)
Capacity variance

Budgeted hours of work	9,000 hours
Actual hours of work	9,400 hours
Capacity variance in hours	400 hours (F)
× standard fixed overhead absorption rate per hour *	× $4
Fixed production overhead capacity variance	$1,600 (F)

* $36,000/9,000 = $4 per hour

Efficiency variance

1,900 units of product should take (× 9,000/1,800 hrs)	9,500 hours
but did take	9,400 hours
Efficiency variance in hours	100 hours (F)
× standard fixed overhead absorption rate per hour *	× $4
Fixed production overhead efficiency variance in $	$400 (F)

* $36,000/9,000 = $4 per hour

14a.7   The correct answer is: (ii) and (iii) only

Statement (i) is not consistent with a favourable labour efficiency variance. Employees of a lower skill level are likely to work less efficiently, resulting in an **adverse efficiency variance**.

Statement (ii) is consistent with a favourable labour efficiency variance. **Time would be saved in processing** if the material was easier to process.

Statement (iii) is consistent with a favourable labour efficiency variance. **Time would be saved in processing** if working methods were improved.

14a.8   The correct answer is: An adverse direct material cost variance can be a combination of a favourable material price variance and an adverse material usage variance

Direct material cost variance = material price variance + material usage variance

The adverse material usage variance could be larger than the favourable material price variance. The total of the two variances would therefore represent a net result of an adverse total direct material cost variance.

14a.9   The correct answer is: $3,500

	$
53,000 kg should cost (× $2.50)	132,500
but did cost	136,000
Material price variance	3,500 (A)

14a.10   The correct answer is: $2,500

	$
27,000 units should use (× 2 kg)	54,000 kg
but did use	53,000 kg
	1,000 kg (F)
× standard cost per kg	2.5
Material usage variance	2,500 (F)

14a.11   The correct answer is: $36,000 Adverse $25,000 Favourable

Labour rate variance

	$
14,000 hours should have cost (× $10 per hour)	140,000
but did cost	176,000
Labour rate variance	36,000 (A)

Labour efficiency variance

	$	
5,500 units should have taken (× 3 hours per unit)	16,500	hrs
but did take	14,000	hrs
Labour efficiency variance (in hours)	2,500	hrs (F)
× standard rate per unit	× $10	
	$25,000	(F)

14a.12   The correct answer is: $5,000 Adverse

Standard fixed overhead absorption rate per hour = $125,000/25,000 = $5 per hour

Fixed overhead volume capacity variance

Budgeted hours of work	25,000 hrs
Actual hours of work	24,000 hrs
Fixed overhead volume capacity variance	1,000 hrs (A)
× standard fixed overhead absorption rate per hour	× $5
Fixed overhead volume capacity variance in $	$5,000 (A)

14a.13   The correct answer is: $10,000 Adverse

The total direct materials variance can be found by comparing the flexed budget figures with the actual figures.

Budgeted material cost per unit	= $110,000/2,200
	= $50
Flexed for 2,000 units	= $50 × 2,000
	= $100,000

Total direct materials variance

	$
Flexed direct material cost	100,000
but did cost	110,000
Total direct materials variance	10,000 (A)

14a.14   The correct answer is: $20,000 Adverse

The total direct labour variance can be found by comparing the flexed budget figures with the actual figures.

Budgeted labour cost per unit	= $286,000/2,200
	= $130
Flexed for 2,000 units	= $130 × 2,000
	= $260,000

Total direct labour variance

	$
Flexed direct labour cost	260,000
but did cost	280,000
Total direct labour variance	20,000 (A)

14a.15   The correct answer is: Nil

The total direct variable overhead variances can be found by comparing the flexed budget figures with the actual figures.

Budgeted variable overhead cost per unit   = $132,000/2,200
                                              = $60

Flexed for 2,000 units   = $60 × 2,000
                                              = $120,000

Total direct variable overhead variance

	$
Flexed direct variable overhead cost	120,000
but did cost	120,000
Total direct variable overhead variance	nil

14a.16   The correct answer is: (i) is true and (ii) is false

Statement (i) is true. Statement (ii) is false. Producing 5,000 standard hours of work in 5,500 hours would give rise to an adverse fixed overhead volume efficiency variance.

14a.17   The correct answer is: Both statements are true.

14a.18   The correct answer is: $10,000 Favourable.

The total direct materials variance can be found by comparing the flexed budget figures with the actual figures.

	$
Total materials cost should have been	150,000
But was	140,000
Variance	10,000 (F)

14a.19   The correct answer is: $2,500 Adverse

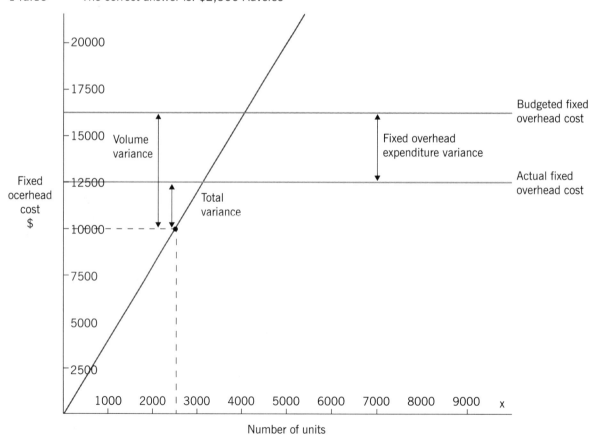

Total fixed overhead variance = $12,500 – $10,000 = $2,500 Adverse.

14b Sales variances and operating statements

14b.1   The correct answer is: Expenditure variance: $5,800 adverse

The only fixed overhead variance in a marginal costing statement is the fixed overhead expenditure variance. This is the difference between budgeted and actual overhead expenditure, calculated in the same way as for an absorption costing system.

There is no volume variance with marginal costing, because under or over absorption due to volume changes cannot arise.

14b.2   The correct answer is: Demand for the product was higher than expected and prices could be raised without adverse effects on sales volumes.

Raising prices in response to higher demand would result in a favourable selling price variance.

14b.3   The correct answer is: 200 units

	$
Total actual direct material cost	2,400
Add back variances: direct material price	(800)
direct material usage	400
Standard direct material cost of production	2,000
Standard material cost per unit	$10
Number of units produced (2,000 ÷ $10)	200

14b.4   The correct answer is: 800 kg

Since there was no change in inventories, the usage variance can be used to calculate the material usage.

$$\text{Saving in material used compared with standard} = \frac{\$400(F)}{\$2 \text{ per kg}} = 200 \text{ kg}$$

Standard material usage for actual production (200 units × 5kg)	1,000 kg
Usage variance in kg	200 kg (F)
Actual usage of material	800 kg

14b.5   The correct answer is: $1,200 (F)

	$
200 units should sell for (× $70)	14,000
but did sell for	15,200
Selling price variance	1,200 (F)

14b.6   The correct answer is: $900 (A)

$$\text{Budgeted sales volume per month} = \frac{\text{Budgeted material cost of sales}}{\text{Standard material cost per unit}}$$

$$= \frac{\$2,300}{\$10} = 230 \text{ units}$$

$$\text{Budgeted profit margin per unit} = \frac{\text{Budgeted monthly profit margin}}{\text{Budgeted monthly sales volume}}$$

$$= \frac{\$6,900}{230} = \$30 \text{ per unit}$$

Budgeted sales volume	230 units
Actual sales volume	200 units
Sales volume variance in units	30 units (A)
Standard profit per unit	× $30
Sales volume variance in $	$900 (A)

14b.7   The correct answer is: 4,200

Actual expenditure = $(48,000 + 2,000) = $50,000
Overhead absorbed = $(50,000 – 8,000) = $42,000
Overhead absorption rate per unit = $48,000 ÷ 4,800 = $10

∴ Number of units produced = $42,000 ÷ $10 = 4,200

14b.8   The correct answer is: $3.40

Total standard cost of material purchased – actual cost of material purchased = Price variance

Total standard cost	=	$21,920 + $1,370
	=	$23,290
Standard price per kg	=	$23,290/6,850
	=	$3.40

14b.9   The correct answer is: Price $1,530 (A)   Volume $2,250 (F)

Actual sales	2,550 units
Budgeted sales	2,400 units
Variance in units	150 units (F)
× standard contribution per unit ($(27 – 12))	× $15
Sales volume variance in $	$2,250 (F)
	$
Revenue from 2,550 units should have been (× $27)	68,850
but was	67,320
Selling price variance	1,530 (A)

14b.10   The correct answer is: $1,000 Adverse

	$	
Budgeted sales volume	10,000	units
Actual sales volume	9,800	units
Sales volume variance (units)	200	units (A)
× standard profit per unit	× $5	
Sales volume profit variance (in $)	$1,000	(A)

14b.11   The correct answer is: $1,200

Direct material price variance

	$
12,000 litres should have cost (× $2.50)	30,000
But did cost (12,000 × $2.50 × 1.04)	31,200
Direct material price variance	1,200 (A)

14b.12   The correct answer is: 1,212

Standard cost per unit = 10.5 litres × $2.50 per litre

= $26.25 per unit

Standard cost of actual production = standard cost + variance
= $(12,000 litres × $2.50) + 1,815
= $(30,000 + 1,815)
= $31,815

∴ Actual production = standard cost of actual production/standard cost per unit

= 31,815/$26.25

= 1,212 units

14b.13   The correct answer is: $4,500 Favourable

	$
Sales revenue for 9,000 units should have been (× $12.50)	112,500
but was	117,000
Sales price variance	4,500 (F)

14b.14 The correct answer is: $17,000

	$
8,500 units should have cost (× $15)	127,500
but did cost (8,500 × $17)	144,500
	17,000 (A)

14b.15 The correct answer is: $2,635 under absorbed

	$
Absorbed overhead (12,400 × 1.02 × $4.25)	53,754
Actual overhead	56,389
Under-absorbed overhead	2,635

14b.16 The correct answer is: $8,500

	$
Standard contribution	10,000
Sales price variance	500
Variable cost variance	(2,000)
	8,500

14b.17 The correct answer is: $12,600 (A)

The sales volume variance in a marginal costing system is valued at standard contribution per unit, rather than standard profit per unit.

Contribution per unit of E = $15 – $8 = $7

Sales volume variance in terms of contribution = $\frac{\$9,000(A)}{\$5} \times \$7 = \$12,600$ (A)

14b.18 The correct answer is: Absorption costing profits will be higher and closing inventory valuations higher than those under marginal costing.

Closing inventory valuation under absorption costing will always be higher than under marginal costing because of the absorption of fixed overheads into closing inventory values.

The profit under absorption costing will be greater because the fixed overhead being carried forward in closing inventory is greater than the fixed overhead being written off in opening inventory.

14b.19 The correct answer is: $2,720 lower

If marginal costing is used to value inventory instead of absorption costing, the difference in profits will be equal to the change in inventory volume multiplied by the fixed production overhead absorption rate = 80 units × $34 = $2,720

Since closing inventory are higher than opening inventories, the marginal costing profit will be lower that the absorption costing profit (so $2,720 higher is incorrect). This is because the marginal costing profit does not 'benefit' from the increase in the amount of fixed production overhead taken to inventory (rather than to the statement of profit or loss).

If you selected $3,400 lower or higher you based the difference on 100 units of opening inventory.

14b.20 The correct answer is: $258,948

Standard marginal costing reconciliation

	$
Original budgeted contribution	290,000
Sales volume variance	(36,250)
Standard contribution from actual sales	253,750
Selling price variance	21,875
	275,625
Variable cost variances	
Total direct material variance	(6,335)
Total direct labour variance	11,323
Total variable overhead variance	(21,665)
Actual contribution	258,948

14b.21   The correct answer is: (i) and (ii) only

ACCA examining team comments

This question relates to study guide heading D1(b).

The correct answer is (i) and (ii) only. In a standard absorption costing system the sales volume margin variance is based upon profit per unit, whereas under a marginal costing system it is based upon contribution per unit. In a standard absorption costing system the total fixed overhead variance includes expenditure and volume variances. Under marginal costing only the expenditure variance is included. Variable cost variances are the same under both systems. Only 15% of candidates selected the correct alternative. The most frequent answers were (i) only (37% of candidates), and (ii) only (30% of candidates). This is essentially a knowledge based question, and the poor results suggest that candidates need to do more work in this area.

14b.22   The correct answer is: $109,000

ACCA examining team comments

The question relates to study guide reference D3a.

The correct answer is $109,000, but was chosen by only a handful of candidates. The correct answer can be obtained by working backwards by adding appropriate adverse variances and subtracting appropriate favourable variances from actual profit. Standard profit on actual sales is exactly what it says, actual units multiplied by standard profit per unit. As it is based on actual units, a profit adjustment for the difference between budgeted and actual volumes is not required, and hence the sales volume variance should be ignored. The calculation can be most easily understood by looking at the standard cost operating statement below.

	$
Budgeted profit	not required
Sales volume variance	not needed
Standard profit on actual	109,000
Sales price variance	5,000 favourable
Total variable cost variance	7,000 adverse
Fixed cost expenditure variance	3,000 favourable
Fixed cost volume variance	2,000 adverse
Actual profit	108,000

If candidates understand how the operating statement works the correct answer can be quickly calculated as $108,000 + $2,000 − $3,000 + $7,000 − $5,000 = $109,000.

Incorrect answers were fairly evenly spread across the other 3 alternatives, suggesting a large amount of guessing by candidates. $115,000 represents the correct calculation of budgeted profit (that is the standard profit figure for budgeted volume). This was not the question asked.

$107,000 represents the answer obtained if candidates added back favourable variances and subtracted adverse variances. Finally $101,000 represents a calculation of budgeted profit if candidates added back favourable variances and subtracted adverse variances.

Performance on another question involving standard cost operating statements in the same exam was also poor.

This suggests a lack of understanding in this area.

14b.23   The correct answer is: $485,000

> **ACCA examining team comments**
>
> This question covers syllabus area D3a. The correct answer can be obtained by working backwards from the actual profit figure. Because we are working backwards, adverse variances must be added back and favourable variances must be deducted to get to the budgeted profit figure. It is also important to remember that the fixed production overhead capacity and efficiency variances are subdivisions of the fixed production overhead volume variance, and it is important to avoid double counting.
>
> The correct answer is therefore
>
> | | $000 |
> | --- | --- |
> | Actual profit | 500 |
> | Add: Sales volume profit variance | 10 adverse |
> | Add: Direct labour efficiency variance | 15 adverse |
> | Add: Fixed production overhead volume variance | 10 adverse |
> | Less: Fixed production overhead expenditure | 50 favourable |
> | Budgeted profit | 485 |
>
> Only 19% of candidates correctly selected this figure, making this question the worst answered in the exam.

14b.24   The correct answer is: $15,000 A $2,000 F $8,000 F

> **ACCA examining team comments**
>
> The correct answer can be arrived at by looking for a combination of variances that satisfy two criteria (i) The total of the variances must add to $5,000 adverse as actual profit is $5,000 less than budgeted profit (ii) As budgeted profit is $30,000 ($25,000 actual plus a $5,000 adverse variance) and standard profit on actual sales is $15,000 (given) then the sales volume variance must be $15,000 adverse. Questions on standard cost operating statements have been mentioned in previous reports and are commonly amongst the worst answered questions in the exam.

14b.25   The correct answer is: $29,000

> **ACCA examining team comments**
>
> I have mentioned in previous reports that candidates appear to experience difficulties with questions involving standard costing operating statements and the reconciliation of budgeted and actual performance. In this question candidates were given an actual profit figure and a list of variances. To get to budgeted profit they needed to (i) add back adverse variances and to deduct favourable variances to actual profit to arrive at budgeted profit. And (ii) in doing so they also needed to avoid double counting. The fixed overhead volume variance ($3,000F) is equal to the sum of the fixed overhead capacity variance ($4,000 F) and the fixed overhead efficiency variance ($1,000 A), so it is important not to include all three and only to deduct $3,000 not $6,000.

14b.26   The correct answer is: $9,000 adverse

> **ACCA examining team comments**
>
> This is calculated by finding the balancing figure. The total variance between budgeted contribution and actual contribution is $5,000 adverse ($20,000 - $15,000). The sales volume and sales price variances sum to $4,000 favourable, so to balance, the variable cost variance must be $9,000 adverse. Questions on the reconciliation of budgeted and actual profits or contributions regularly cause candidates difficulty in this exam and future candidates are recommended to study this area carefully.

14b.27   The correct answer is: $213,000

> **ACCA examining team comments**
>
> This question tests syllabus area D3b , the reconciliation of budgeted and actual contribution under standard marginal costing. It is an area that candidates have found difficult in the past, and once again it generated the worst answered question in the exam. The safest way to answer this type of question is to layout the relevant section of the standard costing operating statement and to "plug in" the figures provided, as shown below:
>
> | | $ |
> | --- | --- |
> | Flexed budget contribution | 200,000 |
> | (= actual sales units x standard contribution) | |
> | Sales price variance | (5,000) |
> | Total variable cost variance | 18,000 |
> | Actual contribution is therefore | 213,000 |
>
> This results in the correct answer, 213,000.

14b.28   The correct answer is: $295,000

> **ACCA examining team comments**
>
> This question covers syllabus area D3b. This is commonly the worst answered section of the exam. The correct answer is $295,000, and was the second most popular choice amongst candidates. This could be arrived at by calculating the standard contribution for actual sales (5,000 units x $60 = $300,000) and then deducting the adverse sales price variance ($300,000 - $5000 = $295,000). $303,000 was the most popular selection. Candidates choosing this alternative incorrectly adjusted standard contribution on actual sales for both the sales price variance and the sales volume contribution variance. This is incorrect because the sales volume contribution variance links standard contribution on budgeted sales with that on actual sales. In other words they were double counting the effect of the sales volume contribution variance.

14b.29   The correct answer is: $21,500

> **ACCA examining team comments**
>
> To arrive at the correct answer candidates had to adjust the budgeted profit for all the variances given. ($25,000 -$1,000 +$2,000- $4,000 -$500 = $21,500.
>
> Some candidates went on to deduct budgeted fixed overheads from this figure to get $9,500. This was incorrect because budgeted fixed overheads would have been already deducted in calculating budgeted profit and hence these candidates were double counting.
>
> Candidates who selected $33,500 adjusted budgeted profit for all of the variances, but then went on to add back fixed overhead figure as if calculating actual contribution.
>
> Lastly candidates who selected $40,000 attempted to calculate actual contribution, but got the variance signage the wrong way round. ($25,000 + $1,000 - $2,000 + $4,000 +$12,000 = $40,000

15 Target setting

15.1   The correct answer is: They should be easily achievable

Attainable (which is part of the SMART objectives framework) is different from 'easily achievable'. The objectives should be motivational which means that they should be at least a little bit challenging.

15.2   The correct answer is: Factors fundamental to strategic success

15.3   The correct answer is: (i), (ii) and (iv) only.

The mission states the aims of the organisation. The strategy outlines what the organisation should be doing; the values and the policies set limits to the ways the strategy may be converted into performance. Profitability is an objective and relates to the critical success factors for business success.

15.4   The correct answer is: (i) only

Reducing training costs may mean that the business is faced with a skills shortage in the long term. (ii) and (iii) should benefit the business in the long term.

15.5   The correct answer is: It is when there is a bias towards short term rather than long term performance.

Longer term objectives are sacrificed.

15.6   The correct answer is: CO_2 emissions

CO_2 emissions are probably more likely to be measured because of government legislation. They are not one of the usual measures of performance (depending on the industry).

15.7   The correct answer is: Both statements are true.

15.8   The correct answer is: Performance measurement involves comparing actual performance against a target and the mission statement represents the organisation's overall target.

15.9   The correct answer is: 'Middle tier' objectives to facilitate the planning and control of individual functions within the organisation

Tactical objectives are middle-tier objectives that facilitate the planning and control of individual functions within the organisation.

15.10   The correct answer is: Sales and revenue are likely to decrease in the second half of the year and performance should be measured in that context.

15.11   The correct answer is: Long-term objectives for the organisation as a whole

Strategic objectives are long-term objectives for the organisation as a whole.

15.12   The correct answers are: A danger of benchmarking is that inappropriate comparisons lead to incorrect conclusions and The ultimate aim of benchmarking is to improve performance.

Benchmarking can be internal, for example comparison against another department. The main aim of benchmarking is improved performance, which could just as readily be in the area of quality as in cost.

15.13   The correct answer is: Functional

This is an example of functional benchmarking.

15.14   The correct answer is: Competitive

This is an example of competitive benchmarking.

15.15   The correct answer is: (iii) only Return on capital employed.

15.16   The correct answer is: Short-termism involves prioritising short-term results above the organisation's long-term prospects.

16 Financial performance measurement

16.1   The correct answer is: Cash flow

Cash flow information is a financial performance measure. The other options are all non-financial indicators (NFIs).

16.2   The correct answer is: 0.6875

$$\text{Acid test ratio} = \frac{\text{Current assets} - \text{inventory}}{\text{Current liabilities}}$$

$$= \frac{40,000 + 1,250}{60,000}$$

$$= 0.6875$$

16.3   The correct answer is: Current ratio: Decrease   Acid test: Decrease

ACCA examining team comments

This question relates to study guide reference E2(a).

The correct answer is - both ratios will decrease. The opening current ratio (current assets/current liabilities) is $1.8m/$1.0m = 1.8, and the opening acid test (current assets less stock/ current liabilities) is $1.3m/$1.0m =1.3. Purchasing (say) $1.0m of inventory on short term credit will decrease the current ratio to ($1.8m + $1m)/ ($1.0m+ $1.0m) = 1.4. The acid test would also decrease to $1.8m/ ($1.0m+ $1.0m) = 0.9. Only 23% of candidates selected this alternative. On this type of question if the answer is not immediately clear candidates should substitute in some simple numbers to test out the effects of a transaction.

16.4   The correct answer is: Return on investment: Decrease   Residual income: Increase

ACCA examining team comments

The question relates to study guide reference E2f. The correct answer is Return on investment: Decrease   Residual income: Increase. The new project's return on investment is less than that of the investment centre and this will result in a reduction in its return on investment. However because the project offers a return higher than the cost of capital it will increase the investment centre's residual income. The most popular answer was Return on investment: Decrease Residual income: Decrease, with 29% of candidates mistakenly believing that the new project would result in a decrease in both return on investment and residual income. This mistake suggests a lack of understanding of residual income.

16.5   The correct answer is: 63.9%

$3,450,000 / $5,400,000 = 63.9%

16.6   The correct answer is: 24.1%

$1,735,000 / $7,200,000 = 24.1%

16.7   The correct answer is: Liquidity

The current ratio measures liquidity.

16.8   The correct answer is: 53.4%

$670,000 / ($670,000 + $585,000) = 53.4%

16.9   The correct answer is: Liquidity

The acid test ratio measures liquidity.

16.10   The correct answer is: Decrease from 20% to 15%

Return on investment $= \dfrac{\text{Profit}}{\text{Capital employed}} \times 100\%$

For 20X7 ROI $= \dfrac{7,500}{37,500} \times 100\% = 20\%$

For 20X8 ROI $= \dfrac{9,000}{60,000} \times 100\% = 15\%$

16.11   The correct answer is: 7.5 times

Asset turnover $= \dfrac{\text{Sales}}{\text{Capital employed}}$

$= \dfrac{450,000}{60,000}$

$= 7.5 \text{ times}$

16.12   The correct answer is: ROI – yes RI – yes

The ROI target is 13% and the cost of capital is 12%. The ROI is calculated as $30,000/$200,000 × 100% = 15% and so the project would be accepted. The RI is calculated as $30,000 – (12% × $200,000) = $6,000. The project would be accepted.

16.13   The correct answer is: (i), (ii) and (iii).

The figures needed to calculate ROI are easily available from the financial accounting records.

16.14   The correct answer is: Work study.

16.15   The correct answer is: Eliminate costs and Reduce costs

Value analysis focuses on costs, not sales volumes or prices.

16.16   The correct answer is: Value analysis considers cost value, exchange value, use value and esteem value.

16.17   The correct answer is: Increase

ACCA examining team comments

This question tests Syllabus heading E2 f. The correct answer was selected by a minority of candidates. A useful way of answering many ratio analysis questions is to substitute some simple numbers into the problem. For example, if the division currently earns an ROI (operating profit over net assets) of 20%, this could be represented by operating profit of $20,000 and net assets of $100,000. Residual income is calculated by operating profit – (net assets x imputed interest rate). A residual income of $1,000 could be represented by an operating profit of $11,000 less an imputed interest charge of $50,000 x 20%. Therefore the new ROI would become (existing operating profit + project operating profit) ÷ (existing net assets + project net assets) = ($20,000 + $11,000) ÷ ($100,000 + $20,000) = 25.83% = an increase in ROI. Far quicker though is to realise that a project offering a positive residual income at an imputed interest rate of 20% must be offering a return higher than 20%, and therefore must improve the existing ROI of 20%.

Alternative 'not possible to tell from this information' was the most popular choice. This possibly says more about candidates' knowledge of residual income than the sufficiency of information in the question. Residual income has been highlighted as an area of weakness in previous reports.

16.18   The correct answer is: Return on capital employed

> **ACCA examining team comments**
>
> Government actions have a huge potential effect on the performance of companies. Government subsidies, such as the rent subsidy in this question, need to be excluded from managerial performance indicators to allow fair comparisons. This is because they are not controllable by shop managers. ROCE would not provide a fair comparison of managerial performance because the operating profit used to calculate return on capital employed, is calculated after deducting rental charges. Managers in the South division would have an in built advantage over those in the North division because of this. None of the other measures include rental cost so would not suffer from this disadvantage.

16.19   The correct answer is: Capital gearing - Increase Current ratio - Increase

> **ACCA examining team comments**
>
> The capital gearing ratio is calculated as non-current liabilities ÷ ordinary shareholders funds (this is sometimes described as the debt to equity ratio) or non-current liabilities ÷ (ordinary shareholders funds + non-current liabilities) (sometimes described as debt to equity + debt ratio) A five year bank loan will increase the company's non-current liabilities. Under either definition above this will increase capital gearing. The current ratio is calculated as current assets ÷ current liabilities. A reduction in overdraft will reduce a company's current liabilities will therefore increase the value of the current ratio.
>
> For those having difficulty in processing the data given in the question I would suggest that they "invent" some simple numbers to represent the existing position and then process the data in the question to see the effect on the ratios. This approach is useful in many ratio analysis problems

17 Assessing non-financial performance

17.1   The correct answer is: Efficiency

17.2   The correct answer is: Both are true.

17.3   The correct answer is: The balanced scorecard approach enables organisations to consider all areas of performance relevant to achieving their strategic goals.

       The Balanced Scorecard approach enables organisations to consider all areas of performance relevant to achieving their strategic goals.

17.4   The correct answer is: To prevent a narrow focus on short-term financial performance.

17.5   The correct answer is: Customer satisfaction, growth, financial success and process efficiency.

17.6   The correct answer is: Achieving agreed targets

       Effectiveness can only be measured in terms of achieved performance. Economy consists of minimising costs, for example, by obtaining suitable inputs at the lowest price. Efficiency, in the narrow sense used here, consists of achieving the greatest output per unit of input: avoiding waste of inputs would contribute to this. Achieving a given level of profit is a measure of overall efficiency in its wider sense and would require proper attention to all three of these matters.

17.7   The correct answer is: Level of refunds given

       The level of refunds given should be used in the customer perspective. If Balance Co has to offer a high level of refunds, this is likely to indicate a low level of customer satisfaction with its product.

17.8   The correct answer is: (i) and (ii)

       The number of customer complaints and the number of repeat orders as a proportion of total orders will reflect the quality of service customers feel they have received from the business. Although sales volume will be affected by the business's ability to retain customers, increasing sales is a more direct measure of the business's marketing effectiveness than its service quality.

17.9   The correct answer is: (ii) and (iii) are non-financial objectives.

17.10   The correct answers are: Net profit margins and Employee absentee rates

Variance analysis and defective units would be more appropriate for manufacturing organisations with large production volumes.

17.11   The correct answer is: (i) and (ii) only

Relative market share is usually a measure of competitiveness. Efficiency and productivity are measures of resource utilisation.

17.12   The correct answer is: Cost per consignment.

Number of customer complaints and client evaluation interviews would be measures of quality. Depot profit league tables is a measure of profit.

18   Mixed Bank 1

18.1   The correct answer is: $286.76

	$ per unit
Material	20.00
Labour	69.40
Production overhead (14 hours × $12.58)	176.12
Total production cost	265.52
General overhead (8% × $265.52)	21.24
	286.76

18.2   The correct answer is: Process 1 Abnormal loss   Process 2 Abnormal loss

		Process 1 kg		Process 2 kg
Input		47,000		42,000
Normal loss	(× 8%)	3,760	(× 5%)	2,100
Expected output		43,240		39,900
Actual output		42,000		38,915
Abnormal loss		1,240		985

18.3   The correct answer is: The actual selling price per unit exceeded the standard selling price per unit.

The actual sales revenue is higher than the flexed budget sales revenue. Since the effect of a sales volume change has been removed from this comparison the higher revenue must be caused by a higher than standard selling price.

18.4   The correct answer is: Be constant per unit of output

Variable costs are conventionally deemed to increase or decrease in direct proportion to changes in output. Therefore the correct answer is Be constant per unit of output. 'Vary per unit of output as production volume changes' and 'Vary, in total, from period to period when production is constant' imply a changing unit rate, which does not comply with this convention. 'Be constant in total when production volume changes' relates to a fixed cost.

18.5   The correct answer is: None of them

None of the criticisms apply in *all* circumstances.

Criticism (i) has some validity but even where output is not standardised it may be possible to identify a number of standard components and activities whose costs may be controlled effectively by the use of standard costs. **Criticism (ii)** also has some validity but the use of information technology means that standards can be updated rapidly and more frequently, so that they may be useful for the purposes of control by comparison. **Criticism (iii)** can also be addressed in some circumstances. The use of ideal standards and more demanding performance levels can combine the benefits of continuous improvement and standard costing control.

18.6   The correct answer is: Cost of acquiring or enhancing non-current assets

Capital expenditure is the cost of acquiring or enhancing non-current assets.

18.7   The correct answer is: Production Cost Centre D

	A	B	C	D
Overhead expenditure	18,757	29,025	46,340	42,293
Direct labour hours	3,080	6,750		
Machine hours			3,380	2,640
Overhead absorption rate	$6.09	$4.30	$13.71	$16.02

18.8   The correct answer is: $113,600

Production cost per unit = $3.60 + ($258,000/60,000) = $7.90

Profit = 700,000 – (56,000 × 7.90) – 144,000 = $113,600

	$	$
Revenue		700,000
Production costs:		
Variable		
(56,000 + 4,000) × $3.60	216,000	
Fixed	258,000	
Closing inventory (4,000 × $7.90)	(31,600)	
		(442,200)
		257,600
Fixed non-production costs		(144,000)
		113,600

18.9   The correct answer is: Profit will be higher; inventory values will be lower

Inventory levels have decreased so marginal costing will result in higher profits and lower inventory values than absorption costing.

18.10   The correct answer is: A product produced at the same time as other products which has a relatively low value compared with the other products

A by-product can be defined as being 'output of some value, produced incidentally while manufacturing the main product'.

'A product produced at the same time as other products which has no value' is incorrect because a by-product has some value.

'A product produced at the same time as other products which requires further processing to put it in a saleable state' is incorrect because this description could also apply to a joint product.

'A product produced at the same time as other products which has a relatively low volume compared with the other products' is incorrect because the value of the product described could be relatively high, even though the output volume is relatively low.

18.11   The correct answer is: $370,300

Direct material cost per 1% activity = $2,000
Direct labour cost per 1% activity = $1,500

Production overhead		$
At	60% activity	54,000
At	80% activity	62,000
Change	20%	8,000

Variable cost per 1% change in activity = $\dfrac{\$8,000}{20}$ = $400

Substituting in 80% activity:

	$
Variable cost = 80 × $400	32,000
Total cost	62,000
∴ Fixed cost	30,000

Other overhead is a wholly fixed cost

Budget flexed at 77% level of activity

	$'000
Direct material 77 × $2,000	154.0
Direct labour 77 × $1,500	115.5
Production overhead:	
Variable 77 × $400	30.8
Fixed	30.0
Other overhead	40.0
	370.3

If you selected $330,300 you did not include a fixed cost allowance for the other overhead. $373,300 ignores the fact that production overhead is a semi-variable cost and $377,300 simply multiplies the total cost for 70% activity by a factor of 1.1. This makes no allowance for the fact that there is an element of fixed costs within production overhead, and other overhead is wholly fixed.

18.12   The correct answer is: 12.1%

$$IRR = a\% + [\frac{A}{A-B} \times (b-a)]\%$$

where a is one interest rate
       b is the other interest rate
       A is the NPV at rate a
       B is the NPV at rate b

$$IRR = 10\% + \left[\frac{2,700}{(2,700+3,740)} \times (15-10)\right]\%$$

$$= 10\% + 2.1\%$$

$$= 12.1\%$$

18.13   The correct answer is: $38,328

Present value = $8,000 + ($8,000 × 3.791) = $38,328

18.14   The correct answer is: Lowering the selling price by 15%

Lowering the selling price by 15% is best described as a short term tactical plan.

18.15   The correct answer is: The absorption costing profit would be $10,000 greater

Fixed costs per unit	= $16 ÷ 4 = $4
Units in closing inventory	= 17,500 – 15,000 = 2,500 units
Profit difference	= inventory increase in units x fixed overhead per unit
	= 2,500 × $4 = $10,000

Inventories increased, therefore fixed overhead would have been carried forward in inventory using absorption costing and the profit would be higher than with marginal costing.

If you selected 'The absorption costing profit would be $10,000 less' you calculated the correct profit difference, but misinterpreted the 'direction' of the difference.

If you selected either of the other two options, you evaluated the inventory difference at variable cost and full cost respectively.

18.16   The correct answer is: $802,000

Total purchase costs = annual demand × purchase price

$$= 20,000 \times \$40 \text{ per unit}$$

$$= \$800,000$$

Order costs

$$\text{Number of orders} = \frac{\text{Annual demand}}{\text{EOQ}} = \frac{20,000 \text{ units}}{500 \text{ units}} = 40 \text{ orders per year}$$

Cost per   = 40 orders x $25 per order

Total order costs = $1,000

Holding costs

Average inventory held = EOQ/2 = 500/2 = 250 units

It costs $4 to hold each unit of inventory

∴ Holding costs = average inventory held × $4 per unit

                    = 250 units × $4 per unit = $1,000

Total annual costs of inventory

	$
Purchase costs	800,000
Order costs	1,000
Holding costs	1,000
Total	802,000

18.17   The correct answer is: a = 28 and b = +2.6

The least squares method of linear regression analysis involves using the following formulae for a and b in Y = a + bX.

$$b = \frac{n\Sigma XY - \Sigma X\Sigma Y}{n\Sigma X^2 - (\Sigma X)^2}$$

$$= \frac{(5 \times 8,104) - (100 \times 400)}{(5 \times 2,040) - 100^2}$$

$$= \frac{40,520 - 40,000}{10,200 - 10,000}$$

$$= \frac{520}{200}$$

$$= 2.6$$

At this stage, you can eliminate options A and C.

$$a = \frac{\Sigma Y}{n} - b\frac{\Sigma X}{b}$$

$$= \frac{400}{5} - 2.6 \times (\frac{100}{5})$$

$$= 28.$$

18.18   The correct answer is: $115,000

	Recruit $'000	Retrain $'000
4 new employees (4 × $40,000)	160	
Training cost		15
Replacements		100
	160	115

The supervision cost would be incurred anyway and is not a relevant cost, since an existing manager is used. Similarly, the salaries of the existing employees are not relevant.

The lowest cost option is to retrain the existing employees, at a total relevant cost of $115,000.

18.19   The correct answer is: 0.17

$$r = \frac{n\sum xy - \sum x \sum y}{\sqrt{[n\sum x^2 - (\sum x)^2][n\sum y^2 - (\sum y)^2]}}$$

$$= \frac{(6\times 14)-(2\times 15)}{\sqrt{\left[6\times 30 - 2^2\right]\left[6\times 130 - 15^2\right]}} = \frac{84-30}{\sqrt{176\times 555}} = \frac{54}{312.54} = 0.172778 = 0.17$$

(to 2 dec places)

18.20   The correct answer is: The total production cost of the job is $440 (to the nearest $)

	$
Direct materials 10 kg × $10	100
Direct labour 20 hours × $5	100
Prime cost	200
Variable production overhead 20 hours × $2	40
Fixed production overhead 20 hours × $10*	200
Total production cost	440
Selling, distribution and administration	50
Total cost	490

* Overhead absorption rate $= \dfrac{\$100,000}{10,000} = \$10$ per labour hour

19   Mixed Bank 2

19.1   The correct answer is: A learning and growth perspective

A target of providing at least 40 hours of training every year to improve skills and productivity has a learning and growth perspective.

19.2   The correct answer is: (i), (ii) and (iii) only

Trend, seasonal variation and cyclical variation.

19.3   The correct answer is: Profit before interest and tax ÷ (Ordinary shareholders' funds + Non-current liabilities) × 100

19.4   The correct answer is: Performance testing.

Re-inspection cost is an internal failure cost. Administration of customer complaints section is an external failure cost and training in quality control is a prevention cost.

19.5   The correct answers are: Direct labour and variable production overhead

19.6   The correct answer is: 3.50

Let x = the number of hours 12,250 units should have taken

12,250 units should have taken	x hrs
but did take	41,000 hrs
Labour efficiency variance (in hrs)	x − 41,000 hrs

Labour efficiency variance (in $)   = $11,250 (F)

∴ Labour efficiency variance (in hrs) $= \dfrac{\$11,250\,(F)}{\$6}$

                         = 1,875 (F)

∴ 1,875 hrs   = (x − 41,000) hrs

∴ standard hours for 12,250 units   = 41,000 + 1,875

                                   = 42,875 hrs

$$\therefore \text{ Standard hours per unit} = \frac{42,875 \text{ hrs}}{12,250 \text{ units}}$$

$$= 3.50 \text{ hrs}$$

19.7 The correct answer is: $300,000

($200,000 + ((100,000 − 80,000) × $5) = $300,000

19.8 The correct answer is: (ii) only

You are not given any information in the question about the actual quantity of fuel used. You are only told about the total cost. Don't be put off by the different number of km – all we want is the difference in fuel quantity.

So, to decide how the quantity has changed from 20 × 8 to 20 × 9 we need to take account of the price increase.

First, we can re-state the 20X9 price in terms of 20X8 prices. This is where the index numbers come in.
$1,440 million × 120/240 = $720

So now we know that in 20X8 prices, the fuel cost $600 in 20X8 and $720 in 20X9. The increase = 720 − 600 = 120. This is a percentage increase of 120/600 ×100% = 20%

19.9 The correct answer is: They are an efficient method of storing text based files

They are *not* an efficient method of storing text based files.

19.10 The correct answer is: $5,000

(6,000 units − 5,000 units) × $25,000 ÷ 5,000 units

19.11 The correct answer is: (i) only

It recognises that overhead costs are not always driven by the volume of production

19.12 The correct answer is: 17.6%

$$\text{IRR} = a\% + [\ \frac{A}{A-B}\ \times (b-a)]\%$$
where a is one interest rate   A is the NPV at rate a
      b is the other interest rate   B is the NPV at rate b

IRR   = 14% + [(16,000/(16,000+10,500)) × 6%
        = 14% + 3.6%
        = 17.6%

19.13 The correct answer is: Adverse fixed overhead capacity variance.

19.14 The correct answer is:

Current ratio   *Quick*
Reduce by 10%   Reduce by 20%

Before the new inventory is bought the current ratio is as follows:

Current assets of $40m divided by current liabilities of $20m = $40/$20 = 2

When the inventory of $5m is purchased, this increases the current assets (inventory) and the current liabilities (payables – because it was bought 'on credit') so the new current ratio =

$$\frac{40+5}{20+5} = 1.8$$

So you can see that the ratio has reduced from 2 to 1.8. A difference of 0.2. As a percentage this is 0.2/2 × 100=10%

The quick ratio involves removing inventory. We are told in the question that after buying $5m, there is $10m so we can deduce that before the new inventory purchase, there is $5m of inventory.

$$\frac{40-5}{20} = 1.75$$

After the purchase, the current liabilities increase by 5 so the quick ratio becomes:

$$\frac{40-5}{25} = 1.4$$

So you can see that the quick ratio has reduced by 0.35. As a percentage this is 0.35/1.75 x 100 = 20%

19.15   The correct answer is: Cluster sampling

19.16   The correct answer is: $18,000

(5,000 × $12 × 20 ÷ 120) + 8,000 = $18,000

19.17   The correct answer is: $5,200 Favourable

$57,200 – (5,200 × $50,000 ÷ 5,000 units) = $5,200 favourable

19.18   The correct answer is: $800 Favourable

(5,200 units – 5,000 units) × $20,000 ÷ 5,000 units = $800

19.19   The correct answer is: The variable cost per unit.

19.20   The correct answer is: RI will increase and ROI will decrease.

20   Mixed Bank 3

20.1   The correct answer is: Multi-stage

The sample is selected in stages, firstly by constituencies. The correct answer is multi-stage sampling as this method involves dividing the population into a number of sub-populations and then selecting a small sample of these sub-populations at random. Each sub-population is then divided further. Stratified sampling involves dividing the population into strata and then taking a random sample from each stratum. Random sampling is where every member of the population has an equal chance of being selected and systematic sampling is where every nth item after a random start is selected.

20.2   The correct answer is: $55,400

Change in inventories	= (8,500 – 7,100) litres
	= 1,400 litres
Difference in profit	= 1,400 × $4
	= $5,600

Absorption costing profit will be lower than marginal costing profits by $5,600.
Therefore absorption costing profit = $61,000 – $5,600
= $55,400

20.3   The correct answer is: Graph C

The cost described is known as a semi-variable cost. Semi-variable costs consist of a fixed amount up to a certain level of activity which is represented by a straight horizontal line on the graph. At a certain point a variable element in introduced and the cost line slopes upwards at a constant rate as the level of activity increases.

20.4   The correct answer is: $88,095

Variable overhead	= ($83,585 − $73,950) / (15,100 − 12,750)
	= $9,635 / 2,350
	= $4.10 per square metre

Fixed overhead	= $73,950 − ($4.10 × 12,750)
	= $73,950 − $52,275
	= $21,675

Overheads for 16,200m^2	= $21,675 + ($4.10 × 16,200)
	= $21,675 + $66,420
	= $88,095

20.5   The correct answer is: $20.50

Actual overheads were $694,075 and under-recovered overheads were $35,000.

So overhead recovered for 32,150 hours at absorption rate x = $(694,075 − 35,000) = $659,075.

∴ 32,150x = $659,075

∴ x = $659,075 / 32,150

    = $20.50

20.6   The correct answer is: 179 degrees

Total cost = $4,630,000
Cat food = $2,300,000 / $4,630,000 × 360 degrees = 179 degrees

20.7   The correct answer is: =SUM(B6:D6)

All formulae in spreadsheets need to start with an equals sign. The SUM function is used to total values in spreadsheets.

20.8   The correct answers are: Statements (iii) and (iv).

ABC is an alternative to traditional volume-based costing models, where production overhead is absorbed on the basis of the volume of direct labour hours or machine hours worked. However, it is still a form of absorption costing because production overheads are absorbed into product costs. ABC identifies costs with support activities and the overhead costs of a product or service could reflect the long-run variable cost of that product or service. ABC can be used for costing services as well as products. Although ABC looks at the costs of activities, it is not a costing method for identifying relevant costs for decision-making.

20.9   The correct answer is: It may lead to excessive investment in short-term projects

It may lead to excessive investment in short-term projects. Focusing on payback will lead to choosing short-term projects. It tends to emphasise those projects which make a quick return.

20.10   The correct answer is: (i), (ii), (iv), (v) esteem value, exchange value, use value, cost value.

20.11   The correct answer is: $5

Whoopie prime cost	$ per unit
Direct material	2.00
Direct labour	2.50
Direct expense	0.50
	5.00

Remember that prime cost is the total of all direct costs. The fixed cost of $3.15 per unit is excluded from the prime cost calculation.

20.12   The correct answers are: (i), (ii), (iii)

Absorption costing and marginal costing will give rise to the same profits if inventory levels do not change, ie, when opening and closing inventory volumes are the same, when no inventory is held as opening inventory and no inventory is held as closing inventory and when inventory levels are constant.

20.13   The correct answer is: Notional whole units which represent incomplete work

Notional whole units which represent incomplete work. A unit of output in relation to which costs may be ascertained describes a cost unit. The quantity of work achievable in one hour at standard levels of performance describes a standard hour. A unit of output which is identical to others previously manufactured in the same process is incorrect because all completed units in process costing are identical.

20.14   The correct answer is: Total cost = $65,000 + ($3 × units produced)

Highest production	3,000 units	$74,000
Lowest production	1,500 units	$69,500
	1,500 units	$4,500

Variable cost per unit	= $4,500 / 1,500 = $3 per unit
Total cost	= fixed cost + ($3 × units produced)
$74,000	= fixed cost + ($3 × 3,000)
Fixed cost	= $74,000 – $9,000
Fixed cost	= $65,000

20.15   The correct answer is: (ii) is true and (i) is false

(i) is false. **Strategic planning** is carried out by senior management. Line managers will be concerned with **operational planning**. (ii) is true. The management accountant may frequently have to take into account non-financial information.

20.16   The correct answer is: (i), (ii) and (iv) only

The only sampling method that does not require a sampling frame is quota sampling, therefore (i), (ii) and (iv) only is the correct option.

20.17   The correct answer is: 1.1

As this is a multiplicative model, the seasonal variations should sum (in this case) to 4 (an average of 1) as there are four quarters.

Let X = seasonal variation in quarter 4

1.2 + 1.3 + 0.4 + X = 4

2.9 + X = 4

X = 4 – 2.9

X = 1.1

20.18   The correct answer is: The trend line for sales decreased between quarter 1 and quarter 2.

For a multiplicative model, the seasonal component S = Y/T

$$\therefore T = Y/S$$

	Quarter	
	1	2
Seasonal component (S)	1.2	1.3
Actual series (Y)	$125,000	$130,000
Trend (T) (= Y/S)	$104,167	$100,000

The trend line for sales has therefore decreased between quarter 1 and quarter 2.

20.19   The correct answer is: Total fixed costs

The intercept is the point at which the line on a graph crosses the y axis. It represents the total fixed costs.

20.20   The correct answer is: (i) and (ii) are true

Flexible budgets help managers to deal with uncertainty by allowing them to see the expected outcomes for a range of activity levels. So Statement (i) is true. A flexed budget provides a more meaningful comparison because it shows what costs should have been for the actual level of activity achieved.

21   Mixed Bank 4

21.1   The correct answer is: Setting cost cutting targets

Short-termism is when there is a bias towards the short-term rather long-term performance. Option A encourages a long-term view and goal congruence. Option B uses multiple targets to encourage a long-term view. If budget targets are unrealistically tough, a manager will be forced to make tread-offs between the short and long-term, therefore option D is useful for encouraging a long-term view. Setting cost cutting targets could lead to a reduction in R&D expenditure, quality control, customer service and staff training. These could all hinder the long-term performance of the business.

21.2   The correct answer is: Applying a zero defect philosophy to the management of all resources and relationships within an organisation

'Identifying the factors which cause the costs of an organisation's major activities' describes ABC. 'Tracking and accumulating costs and revenues attributable to each product over its life' describes life-cycle costing and 'Estimating product costs by subtracting a desired profit margin from a selling price' describes target costing.

21.3   The correct answer is: Normal loss = $840 Abnormal loss = $880

Step 1 Determine output and losses

Input	15,000	kg
Normal loss (10%)	1,500	kg
Expected output	13,500	kg
Actual output	13,000	kg
Abnormal loss	500	kg

Step 2 Calculate cost per unit of output and losses

Scrap value of normal loss (1,500 × $0.56)	$840
Scrap value of abnormal loss (500 × $0.56)	$280
	$1,120

$$\text{Cost per expected unit} = \frac{\$22,500 + \$2,100 - \$840}{13,500} = \$1.76$$

Step 3 Calculate total cost of output and losses

Output	(13,000 × $1.76)	$22,880
Normal loss	(1,500 × $0.56)	$840
Abnormal loss	(500 × $1.76)	$880
		$24,600

21.4   The correct answer is: $106,700

Statement of profit or loss for May under marginal costing

		May	
		$	$
Sales	A (4,300 × $85)		365,500
	U (2,600 × $60)		156,000
			521,500
Opening inventory	A		0
	U		0
			0
Variable costs	A (4,500 × $50)	225,000	
	U (3,100 × $48)	148,800	
		373,800	
Less closing inventory	A (200 × $50)	(10,000)	
	U (500 × $48)	(24,000)	
Variable cost of goods sold			339,800
Contribution			181,700
Fixed costs			75,000
Profit			106,700

21.5   The correct answer is: $19.50

This is a question in which you have to work backwards.

750 kg should have cost (× $p)	?
But did cost	$13,500
Material price variance	$1,125 (F)

The 750 kg should have cost $13,500 + $1,125 = $14,625

The standard cost per kg is therefore $14,625/750 = $19.50

21.6   The correct answer is: Stratified

Stratified sampling is a method of sampling which involves dividing the population into strata or categories.

21.7   The correct answer is: $25.20

$$100 \times \frac{P_1}{P_0} = 125$$

$$P_1 = \$31.50$$

$$\therefore \frac{100 \times \$31.50}{P_0} = 125$$

$$\therefore \frac{100 \times \$31.50}{125} = P_0 = \$25.20$$

21.8   The correct answer is: Both statements are true.

21.9   The correct answer is: 5

The point at which the straight line crosses the y axis is the intercept and this is the value of a. The gradient is b.

y = a + bx
$270 = $20 + (b × 50)
$270 – $20 = 50b

$$\frac{$250}{50} = b$$

b = 5

21.10   The correct answer is: $318,000

Marginal costing:

	$'000	$'000
Sales (25,000 × $80)		2,000
Opening inventory	0	
Variable production overhead (W1)	1,560	
	1,560	
Less closing inventory (W2)	(60)	
Variable cost of sales		1,500
Contribution		500
Less fixed costs (W3)		182
Profit		318

Workings

(1)   26,000 units × $60 = $1,560,000

(2)   Production units + opening inventory – sales   = closing inventory
                                                      = 26,000 + 0 – 25,000 = 1,000 units

         Valued at marginal cost: 1,000 × $60   = $60,000

(3)   Fixed production overhead + fixed selling costs   = $113,000 + $69,000 = $182,000

21.11   The correct answer is: $323,500

Absorption costing

OAR = Budgeted overhead / budgeted production = $143,000/26,000 = $5.5/unit

As inventory has increased, absorption costing will report a higher profit than marginal costing.

The difference in profit   =   change in inventory volume × fixed production overhead per unit
                                  =   1,000 × $5.5
                                  = $5,500

Marginal profit   = $318,000
∴ absorption profit   = $318,000 + $5,500 = $323,500

21.12   The correct answer is:

29,000 units   *35,000 units*

$163,000 $211,000

Step 1 Find the highest and lowest levels of activity (note that this is the activity level and is not necessarily the highest and lowest cost).

In this case we only have two levels of activity so we have to use those.

Step 2 Compare the activity level and costs for each of these but deduct the extra step up fixed cost for 34,000 units

	Number of units	*Cost $*
Highest	34,000	208,000 – 30,000=178,000
Lowest	28,000	160,000
Increase	6,000	18,000

This shows that for an increase in 6,000 units there has been a cost increase of $18,000. Therefore the variable cost per unit can be estimated as:

Variable rate of increase	=	$18,000/6,000 units
	=	$3 per unit

Step 3 We can now find the fixed element of the cost at each activity level, by substituting the variable rate into the activity levels, with the fixed element appearing as the balancing figure.

Fixed cost at 28,000 units = $160,000 – (28,000 × $3) = $76,000

Fixed cost at 34,000 units = $208,000 – (34,000 × $3) = $106,000

Notice that the fixed cost at 34,000 units is $30,000 higher than at 28,000 units. This is reassuring as we were told this originally. Alternatively to find the fixed cost at 34,000 units we could have just calculated the fixed cost at 28,000 units and then added on the extra $30,000.

Cost at 29,000 units = $76,000 + (29,000 × $3) = $163,000

Cost at 35,000 units = $106,000 + (35,000 × $3) = $211,000

21.13   The correct answer is: $4,250 Favourable

	$
9,200 hours should have cost (× $12.50)	115,000
but did cost	110,750
Direct labour rate variance	4,250 (F)

21.14   The correct answer is: $5,250 Adverse

2,195 units should have taken (× 4 hours)	8,780 hours
but did take	9,200 hours
Direct labour efficiency variance (in hours)	420 hours (A)
x standard rate pre hour	× 12.50
	5,250 (A)

21.15   The correct answer is: 953

$$EOQ = \sqrt{\frac{2CoD}{Ch}} = \sqrt{\frac{2 \times 15 \times (2 \times 50,000)}{110 \times 3\%}} = \sqrt{\frac{3,000,000}{3.3}} = 953 \text{ (to the nearest whole unit)}$$

22 Mixed Bank 5

22.1   The correct answer is:

19,000 units   *21,000 units*

$210,000 $235,000

Step 1 We have been told what the fixed cost element is for 22,000 units so we can break the total cost into its fixed and variable elements and then find the variable cost per unit from this. Variable cost of 22,000 units = $245,000 – $25,000

$$\text{Variable cost per unit} = \frac{\$245,000 - \$25,000}{22,000} = \$10$$

Step 2 Now that we have the variable cost per unit, we can substitute this into the lower level activity to find the fixed element for an activity level below 20,000.

Fixed element for lower activity level = $200,000 – (18,000 × $10) = $20,000.

Step 3 We can now find the cost at activity levels of 19,000 and 21,000 units. Remember the fixed element will be different in each case because of the step.

Cost at 19,000 units = $20,000 + (19,000 × $10) = $210,000

Cost at 21,000 units = $25,000 + (21,000 × $10) = $235,000

22.2   The correct answer is: 20%

Return on investment	= Profit/capital employed
Profit	= $30,000 + ($300,000 × 10%)
	= $60,000
ROI	= $60,000/$300,000
	= 20%

22.3   The correct answer is:

Statement (i)   *Statement (ii)*

False   True

A purchase requisition is completed in the department which requires the goods and then sent to the purchasing department where a purchase order is raised to send to the supplier. Therefore statement (i) is false. Statement (ii) is true.

22.4   The correct answer is: $41,000

The fixed overhead expenditure variance is not relevant to a reconciliation of budgeted and actual contributions. Fixed costs are deducted afterwards from contribution to arrive at profit. The figure of $40,000 given in the question as the 'standard contribution on actual sales' means that the effect of the sales volume contribution variance has already been taken into account in arriving at that figure of $40,000. Budgeted contribution is adjusted for the sales volume contribution variance to arrive at the figure for 'standard contribution on actual sales'. Therefore the only variance that needs to be taken into account in this particular question is the favourable sales price variance as follows: [40,000 + 1,000] = $41,000.

22.5   The correct answer is: 91.2%

The actual costs were $93,600 and when compared with the flexed budget this gave an **adverse** variance of $2,400. Therefore the flexed budget was [93,600 − 2,400] = $91,200. Budgets are flexed based on **activity** levels. As $100,000 of direct costs represented a 100% activity level then flexed budget direct costs of $91,200 represents a 91.2% level of activity [actual activity as a % of the fixed budget].

22.6   The correct answer is: $13,800

Step 1 Determine output and losses

Input   10,000 litres
Normal loss (5%)   500 litres
Expected output   9,500 litres
Actual output   9,200 litres
Abnormal loss   300 litres

Step 2 Calculate cost per unit of output and losses

Scrap value of normal loss (500 × $38) $19,000
Scrap value of abnormal loss (300 × $38) $11,400
                                            $30,400

$$\text{Cost per expected unit} = \frac{\$456{,}000 - \$19{,}000}{9{,}500} = \$46$$

Step 3 Calculate total cost of output and losses

Output   (9,200 × $46) $423,200
Normal loss   (500 × $38) $19,000
Abnormal loss (300 × $46) $13,800
                              $456,000

22.7   The correct answer is: $52.97

$$100 \times \frac{P_1}{P_0} = 175$$

$$P_1 = \$92.70$$

$$\therefore \frac{100 \times \$92.70}{P_0} = 175$$

$$\therefore \frac{100 \times \$92.70}{175} = P_0 = \$52.97$$

22.8   The correct answer is: $600,000

$$\$200{,}000 \div \frac{120}{360} = \$600{,}000$$

22.9   The correct answer is: 300

The point at which the straight line crosses the y axis is the intercept and this is the value of a. The gradient is b = $40.

y = a + bx
$1,100 = a + ($40 × 20)
$1,100 − $800 = a
a = 300

22.10   The correct answer is: $47,500

	$
Actual fixed production overheads	X
Absorbed fixed production overheads (5,500 × $7)	38,500
Under-absorbed fixed production overheads	9,000

Actual fixed production overheads   = $38,500 + $9,000
                                    = $47,500

23 Budgeting

23.1 **Task 1**

(i)   January closing inventory units = 880 units (4,400 units × 20%)

(ii)   March sales units = 4,840 units (4,400 × 1.1)

(iii)   May production units = 5,856 units (5,324 × 1.1), as sales for June are the same as May there will not be any change in inventory levels (given that closing inventory is to remain at 20% of sales) so sales equal production.

	Jan	Feb	Mar	Apr	May	Jun
Sales of M (units)	4,000	4,400	**4,840**	5,324	5,856	5,856
Opening inventory	500	880	968	1065	1,171	1,171
Closing inventory	**880**	968	1065	1,171	1,171	1,171
Production	4,380	4,488	4937	5,430	**5,856**	5,856

Task 2

The correct answer is: $151,250

	Kg
Material G required for production: 20,000 units × 3kg	60,000
Opening inventory	(3,000)
Closing inventory	3,500
Purchases	60,500
Costs of purchases @ $2.50 per kg	$151,250

Task 3

The correct answer is: Time delays with the issue of bank statements

Purchase of non-current assets

For example, suppose an asset is purchased for $20,000 and depreciation is charged at 10% of the original cost. The cash outflow during the year is $20,000 (and this does not appear in the statement of profit or loss). The depreciation charge = 10% × $20,000 = $2,000. This is charged to the statement of profit or loss and will reduce overall profits.

Sale of non-current assets

When an asset is sold there is usually a profit or loss on sale. For example, an asset with a net book value of $15,000 could be sold for $11,000, giving rise to a loss on disposal of $4,000.

The increase in cash flow during the year = $11,000 sale proceeds. There will be no effect on the statement of profit or loss.

The loss on sale of non-current assets = $4,000. This will be recorded in the firm's statement of profit or loss and will reduce overall profits.

Depreciation of non-current assets

Depreciation is a non-cash item and will therefore be a reason why profit and cash flow differ.

23.2 **Task 1**

	$'000
Sales receipts	820
Purchase payments	575
Overhead payments	95

Workings

Sales receipts	= 860 + 45 – 85	= 820
Purchase payments	= 600 + 75 – 100	= 575
Overhead payments	= 100 + 40 – 45	= 95

Task 2

	$
Receipts in March relating to January sales 21,000 × $30 × 60%	378,000
Receipts in March relating to February sales 22,000 × $30 × 1.04 × 40%	274,560
Total March receipts	652,560

Task 3

The correct answer is:

It is amended in response to changes in the level of activity

A flexible budget is a budget which is designed to change as volumes of output change.

23.3 **Task 1**

> **Top tips.** Make sure that you always read the question carefully. Note that sales are invoiced at the **end** of the month.

	Nov $'000	Dec $'000	Jan $'000
Class A (W1)		50	105
Class B (W2)	36	63	50

Workings

(1) *Class A customers*

October sales
50% received December $100,000 × 50% = $50,000
30% received January $100,000 × 30% = 30,000

November sales
50% received January $150,000 × 50% = $75,000

(2) *Class B customers*

October sales
60% received November $60,000 × 60% = $36,000
25% received December $60,000 × 25% = $15,000
10% received January $60,000 × 10% = $6,000

November sales
60% received December $80,000 × 60% = $48,000
25% received January $80,000 × 25% = $20,000

December sales
60% received January $40,000 × 60% = $24,000

Task 2 The correct answer is: $22,000

Only items of cash outflows should be included in the cash budget. For fixed overheads at HM Co this is comprises: $10,000 rent, $1,000 vehicle running costs and $11,000 wages.

Deprecation is not a cash flow.

Task 3 The correct answer is: Annual overhead charge from Head Office based on the floor space occupied by the machine

This is not a cash flow, whereas the purchase price of the asset along with the delivery costs are cash out flows and the proceeds from the sale of the old asset is a cash inflow.

23.4 **Task 1**

	Price index	Working
Material A	143	(1.40/0.98) × 100
Material B	116	(1.10/0.95) × 100
Material C	77	(0.92/1.20) × 100
Material D	104	(1.14/1.10) × 100

Task 2

The correct answer is: $20,000

Using the high-low method:

	Units	$
High	14,000	72,500
Low	10,000	57,500
Difference	4,000	15,000

Variable cost per unit: $15,000/4,000 = $3.75

Substitute variable cost into total cost equation to give fixed cost

72,500 – (3.75 × 14,000) = 20,000

Task 3

The correct answer is: 11,000 units of Product J being manufactured in July

The high-low equation should be used for activity levels within the range of data levels already observed. If RJM made 15,000 units, the forecast using the high low equation would be less accurate because it would involve extrapolation, whereas 11,000 units would not. Similarly making a different product (R) or producing them in a different factory would be likely to alter the cost structure.

23.5 **Task 1**

The correct answer is: = (E2 – B2) / (E3 – B3)

If brackets are NOT used ie E2 – B2 / E3 – B3 then the division ie B2 / E3 will be done before the subtraction and this will give the wrong answer.

Task 2

The correct answer is: y = $79,739 + 2.1x

	$		Units	
High	259,541		85,620	
Low	(214,559)		(64,200)	
Variable cost =	44,982	÷	21,420	= $2.1/unit

Fixed cost = $259,541 – (85,620 × $2.1) = $79,739

Task 3

The correct answer is: = SUM(E4:E8)

This formula will add up the values of XY in the column above to give a total.

Task 4

Cash flow forecasting	✓
Monthly sales analysis by market	✓
Writing a memo	
Calculation of depreciation	✓

BPP
LEARNING MEDIA

Spreadsheets are useful for many types of calculation, but are not generally used for memoranda or report writing, except as an import (eg a table of data).

23.6 **Task 1**

The correct answer is:

C2: $250,000
H3: $60,000
D4: $75,000 (w1)
D5: $15,000 (w2)
D6: 0 – depreciation is not a cash flow and should therefore not be included
E8: 0.826

Workings

1 Extra contribution per unit $6-$4.50 = $1.50

$1.50 × 50,000 units = $75,000

2 Extra fixed costs attributable to new technology are $15,000 per year (75% × $20,000)

Task 2

The correct answer is:

- It takes into account the time value of money
- It does not require the company's cost of capital

As IRR discounts future cash flows it takes into account the time value of money. The IRR calculates the breakeven cost of capital, which means that it does not require a cost of capital to be calculated. This is a benefit as in reality calculating a cost of capital can be complicated and time consuming.

It is NPV, not IRR which is considered to be the superior investment appraisal technique because NPV always correctly ranks projects

IRR is not quick and simple to calculate compared to techniques such as the payback period and it is based on cash flows and not profits.

23.7 **Task 1**

	Relevant	Irrelevant
Investment of $450,000 in the new equipment	X	
Depreciation of $90,000 over each of the five years		X
Staff training costs of $20,000	X	
Temporary manager's salary of $4,000		X
Conference costs of $3,000		X
Interest costs of $6,000 per year		X

Investment of $450,000 in the new equipment is relevant – because if the investment is not made this equipment would not be purchased.

Depreciation of $90,000 over each of the five years is irrelevant – depreciation is a notional amount (ie an accounting entry) and not a cash flow, therefore it is never a relevant cost.

Staff training costs of $20,000 are relevant – this training is a future cost because it will only need to be incurred if the equipment is purchased.

Temporary manager's salary of $4,000 is irrelevant – the manager is not going to be paid any extra salary as a result of the project. As there is no incremental cost to the company as a whole, this is not a relevant cost.

Conference costs of $3,000 are irrelevant – the conference and this training has already happened and the cost of it is a sunk cost. The company will not get the money back if the equipment is not purchased.

Interest costs of $6,000 per year are irrelevant – interest is a finance cost. The discount rate provides the investor compensation for interest, which means that interest is never a relevant cost.

Task 2

Incremental sales in Year 1 = $90,000
PV of maintenance costs over the life of the contract = $37,910
Additional electricity costs = $27,500

Workings

1   Increase in sales = ($550,000 - $500,000) = $50,000
      Increase due to the project = ($50,000 + $40,000) = $90,000

2   Annuity factor for five years at 10% = 3.791
      Present value = (3.791 × $10,000) = $37,910

3   Total sales in Year 1 = $550,000
      Additional electricity = ($550,000 × 0.05) = $27,500

23.8 Task 1

Expenditure	Capital	Revenue
Purchase of new delivery van	x	
Road tax for new delivery van		x
Repairs to customer toilets		x
Extension of customer car park	x	

The purchase of the new delivery van and the extension to the customer car park are both classified as capital expenditure because they will deliver benefits to the company, for more than one year.

The road tax is a running cost of the van and should be treated as revenue for the period, along with the repairs to the toilets. The toilets have not been improved or enhanced by the expenditure, their use has merely been maintained.

Task 2

The correct answer is: 235

	Units
Sales	200
Less: opening inventory	(15)
Add: closing inventory (W1)	50
Manufacture	235

W1: Sales for July: 200 × 1.25 = 250 units

Closing inventory is 20% July's sales = 0.2 × 250 = 50 units

Task 3

(i)   1,000 m²

	m²
Required for production (90 × 10m²)	900
Plus waste	100
Purchase	1,000

(ii) $10,800

      90 units × 8 hours × $15 per hour = $10,800

23.9 **Task 1**

		$
Total cost of 9,800 units	=	44,400
Total cost of 7,700 units	=	38,100
Variable cost of 2,100 units	=	6,300

The variable cost per unit is $3.

		$
Total cost of 9,800 units	=	44,400
Variable cost of 9,800 units (9,800 × $3)	=	29,400
Fixed costs	=	15,000

Task 2

The correct answer is $3,000

	Budget 9,000 units $
Sales (× $5)	45,000
Variable costs (× $3)	27,000
Contribution	18,000
Fixed costs	15,000
Profit	3,000

Task 3

80% of capacity = 8,000 units

100% of capacity = 10,000 units

	Flexible budget 8,000 units $	Flexible budget 10,000 units $
Sales (× $5)	40,000	50,000
Variable costs (× $3)	24,000	30,000
Contribution	16,000	20,000
Fixed costs	15,000	15,000
Profit	1,000	5,000

23.10 **Task 1**

The payback period	X
Net present value	
Discounted payback period	
Internal rate of return	
Return on capital employed	X

Return on capital employed and payback take no account of when costs or revenues are incurred or received when determining their value. Approaches that use discounted cash flow (net present value, IRR and discounted payback) are considered to be more sophisticated, based on the principle that cash received in the future is not worth as much as cash received today.

Task 2

The correct answer is: 2.25 years

20,000 + 30,000 = 50,000 will be paid back at the end of year 2, leaving 10,000 to be repaid in year 3.10,000/40,000 = 0.25, so payback occurs after 2.25 years

Task 3

NPV $ | 35,000 |

Discounted payback | 2.76 | years

Year	Cash flow	15%	NPV	Cumulative PV
0	(60,000)	1	(60,000)	(60,000)
1	20,000	0.870	17,400	(42,600)
2	30,000	0.756	22,680	(19,920)
3	40,000	0.658	26,320	6,400
4	50,000	0.572	28,600	35,000
			35,000	

Discounted payback period   =   2 + (19,920/26,320) years

                                          =   2.76 years (approximately 2 years and 9 months)

This compares with a non-discounted payback period of 2.25 years for the same project.

Task 4

The correct answer is: True

24   Standard costing

24.1   **Task 1**

The correct answer is: $20,000 Adverse

The sales volume variance in a marginal costing system is valued at standard contribution per unit rather than standard profit per unit.

Contribution per unit of DG = $22 – $12 = $10

Sales volume variance in terms of contribution = $\dfrac{\$12,000}{\$6}$ × $10 = $20,000 Adverse.

Task 2

The correct answer is:

The difference between actual and budgeted volume multiplied by the standard absorption rate per unit.

Incorrect answers:

The difference between budgeted hours of work and the actual hours of work multiplied by the standard absorption rate per unit – this is the fixed overhead volume capacity variance

The difference between the fixed overhead incurred and the fixed overhead absorbed – this is how to calculate the fixed overhead **total** variance

The difference between the budgeted fixed overhead expenditure and the actual fixed overhead expenditure – this is how to calculate the fixed overhead **expenditure** variance

Task 3

The correct answers are:

Offer overtime pay to the company's existing skilled employees on a piecework basis – this would encourage existing employees to work more efficiently.
Implement training for the temporary employees – this would enable temporary employees to work more efficiently.

Incorrect answers

Increase the hourly rate paid to temporary workers – increasing the hourly pay will not directly increase efficiency.

Reduce the number of supervisors – this could in fact reduce efficiency if employees are not being monitored.

Task 4 $3,500 (A)

	$
53,000 kg should have cost ($\times$ $2.50*)	132,500
But was	136,000
Material price variance	3,500(A)

*Budgeted material cost per kg = $125,000/(25,000 units $\times$ 2 kg)

24.2 **Task 1**

The correct answer is:

Connolly uses standard **absorption** costing. In the last month actual selling price was **higher than** standard.

Actual units sold were **1,000 less than** budgeted and actual sales revenue was **$910,000**

Production was **100 units less than** budgeted.

Materials caused the biggest cost variance, where a decision to pay **less than** standard price resulted in the company using **800kg more than flexed** budget.

Explanation of answers

Absorption costing – fixed overheads are included in the standard cost card.

Selling price was higher than standard due to the favourable selling price variance.

Actual units sold were 1,000 less than budget due to the adverse sales volume variance of $50,000 ($50,000/$50 standard profit = 1,000 units).

Sales revenue = $910,000. This can be calculated by taking the actual units x the budgeted SP (9,000 x $100) and adding the $10,000 favourable sales price variance.

Production of 100 units less than budget can be calculated by taking the fixed overhead volume variance and dividing it by the fixed overhead standard cost per unit ($1,000/$10) = 100 units

Materials price was favourable therefore Connolly must have paid less than standard price.

800kg more than flexed budget can be calculated by taking the $8,000 material usage variance and dividing it by the $10 standard cost per kg.

24.3 **Task 1**

Sales volume variance	$75,000 Favourable
	(21,500–20,000) × $50
Standard contribution on actual sales	$1,075,000
	($1,000,000 + $75,000)
Sales price variance	$21,500 Adverse
Actual sales revenue generated from actual sales units	$2,128,500
Actual sales units should have generated revenue of	$2,150,000 (21,500 × $100)
Therefore an adverse variance of	$21,500
Actual contribution	$1,053,500

Budgeted contribution (20,000 × $50)	1,000,000	
Sales volume variance	75,000	F
Standard contribution on actual sales	1,075,000	
Sales price variance	21,500	A
	1,053,500	

Cost variances

Total direct material variances	15,000	Adverse
Total direct labour variances	10,000	Favourable
Total variable production overhead variances	5,000	Favourable
Actual contribution	1,053,500	

Alternative method:

Actual sales revenue and costs per unit

	$ per unit	$ per unit	
Sales		99.00	(2,128,500/21,500)
Direct materials	25.68		(565,000/22,000)
Direct labour	9.55		(210,000/22,000)
Variable overheads	14.77	(50.00)	(325,000/22,000)
Contribution		49.00	

Actual contribution:

	$	$
Sales 21,500 @ $99		2,128,500
Opening inventory	–	
Variable production cost		
22,000 @ $50	1,100,000	
Less closing inventory		
22,000–21,500 @ $50	25,000	(1,075,000)
Contribution		**1,053,500**

Task 2

The correct answer is:

Actual sales units were greater than budgeted sales units

Sales volume variance looks at the difference between actual sales units and budgeted sales units multiplied by budgeted contribution.

24.4 **Task 1**

High-low method

Budgeted variable overhead per tonne

Using the high-low technique:

$$\text{Budgeted variable overhead per tonne} = \frac{\text{Change in total budgeted overhead}}{\text{Change in volume}}$$

$$= \frac{(\$264{,}000 - \$200{,}000)}{(9{,}000 - 5{,}000 \text{ tonnes})}$$

$$= \mathbf{\$16 \text{ per tonne}}$$

Budgeted fixed overhead for the period

	$
If total overhead at 9,000 tonnes =	264,000
Variable overhead = 9,000 tonnes × $16 per tonne =	(144,000)
Budgeted fixed overheads	120,000

Task 2

Variances

Fixed overhead expenditure variance

Budgeted expenditure	$120,000
Actual expenditure	$125,000
Fixed overhead expenditure variance	$5,000 (A)

Fixed overhead volume variance

Actual production at standard rate (6,500 × $24)	$156,000
Budgeted production at standard rate	$120,000
Fixed overhead volume variance	$ 36,000 (F)

Task 3

The correct answer is: Absorbed overheads exceed actual overheads

Over absorption will occur when the amount of overheads absorbed exceed the actual amount of overheads.

24.5 **Task 1**

Variances

Variance	$	Favourable or Adverse
Fixed overhead expenditure	3,000 (W1)	F
Fixed overhead efficiency	4,000 (W2)	A
Fixed overhead capacity	6,000 (W3)	F

(W1) Fixed overhead expenditure variance

	$	
Budgeted fixed overheads	26,000	
Actual fixed overheads	23,000	
Fixed overhead expenditure variance	3,000	F

(W2) Fixed overhead efficiency variance

14,000 sets should have taken (× 0.5 hrs)	7,000 hrs	
But did take	8,000 hrs	
	1,000 hrs	A
× std fixed overhead abs rate per hour	× $4	
	$4,000	A

(W3) Fixed overhead capacity variance

Budgeted hours of work (13,000 × 0.5 hrs)	6,500 hrs
Actual hours of work	8,000 hrs
	1,500 hrs F
× std fixed overhead abs rate per hour	× $4
	6,000 F

Task 2

Volume variance	Over-absorption of fixed overheads
Efficiency variance	Labour productivity was lower than expected
Expenditure variance	Fixed overhead expenditure was lower than expected
Capacity variance	Labour worked more hours than expected

The **capacity and efficiency variances** attempt to explain the cause of over-absorption indicated by the volume variance.

The higher number of labour hours worked compared to budget resulted in $6,000 more overhead absorbed than budgeted. However, the higher hours of labour worked were a result of inefficient labour use as indicated by the labour efficiency variance. This resulted in the $4,000 adverse fixed overhead efficiency variance. Therefore the overall volume variance is only $2,000 favourable.

24.6 Task 1

The direct material total variance

	$
2,500 units should have cost	225,000
but did cost	175,000
Direct material total variance	50,000 (F)

The direct material price variance

	$
12,000 kg of W should have cost	180,000
but did cost	175,000
Material W price variance	5,000 (F)

The direct material usage variance

2,500 units should have used (× 6 kg)	15,000 kg
but did use	12,000 kg
Usage variance in kg	3,000 kg (F)
Standard cost per kg	× $15
Usage variance in $	$45,000 (F)

Summary

	$
Price variance	5,000 (F)
Usage variance	45,000 (F)
Total variance	50,000 (F)

Task 2

The correct answer is: $15,000 adverse.

This is calculated by finding the balancing figure. The total variance between budgeted contribution and actual contribution is $10,000 adverse ($30,000 – $20,000). The sales volume and sales price variances sum to $5,000 favourable, so to balance, the variable cost variance must be $15,000 adverse.

Task 3

The correct answers are:

An increase in direct material prices
An increase in raw material usage per unit

Incorrect answers:

Units produced being greater than budgeted – this would not cause the variance due to the variance being based on the flexed budget

Units sold being greater than budgeted – units sold are not a cause of a direct material variance, it would be based on units produced.

24.7 **Task 1**

Total labour variance $1,000 Adverse (W1)
Labour rate variance $4,250 Favourable (W2)
Labour efficiency variance $5,250 Adverse (W3)

W1 Total labour variance

Actual units should cost 2,195 × 4 hours × $12.20 = $109,750
Actual labour did cost = $110,750
Therefore $1,000 Adverse variance

W2 Labour rate variance

Actual hours paid should cost 9,200 × $12.50 = $115,500
Actual labour did cost = $110,750.
Therefore $4,250 favourable

W3 Labour efficiency variance

Actual production should use 2,195 x 4 hours = 8,780 hours
Actual production did use 9,200 hours
Therefore 420 hours adverse variance valued at standard cost of $12.50 = $5,250

Task 2

The correct answer is:

Actual production took longer than expected

Incorrect answers:

The rate actually paid to workers was higher than the standard – this would not impact on the efficiency variance as the difference in production time is valued at the standard rate per hour.

The rate actually paid to workers was lower than the standard - this would not impact on the efficiency variance as the difference in production time is valued at the standard rate per hour.

Actual production was quicker than expected – this would result in a favourable efficiency variance

Task 3

The correct answer is:

Sales volume variance

The sales volume variance would be valued at standard contribution under marginal costing but at standard profit under absorption costing.

24.8 **Task 1**

STANDARD COST CARD FOR A WIDGET

	$	$
Direct materials		
X – 5 kg × $2	10	
Z – 2 metres × $5	10	
		20
Direct labour		
Skilled – 3 × $15	45	
Unskilled – 6 × $3	18	
		63
Standard direct cost		83
Variable production overhead – 3 × $3.00		9
Standard variable cost of production		92
Fixed production overhead – 3 × $3.33 (W)		10
Standard full production cost		102
Administration, selling and distribution overhead		20
Standard cost of sale		**122**
Standard profit (15% × 122)		18.30
Standard sales price		**140.30**

Working

Fixed overhead absorption rate = ($100,000/(10,000 × 3)) = $3.33 per skilled labour hour

Task 2

The correct answer is:

The difference between what the sales revenue should have been for the quantity sold, and what it was

24.9 **Task 1**

Direct labour total variance

This is the difference between what 3,000 units should have cost and what they did cost.

	$
3,000 units should have cost (× 3 hrs × $5)	45,000
but did cost	43,700
Direct labour total variance	1,300 (F)

The total variance can then be analysed into the rate variance and the efficiency variance as follows:

Direct labour rate variance

	$
10,000 hours of work should have cost	50,000
but did cost	43,700
Direct labour rate variance	6,300 (F)

Direct labour efficiency variance	
3,000 units of Fab should have taken (× 3 hrs)	9,000 hrs
but did take	10,000 hrs
Efficiency variance in hours	1,000 hrs (A)
× standard rate per hour	× $5
Efficiency variance in $	$5,000 (A)

	$
Rate variance	6,300 (F)
Efficiency variance	5,000 (A)
Total variance	1,300 (F)

Task 2

The direct labour rate variance is the difference between the **standard** cost and the **actual** cost for the **actual** number of **hours** paid for.

Task 3

The correct answer is: $31

	$
Actual material cost	96,000
Variance	(3,000) (A)
Should have cost	93,000

$93,000 / 3,000 units = $31 per unit

24.10 **Task 1**

The correct answer is $7.45

12,600 hrs should have cost ($\times$ $7.50) = $94,500

But did cost $93,825 ($94,500 – $675)

Cost per hr = $93,825 / 12,600 = $7.446 ($7.45)

$7.75 and $7.60 are incorrect because they are both above the standard rate per hour, and the rate variance was favourable. If the rate variance is favourable, then the actual rate must be below standard. $7.44 is incorrect because it results from using 10,800 hours in the calculations, rather than the actual hours.

Task 2

The correct answer is: 30,500 kg

Quantity of Sparkle used = Y	
6,000 units should have used ($\times$ 5 kg)	30,000 kg
but did use	Y kg
Usage variance in kg	(Y – 30,000) kg
$\times$ standard price per kg	$\times$ $20
Usage variance in $	$10,000 (A)

$\therefore$ 20(Y – 30,000)   = 10,000
         Y – 30,000   = 500
$\therefore$ Y   = 30,500 kg

Task 3

The correct answer is: $139,500

The correct answer is arrived at by deducting appropriate adverse variances and adding appropriate favourable variances from standard profit. A profit adjustment for the difference between budgeted and actual volumes is not required, and so the sales volume variance should be ignored. The answer can therefore be calculated as:

$135,000 - $4,000 + $5,500 - $7,500 + $10,500 = $139,500.

Task 4

The correct answers are:

The sales volume variance will be valued at standard contribution margin.

There will be no fixed cost volume variance.

The sales volume variance will be valued at standard contribution margin (sales price per unit minus variable costs of sale per unit), not standard profit margin.

In marginal costing, fixed costs are not absorbed into product costs and so there are no fixed cost variances to explain under- or over-absorption of overheads. There is therefore no fixed cost volume variance (although there will be a fixed cost expenditure variance).

25 Performance measurement

25.1 **Task 1**

Return on capital employed	20.0% ($22 million/$110 million)
Operating profit margin	8.8% ($22 million/$250 million)
Asset turnover	2.3 times ($250 million/$110 million)
Percentage of sales attributable to new routes	5.2% ($13 million/$250 million)

Task 2

Percentage of customer who make a complaint	3% (37,500/1,250,000)
Percentage of flights delayed	15% (375,000/2,500,000)

Task 3

A balanced scored card measures performance from four perspectives: financial success, process efficiency, growth and **customer satisfaction.**

Flyrite's performance measure of **percentage of sales attributable to new routes** would be categorised under the growth perspective of the balanced scorecard.

25.2 **Task 1**

Return on sales	5%	($5,000/$100,000)
Asset turnover	5 times	($100,000/$20,000)
Market share	10%	($100,000/$1,000,000)
Return on investment	25%	($5,000/$20,000)
Residual income	$3,000	$5,000 – (10% × $20,000)

Task 2

The correct answers are:

It makes division managers aware of the cost of financing their divisions – this is correct as imputed interest is deducted from profit

It gives an absolute measure of performance – this is correct as it provides a monetary measure in $'s

Incorrect answers:

It enables the performance of divisions of different sizes to be compared – this is and advantage of ROI not RI

It relates the size of the division's income to the size of the investment – this is an advantage of ROI not RI

Task 3

The correct answers are:

Number of new products launched – this is a measure of growth
Number of customer complaints – this is a measure of customer satisfaction

Incorrect answers:

Profit per product and Sales revenue per product these are measures of financial success.

25.3 **Task 1**

Performance measure	20X1
Return on capital employed (to two decimal places)	31.25% (3,500 – 1,750-500)/(3,200+800)
Operating profit margin (to two decimal places)	35.71% (3,500 – 1,750-500)/3,500
Asset turnover (to two decimal places)	0.875 times 3,500/(3,200 + 800)
Interest cover (to two decimal places)	15.63 (3,500 – 1,750 – 500)/80
Gearing (debt/debt + equity) (to two decimal places)	20.00% 800/(3,200+800)
Inventory days (to the nearest whole day)	52 days (250/1,750) × 365
Receivables days (to the nearest whole day)	42 days (400/3,500) × 365
Payables day (to the nearest whole day)	38 days (180/1,750) × 365

Task 2

The correct answer is: Non-financial success. This is not a perspective of the balanced scorecard. The four perspectives are:

Financial success
Growth
Process efficiency
Customer satisfaction

25.4 **Task 1**

ROI = $10m/$40m = 25%

RI = $10m – (10% × $40m) = $6m

Task 2

The correct answers are:

Proposal 1 will increase ROI - false
Proposal 1 will increase RI - true
Proposal 2 will decreased ROI - false
Proposal 2 will decrease RI - true

Proposal 1

New profit = $10m + $1m = $11m
New capital employed = $40m + $5m = $45m
New ROI = 11/45 = 24% therefore ROI will decrease
New RI = $11m – (10% × $45m) = $6.5m therefore RI will increase

Proposal 2

New profit = $10m – $1.5 m = $8.5m
New capital employed = $40m – $10m = $30m
New ROI = $8.5/$30 = 28% – therefore ROI will increase
New RI = $8.5 – (10% × $30m) = $5.5m – therefore RI will decrease

Task 3

The correct answers are:

It is more easily understood by divisional managers. – This is true as it is quoted as a simple % return as opposed to dealing with an applied financing cost in RI

It helps in comparing the performance of the managers of divisions of different sizes. – This is true due to the fact that ROI is a relative measure showing profit as a percentage of the investment.

Incorrect answers:

It gives an absolute measure of performance. – This is not true as it gives a percentage return. RI gives an absolute measure of performance

It makes manages aware of the cost of financing their division. – This is not true. This is an advantage of RI

25.5 **Task 1**

Return on investment for division JC	20% (700/3,500)
Return on investment for division GC	15% (675/4,500)
Residual income for division JC	$350 ($700 – (10% × $3,500))
Residual income for division GC	$225 ($675 – (10% × $4,500))
Market share for division JC	2% ($50,000/$2,500,000)
Asset turnover for division GC	13 times ($60,000/$4,500)

Task 2

The correct answers are:

Comparisons between divisions of different sizes is difficult - For example one division may have a higher RI, but this could be because it's larger a larger division.

It does not relate the size of the centres income to the size of the investment

Incorrect answers:

It does not make divisional managers aware of the cost of financing their divisions – it does by applying an imputed interest charge

It is not directly related to net present value (NPV) – it is by incorporating the cost of capital via the imputed interest charge.

Task 3

The correct answers are:

Number of new customers – this is a measure of growth
% increase in market share – this is also a measure of growth

Incorrect answers

Return on sales
Sales to each new customer

These are both examples of financial performance measures.

25.6 **Task 1**

		20X6
(i)	Gross profit margin	43.90%
(ii)	Return on capital employed	27.18%
(iii)	Asset turnover	1.34 times
(iv)	Current ratio	1.77
(v)	Quick ratio	1.20
(vi)	Inventory holding period in days	46.11 days
(vii)	Payables payment period in days	81.45 days
(viii)	Receivables period in days	49.86 days

Workings

		20X6
(i)	Gross profit margin	(2,540 – 1,425/2,540) × 100% = 43.90
(ii)	Return on capital employed	(2,540 –1,425 – 600)/(1,650 + 36 + 347+ 180 – 318) × 100% = 27.18
(iii)	Asset turnover	(2,540/1,650 + 36 + 347 +180 - 318) = 1.34
(iv)	Current ratio	(347 + 180 + 36/318) = 1.77
(v)	Quick ratio	(347 + 36/318) = 1.20
(vi)	Inventory holding period in days	(180/1,425) × 365 = 46.11
(vii)	Payables payment period in days	(318/1,425) × 365 = 81.45
(viii)	Receivables period in days	(347/2,540) × 365 = 49.86

Task 2

The correct answer is:

Internal business processes

The quality of products or services is an aspect of operational performance. Quality affects customer perceptions, but is under the control of management.

25.7 **Task 1**

The correct answer is: W

Level	Maintenance cost	Sales value lost	Total cost
	$	$	$
W	10,000	15 × $1,000	25,000
X	8,000	21 × $1,000	29,000
Y	9,750	19 × $1,000	28,750
Z	7,500	27 × $1,000	34,500

Level W should be chosen given that it is the lowest cost option.

Task 2

Measure	CSF	KPI
95% customer complaint resolution		X
Successful relationships with key suppliers	X	
Negotiation of favourable terms for new project finance	X	
Gain in market share by 2% each month		X
Lower the cost of capital by 1.5%		X

Task 3

The correct answer is: A performance requirement that is fundamental to competitive success – this describes a CSF.

Incorrect answers:

A statement of what the organisation intends to achieve over a period of time - describes strategic objectives.

A measurable indicator of organisational performance - describes a KPI.

A basic belief of the people who work in the organisation - describes organisational values and culture.

25.8 **Task 1**

Asset turnover	2.26 times
Inventory days	6.96 days
Payables days	50.38 days
Current ratio	0.86
Quick ratio	0.78
Return on capital employed	24.81%

Task 2

X	A slowdown in trading
	A lengthening of the time taken by customers to pay for their goods
X	A build-up in inventory levels
	A reduction in inventory levels
	A lengthening of the average time taken to pay suppliers

A lengthening inventory turnover period from one year to the next indicates either a slowdown in trading or a build-up in inventory levels, suggesting that investment in inventories is becoming excessive. Payments from customers and payments to suppliers are not relevant to inventory ratio calculations.

Task 3

The correct answer is:

They give early warning signs of problems

An important reason for the use of non-financial performance measures is that they give early warning signals of problems. For this reason, they are often referred to as 'leading indicators'.

Incorrect answers:

Financial performance measures are often described as 'lagging indicators'; that is, they tell the firm that something has gone wrong after it has gone wrong. It is not necessarily true that non-financial indicators are more important than financial ones, but the use of non-financial performance measures gives a firm a chance of correcting problems before they go too far. They may be more understandable for non-financial staff, but that is not the reason why they are termed 'leading indicators'.

25.9 **Task 1**

Indicator	Financial	Non-financial
Number of customer complaints		X
Market share	X	
Earnings per share	X	
Machine down time		X
Employee attitudes		X
Residual income	X	

Task 2

The correct answer is: 25%

($150,000 – $25,000) / $500,000 = 25%

Task 3

The correct answer is: $15,000

Residual income (RI) = profit – imputed interest charge on investment

We need to find the level of investment

If the return on investment = 20%, then $60,000 represents 20%, so the investment must be $60,000/20% = $300,000.

Therefore RI = $60,000 – ($300,000 × 0.15) = ($60,000 – $45,000) = $15,000

Task 4

Residual income is an absolute measure

Return on equity is a relative measure

25.10 **Task 1**

$$\text{Capacity ratio} = \frac{\text{Actual hours worked}}{\text{Budgeted hours}} \times 100\% = \frac{1,200}{1,000} \times 100\% = 120\%$$

$$\text{Activity ratio} = \frac{\text{Standard hours produced}}{\text{Budgeted hours}} \times 100\% = \frac{1,225}{1,000} \times 100\% = 123\%$$

$$\text{Efficiency ratio} = \frac{\text{Standard hours produced}}{\text{Actual hours worked}} \times 100\% = \frac{1,225}{1,300} \times 100\% = 94\%$$

Task 2

	More labour hours were worked than budgeted	Labour hours produced fewer units per hour than budgeted	Labour hours produced more units per hour than budgeted	Fewer labour hours were worked than budgeted
Capacity ratio	X			
Efficiency ratio			X	

A capacity ratio of over 100% means that more labour hours were worked than budgeted.

An efficiency ratio of over 100% means that efficiency was greater than budgeted ie the labour force produced more units per hour than budgeted.

Task 3

The correct answers are: The ultimate aim of benchmarking is to improve performance and Benchmarking is suitable for non-profit seeking entities.

'Competitive benchmarking can be used to compare internal departments' is incorrect. Competitive benchmarking is used to compare measures with a competitor's (ie it is external to the company as opposed to being internal).

'Benchmarking is quick and straightforward' is incorrect. There are several limitations to benchmarking including the difficulty in deciding which activities to benchmark. It can therefore be time consuming.

Appendix – Formula sheet and tables

Formula sheet given in the exam

Regression analysis

$y = a + bx$

$$a = \frac{\Sigma Y}{n} - \frac{b\Sigma x}{n}$$

$$b = \frac{n\Sigma xy - \Sigma x\Sigma y}{n\Sigma x^2 - (\Sigma x)^2}$$

$$r = \frac{n\Sigma xy - \Sigma x\Sigma y}{\sqrt{(n\Sigma x^2 - (\Sigma x)^2)(n\Sigma y^2 - (\Sigma y)^2)}}$$

Economic order quantity

$$\sqrt{\frac{2C_0 D}{C_h}}$$

Economic batch quantity

$$\sqrt{\frac{2C_0 D}{C_h(1 - \frac{D}{R})}}$$

Present value table

Present value of £1 ie $(1+r)^{-n}$

where r = interest rate,

n = number of periods until payment

Periods Discount rates (r)

(n)	1%	2%	3%	4%	5%	6%	7%	8%	9%	10%
1	0.990	0.980	0.971	0.962	0.952	0.943	0.935	0.926	0.917	0.909
2	0.980	0.961	0.943	0.925	0.907	0.890	0.873	0.857	0.842	0.826
3	0.971	0.942	0.915	0.889	0.864	0.840	0.816	0.794	0.772	0.751
4	0.961	0.924	0.888	0.855	0.823	0.792	0.763	0.735	0.708	0.683
5	0.951	0.906	0.863	0.822	0.784	0.747	0.713	0.681	0.650	0.621
6	0.942	0.888	0.837	0.790	0.746	0.705	0.666	0.630	0.596	0.564
7	0.933	0.871	0.813	0.760	0.711	0.665	0.623	0.583	0.547	0.513
8	0.923	0.853	0.789	0.731	0.677	0.627	0.582	0.540	0.502	0.467
9	0.914	0.837	0.766	0.703	0.645	0.592	0.544	0.500	0.460	0.424
10	0.905	0.820	0.744	0.676	0.614	0.558	0.508	0.463	0.422	0.386
11	0.896	0.804	0.722	0.650	0.585	0.527	0.475	0.429	0.388	0.350
12	0.887	0.788	0.701	0.625	0.557	0.497	0.444	0.397	0.356	0.319
13	0.879	0.773	0.681	0.601	0.530	0.469	0.415	0.368	0.326	0.290
14	0.870	0.758	0.661	0.577	0.505	0.442	0.388	0.340	0.299	0.263
15	0.861	0.743	0.642	0.555	0.481	0.417	0.362	0.315	0.275	0.239

(n)	11%	12%	13%	14%	15%	16%	17%	18%	19%	20%
1	0.901	0.893	0.885	0.877	0.870	0.862	0.855	0.847	0.840	0.833
2	0.812	0.797	0.783	0.769	0.756	0.743	0.731	0.718	0.706	0.694
3	0.731	0.712	0.693	0.675	0.658	0.641	0.624	0.609	0.593	0.579
4	0.659	0.636	0.613	0.592	0.572	0.552	0.534	0.516	0.499	0.482
5	0.593	0.567	0.543	0.519	0.497	0.476	0.456	0.437	0.419	0.402
6	0.535	0.507	0.480	0.456	0.432	0.410	0.390	0.370	0.352	0.335
7	0.482	0.452	0.425	0.400	0.376	0.354	0.333	0.314	0.296	0.279
8	0.434	0.404	0.376	0.351	0.327	0.305	0.285	0.266	0.249	0.233
9	0.391	0.361	0.333	0.308	0.284	0.263	0.243	0.225	0.209	0.194
10	0.352	0.322	0.295	0.270	0.247	0.227	0.208	0.191	0.176	0.162
11	0.317	0.287	0.261	0.237	0.215	0.195	0.178	0.162	0.148	0.135
12	0.286	0.257	0.231	0.208	0.187	0.168	0.152	0.137	0.124	0.112
13	0.258	0.229	0.204	0.182	0.163	0.145	0.130	0.116	0.104	0.093
14	0.232	0.205	0.181	0.160	0.141	0.125	0.111	0.099	0.088	0.078
15	0.209	0.183	0.160	0.140	0.123	0.108	0.095	0.084	0.074	0.065

Annuity table

Present value of an annuity of 1 ie $\dfrac{1-(1+r)^{-n}}{r}$

where r = interest rate,

n = number of periods

Periods **Discount rates (r)**

(n)	1%	2%	3%	4%	5%	6%	7%	8%	9%	10%
1	0.990	0.980	0.971	0.962	0.952	0.943	0.935	0.926	0.917	0.909
2	1.970	1.942	1.913	1.886	1.859	1.833	1.808	1.783	1.759	1.736
3	2.941	2.884	2.829	2.775	2.723	2.673	2.624	2.577	2.531	2.487
4	3.902	3.808	3.717	3.630	3.546	3.465	3.387	3.312	3.240	3.170
5	4.853	4.713	4.580	4.452	4.329	4.212	4.100	3.993	3.890	3.791
6	5.795	5.601	5.417	5.242	5.076	4.917	4.767	4.623	4.486	4.355
7	6.728	6.472	6.230	6.002	5.786	5.582	5.389	5.206	5.033	4.868
8	7.652	7.325	7.020	6.733	6.463	6.210	5.971	5.747	5.535	5.335
9	8.566	8.162	7.786	7.435	7.108	6.802	6.515	6.247	5.995	5.759
10	9.471	8.983	8.530	8.111	7.722	7.360	7.024	6.710	6.418	6.145
11	10.368	9.787	9.253	8.760	8.306	7.887	7.499	7.139	6.805	6.495
12	11.255	10.575	9.954	9.385	8.863	8.384	7.943	7.536	7.161	6.814
13	12.134	11.348	10.635	9.986	9.394	8.853	8.358	7.904	7.487	7.103
14	13.004	12.106	11.296	10.563	9.899	9.295	8.745	8.244	7.786	7.367
15	13.865	12.849	11.938	11.118	10.380	9.712	9.108	8.559	8.061	7.606

(n)	11%	12%	13%	14%	15%	16%	17%	18%	19%	20%
1	0.901	0.893	0.885	0.877	0.870	0.862	0.855	0.847	0.840	0.833
2	1.713	1.690	1.668	1.647	1.626	1.605	1.585	1.566	1.547	1.528
3	2.444	2.402	2.361	2.322	2.283	2.246	2.210	2.174	2.140	2.106
4	3.102	3.037	2.974	2.914	2.855	2.798	2.743	2.690	2.639	2.589
5	3.696	3.605	3.517	3.433	3.352	3.274	3.199	3.127	3.058	2.991
6	4.231	4.111	3.998	3.889	3.784	3.685	3.589	3.498	3.410	3.326
7	4.712	4.564	4.423	4.288	4.160	4.039	3.922	3.812	3.706	3.605
8	5.146	4.968	4.799	4.639	4.487	4.344	4.207	4.078	3.954	3.837
9	5.537	5.328	5.132	4.946	4.772	4.607	4.451	4.303	4.163	4.031
10	5.889	5.650	5.426	5.216	5.019	4.833	4.659	4.494	4.339	4.192
11	6.207	5.938	5.687	5.453	5.234	5.029	4.836	4.656	4.486	4.327
12	6.492	6.194	5.918	5.660	5.421	5.197	4.988	4.793	4.611	4.439
13	6.750	6.424	6.122	5.842	5.583	5.342	5.118	4.910	4.715	4.533
14	6.982	6.628	6.302	6.002	5.724	5.468	5.229	5.008	4.802	4.611
15	7.191	6.811	6.462	6.142	5.847	5.575	5.324	5.092	4.876	4.675

Area under the normal curve

This table gives the area under the normal curve between the mean and the point Z standard deviations above the mean. The corresponding area for deviations below the mean can be found by symmetry.

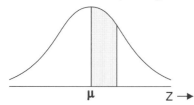

$Z = \dfrac{(x - \mu)}{\sigma}$	0.00	0.01	0.02	0.03	0.04	0.05	0.06	0.07	0.08	0.09
0.0	.0000	.0040	.0080	.0120	.0160	.0199	.0239	.0279	.0319	.0359
0.1	.0398	.0438	.0478	.0517	.0557	.0596	.0636	.0675	.0714	.0753
0.2	.0793	.0832	.0871	.0910	.0948	.0987	.1026	.1064	.1103	.1141
0.3	.1179	.1217	.1255	.1293	.1331	.1368	.1406	.1443	.1480	.1517
0.4	.1554	.1591	.1628	.1664	.1700	.1736	.1772	.1808	.1844	.1879
0.5	.1915	.1950	.1985	.2019	.2054	.2088	.2123	.2157	.2190	.2224
0.6	.2257	.2291	.2324	.2357	.2389	.2422	.2454	.2486	.2517	.2549
0.7	.2580	.2611	.2642	.2673	.2704	.2734	.2764	.2794	.2823	.2852
0.8	.2881	.2910	.2939	.2967	.2995	.3023	.3051	.3078	.3106	.3133
0.9	.3159	.3186	.3212	.3238	.3264	.3289	.3315	.3340	.3365	.3389
1.0	.3413	.3438	.3461	.3485	.3508	.3531	.3554	.3577	.3599	.3621
1.1	.3643	.3665	.3686	.3708	.3729	.3749	.3770	.3790	.3810	.3830
1.2	.3849	.3869	.3888	.3907	.3925	.3944	.3962	.3980	.3997	.4015
1.3	.4032	.4049	.4066	.4082	.4099	.4115	.4131	.4147	.4162	.4177
1.4	.4192	.4207	.4222	.4236	.4251	.4265	.4279	.4292	.4306	.4319
1.5	.4332	.4345	.4357	.4370	.4382	.4394	.4406	.4418	.4429	.4441
1.6	.4452	.4463	.4474	.4484	.4495	.4505	.4515	.4525	.4535	.4545
1.7	.4554	.4564	.4573	.4582	.4591	.4599	.4608	.4616	.4625	.4633
1.8	.4641	.4649	.4656	.4664	.4671	.4678	.4686	.4693	.4699	.4706
1.9	.4713	.4719	.4726	.4732	.4738	.4744	.4750	.4756	.4761	.4767
2.0	.4772	.4778	.4783	.4788	.4793	.4798	.4803	.4808	.4812	.4817
2.1	.4821	.4826	.4830	.4834	.4838	.4842	.4846	.4850	.4854	.4857
2.2	.4861	.4864	.4868	.4871	.4875	.4878	.4881	.4884	.4887	.4890
2.3	.4893	.4896	.4898	.4901	.4904	.4906	.4909	.4911	.4913	.4916
2.4	.4918	.4920	.4922	.4925	.4927	.4929	.4931	.4932	.4934	.4936
2.5	.4938	.4940	.4941	.4943	.4945	.4946	.4948	.4949	.4951	.4952
2.6	.4953	.4955	.4956	.4957	.4959	.4960	.4961	.4962	.4963	.4964
2.7	.4965	.4966	.4967	.4968	.4969	.4970	.4971	.4972	.4973	.4974
2.8	.4974	.4975	.4976	.4977	.4977	.4978	.4979	.4979	.4980	.4981
2.9	.4981	.4982	.4982	.4983	.4984	.4984	.4985	.4985	.4986	.4986
3.0	.49865	.4987	.4987	.4988	.4988	.4989	.4989	.4989	.4990	.4990
3.1	.49903	.4991	.4991	.4991	.4992	.4992	.4992	.4992	.4993	.4993
3.2	.49931	.4993	.4994	.4994	.4994	.4994	.4994	.4995	.4995	.4995
3.3	.49952	.4995	.4995	.4996	.4996	.4996	.4996	.4996	.4996	.4997
3.4	.49966	.4997	.4997	.4997	.4997	.4997	.4997	.4997	.4997	.4998
3.5	.49977									

Mock Exam 1
(Specimen Exam)

Foundations in Accountancy /ACCA

FMA/MA

Management Accounting

Mock Examination 1 (Specimen exam)

Questions	
Time allowed	2 hours
This examination is divided into two sections:	
Section A – 35 questions, each worth 2 marks	
Section B – 3 questions, each worth 10 marks	
All questions within each section are compulsory	

DO NOT OPEN THIS EXAMINATION UNTIL YOU ARE READY TO START UNDER EXAMINATION CONDITIONS

Section A – ALL 35 questions are compulsory and MUST be attempted

1   A manufacturing company benchmarks the performance of its accounts receivable department with that of a leading credit card company.

What type of benchmarking is the company using?

○   Internal benchmarking
○   Competitive benchmarking
○   Functional benchmarking
○   Strategic benchmarking   **(2 marks)**

2   Which of the following BEST describes target costing?

○   Setting a cost by subtracting a desired profit margin from a competitive market price
○   Setting a price by adding a desired profit margin to a production cost
○   Setting a cost for the use in the calculation of variances
○   Setting a selling price for the company to aim for in the long run   **(2 marks)**

3   Information relating to two processes (F and G) was as follows:

Process	Normal loss as % of input	Input (litres)	Output (litres)
F	8	65,000	58,900
G	5	37,500	35,700

For each process, was there an abnormal loss or an abnormal gain?

	Abnormal loss	Abnormal gain
Process F	○	○
Process G	○	○

(2 marks)

4   The following budgeted information relates to a manufacturing company for next period:

	Units		$
Production	14,000	Fixed production costs	63,000
Sales	12,000	Fixed selling costs	12,000

The normal level of activity is 14,000 units per period.

Using absorption costing the profit for next period has been calculated as $36,000

What would be the profit for next period using marginal costing?

$ [   ]

(2 marks)

5   The Eastland Postal Service is government owned. The government requires it to provide a parcel delivery service to every home and business in Eastland at a low price which is set by the government. Express Couriers Co is a privately owned parcel delivery company that also operates in Eastland. It is not subject to government regulation and most of its deliveries are to large businesses located in Eastland's capital city. You have been asked to assess the relative efficiency of the management of the two organisations.

Which of the following factors should NOT be allowed for when comparing the ROCE of the two organisations to assess the efficiency of their management?

○   Differences in prices charged
○   Differences in objectives pursued
○   Differences in workforce motivation
○   Differences in geographic areas served   **(2 marks)**

6   Under which sampling method does every member of the target population have an equal chance of being in the sample?

       O   Stratified sampling
       O   Random sampling
       O   Systematic sampling
       O   Cluster sampling   **(2 marks)**

7   A Company manufactures and sells one product which requires 8 kg of raw material in its manufacture. The budgeted data relating to the next period are as follows:

	Units
Sales	19,000
Opening inventory of finished goods	4,000
Closing inventory of finished goods	3,000

	Kg
Opening inventory of raw materials	50,000
Closing inventory of raw materials	53,000

What is the budgeted raw material purchases for next period?

☐ kg

(2 marks)

8   Up to a given level of activity in each period the purchase price per unit of a raw material is constant. After that point a lower price per unit applies both to further units purchased and also retrospectively to all units already purchased.

Which of the following graphs depicts the total cost of the raw materials for a period?

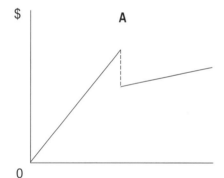

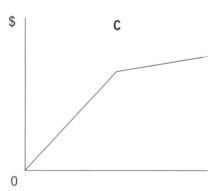

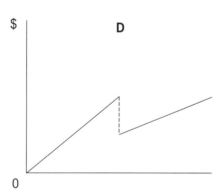

       O   Graph A
       O   Graph B
       O   Graph C
       O   Graph D   **(2 marks)**

9   Which TWO of the following are benefits of budgeting?

☐   It helps coordinate the activities of different departments

☐   It fulfils legal reporting obligations

☐   It establishes a system of control

☐   It is a starting point for strategic planning   **(2 marks)**

10   The following statements relate to the participation of junior management in setting budgets:

1   It speeds up the setting of budgets
2   It increases the motivation of junior managers
3   It reduces the level of budget padding

Which of the above statements are true?

○   1 only
○   2 only
○   2 and 3 only
○   1, 2 and 3   **(2 marks)**

11   A company has a capital employed of $200,000. It has a cost of capital of 12% per year. Its residual income is $36,000.

What is the company's return on investment?

☐____%   **(2 marks)**

12   A company has calculated a $10,000 adverse direct material variance by subtracting its flexed budget direct material cost from its actual direct material cost for the period.

Which TWO of the following could have caused the variance?

☐   An increase in direct material prices

☐   An increase in raw material usage per unit

☐   Units produced being greater than budgeted

☐   Units sold being greater than budgeted   **(2 marks)**

13   A company has recorded the following variances for a period:

Sales volume variance $10,000 Adverse
Sales price variance $5,000 Favourable
Total cost variance $12,000 Adverse

Standard profit on actual sales for the period was $120,000.
What was the fixed budget profit for the period?

○ $137,000
○ $103,000
○ $110,000
○ $130,000   **(2 marks)**

14 Which of the following are suitable measures of performance at the strategic level?

1 Return on investment
2 Market share
3 Number of customer complaints

○ 1 and 2
○ 2 only
○ 2 and 3
○ 1 and 3   **(2 marks)**

---

15 Which TWO of the following are feasible values for the correlation coefficient?

☐ +1.40

☐ +1.04

☐ 0

☐ −0.94   **(2 marks)**

---

16 A company's operating costs are 60% variable and 40% fixed.

Which of the following variances' values would change if the company switched from standard marginal costing to standard absorption costing?

○ Direct material efficiency variance
○ Variable overhead efficiency variance
○ Sales volume variance
○ Fixed overhead expenditure variance   **(2 marks)**

---

17 ABC Co has a manufacturing capacity of 10,000 units. The flexed production cost budget of the company is as follows:

Capacity	60%	100%
Total production costs	$11,280	$15,120

What is the budgeted total production cost if it operates at 85% capacity?

$ ☐   **(2 marks)**

---

18 Using an interest rate of 10% per year the net present value (NPV) of a project has been correctly calculated as $50. If the interest rate is increased by 1% the NPV of the project falls by $20.

What is the internal rate of return (IRR) of the project?

○ 7.5%
○ 11.7%
○ 12.5%
○ 20.0%   **(2 marks)**

19   A factory consists of two production cost centres (P and Q) and two service cost centres (X and Y). The total allocated and apportioned overhead for each is as follows:

P	Q	X	Y
$95,000	$82,000	$46,000	$30,000

It has been estimated that each service cost centre does work for other cost centres in the following proportions:

	P	Q	X	Y
Percentage of service cost centre X to	50	50	–	–
Percentage of service cost centre Y to	30	60	10	–

The reapportionment of service cost centre costs to other cost centres fully reflects the above proportions.

After the reapportionment of service cost centre costs has been carried out, what is the total overhead for production cost centre P?

O $124,500
O $126,100
O $127,000
O $128,500   **(2 marks)**

20   A company always determines its order quantity for a raw material by using the Economic Order Quantity (EOQ) model.

What would be the effects on the EOQ and the total annual holding cost of a decrease in the cost of ordering a batch of raw material?

	Higher	Lower
EOQ	O	O
Annual holding cost	O	O

(2 marks)

21   A company which operates a process costing system had work-in-progress at the start of last month of 300 units (valued at $1,710) which were 60% complete in respect of all costs. Last month a total of 2,000 units were completed and transferred to the finished goods warehouse. The cost per equivalent unit for costs arising last month was $10. The company uses the FIFO method of cost allocation.

What was the total value of the 2,000 units transferred to the finished goods warehouse last month?

O $19,910
O $20,000
O $20,510
O $21,710   **(2 marks)**

22   Identify whether each of the following statements about the uses of Big Data analytics in organisations is true or false.

	True	False
It helps to better understand customer behaviour and preferences	O	O
It helps to analyse the efficiency of business processes in real time	O	O

(2 marks)

23   The number of daily complaints to a local government office has a mean of 12 and a standard deviation of 3 complaints.

What is the coefficient of variation as a %?

[   ] %

(2 marks)

24   Under which of the following labour remuneration methods will direct labour cost always be a variable cost?

- O   Day rate
- O   Piece rate
- O   Differential piece rate
- O   Group bonus scheme

(2 marks)

25   A company manufactures and sells a single product. In two consecutive months the following levels of production and sales (in units) occurred:

	Month 1	Month 2
Sales	3,800	4,400
Production	3,900	4,200

The opening inventory for Month 1 was 400 units. Profits or losses have been calculated for each month using both absorption and marginal costing principles.

Which of the following combinations of profits and losses for the two months is consistent with the above data?

	Absorption costing profit/(loss)		Marginal costing profit/(loss)	
	Month 1	Month 2	Month 1	Month 2
	$	$	$	$
O	200	4,400	(400)	3,200
O	(400)	4,400	200	3,200
O	200	3,200	(400)	4,400
O	(400)	3,200	200	4,400

(2 marks)

26   The following statements relate to the advantages that linear regression analysis has over the high low method in the analysis of cost behaviour:

1   The reliability of the analysis can be statistically tested
2   It takes into account all of the data
3   It assumes linear cost behaviour

Which of the above statements are TRUE?

- O   1 only
- O   1 and 2 only
- O   2 and 3 only
- O   1, 2 and 3

(2 marks)

27   A company operates a process in which no losses are incurred. The process account for last month, when there was no opening work-in-progress, was as follows:

Process account

	$		$
Costs arising	624,000	Finished output (10,000 units)	480,000
		Closing work-in-progress (4,000 units)	144,000
	624,000		624,000

The closing work in progress was complete to the same degree for all elements of cost.

What was the percentage degree of completion of the closing work-in-progress?

   O   12%
   O   30%
   O   40%
   O   75%   **(2 marks)**

28   Which of the following would NOT be expected to appear in an organisation's mission statement?

   O   The organisation's values and beliefs
   O   The products or services offered by the organisation
   O   Quantified short term targets the organisation seeks to achieve
   O   The organisation's major stakeholders   **(2 marks)**

29   An organisation operates a piecework system of remuneration, but also guarantees its employees 80% of a time-based rate of pay which is based on $20 per hour for an eight hour working day. Three minutes is the standard time allowed per unit of output. Piecework is paid at the rate of $18 per standard hour.

   If an employee produces 200 units in eight hours on a particular day, what is the employee's gross pay for that day?

   $ [   ]   **(2 marks)**

30   A company uses an overhead absorption rate of $3.50 per machine hour, based on 32,000 budgeted machine hours for the period. During the same period the actual total overhead expenditure amounted to $108,875 and 30,000 machine hours were recorded on actual production.

   By how much was the total overhead under or over absorbed for the period?

   O   Under absorbed by $3,875
   O   Under absorbed by $7,000
   O   Over absorbed by $3,875
   O   Over absorbed by $7,000   **(2 marks)**

31   Which TWO of the following statements relating to management information are true?

   ☐   It is produced for parties external to the organisation

   ☐   There is usually a legal requirement for the information to be produced

   ☐   No strict rules govern the way in which the information is presented

   ☐   It may be presented in monetary or non monetary terms   **(2 marks)**

32 A company's sales in the last year in its three different markets were as follows

	$
Market 1	100,000
Market 2	149,000
Market 3	51,000
Total	300,000

In a pie chart representing the proportion of sales made by each region what would be the angle of the section representing Market 3?

○   17 degrees
○   50 degrees
○   61 degrees
○   120 degrees   **(2 marks)**

33 The results of a chemistry examination are normally distributed with a mean score of 56 and a standard deviation of 12.

What is the percentage probability that a student will score more than 80?

☐ %

(2 marks)

34 The purchase price of an item of inventory is $25 per unit. In each three month period the usage of the item is 20,000 units. The annual holding costs associated with one unit equate to 6% of its purchase price. The cost of placing an order for the item is $20.

What is the economic order quantity for the inventory item (to the nearest whole unit)?

☐

(2 marks)

35 A company uses marginal costing. The following variances occurred in the last period when the actual net profit was $40,000.

Materials	$900 adverse
Labour	$1,000 favourable
Overheads	$700 adverse
Sales price	$500 favourable
Sales volume contribution	$900 favourable

What was the budgeted net profit for the last period?

○ $41,500
○ $40,800
○ $38,500
○ $39,200   **(2 marks)**

Section B – ALL THREE questions are compulsory and MUST be attempted

36   Cab Co owns and runs 350 taxis and had sales of $10 million in the last year. Cab Co is considering introducing a new computerised taxi tracking system.

The expected costs and benefits of the new computerised tracking system are as follows:

(i)   The system would cost $2,100,000 to implement.

(ii)   Depreciation would be provided at $420,000 per year.

(iii) $75,000 has already been spent on staff training in order to evaluate the potential of the new system. Further training costs of $425,000 would be required in the first year if the new system is implemented.

(iv)   Sales are expected to rise to $11 million in Year 1 if the new system is implemented, thereafter increasing by 5% per year. If the new system is not implemented, sales would be expected to increase by $200,000 per year.

(v)   Despite increased sales, savings in vehicle running costs are expected as a result of the new system. These are estimated at 1% of total sales.

(vi)   Six new members of staff would be recruited to manage the new system at a total cost of $120,000 per year.

(vii)   Cab Co would have to take out a maintenance contract for the new system at a cost of $75,000 per year for five years.

(viii) Interest on money borrowed to finance the project would cost $150,000 per year.

(ix)   Cab Co's cost of capital is 10% per year.

Task 1

In order to determine whether a computerised tracking system should be introduced, indicate whether each of the following is a relevant or an irrelevant cost for a net present value (NPV) evaluation.

Computerised tracking system investment of $2,100,000	▼
Depreciation of $420,000 in each of the five years	▼
Staff training costs of $425,000	▼
New staff total salary of $120,000 per annum	▼
Staff training costs of $75,000	▼
Interest cost of $150,000 per annum	▼

Picklist
Relevant
Irrelevant

(5 marks)

Task 2

Calculate the following values if the computerised tracking system is implemented.

Incremental sales in Year 1 $☐

Savings in vehicle running costs in Year 1 $☐

Present value of the maintenance costs over the life of the contract $☐

(3 marks)

Task 3

Cab Co wishes to maximise the wealth of its shareholders. It has correctly calculated the following measures for the proposed computerised tracking system project:

–   The internal rate of return (IRR) is 14%
–   The return on average capital employed (ROCE) is 20%
–   The payback period is four years

Required

Which of the following is TRUE?

O   The project is worthwhile because the IRR is a positive value
O   The project is worthwhile because the IRR is greater than the cost of capital
O   The project is not worthwhile because the IRR is less than the ROCE
O   The project is not worthwhile because the payback is less than five years   **(2 marks)**

37   Castilda Co manufactures toy robots. The company operates a standard marginal costing system and values inventory at standard cost.

The following is an extract of a partly completed spreadsheet for calculating variances.

	A	B	C
1	**Standard Cost Card – Toy Robot**		$ per robot
2	Selling price		120
3	Direct material	1 material per unit	20
4	Direct labour	6 hours @ $8 per hour	48
5	Production overhead		24
6	Standard contribution		28
7	**Actual and budgeted activity levels in units**	**Budget**	**Actual**
8	Sales	25,000	25,600
9	Production	25,000	26,000
10	**Actual sales revenue and variable costs**	$	
11	Sales	3,066,880	
12	Direct material (purchased and used)	532,800	
13	Direct labour (150,000 hours)	1,221,000	
14	Variable production overhead	614,000	
15	**Variances**	$	
16	Total direct materials variances	12,800	Adverse
17	Direct labour rate variances	21,000	Adverse
18	Direct labour efficiency variances	48,000	Favourable
19	Total variable production overhead variances	10,000	Favourable

Task 1

Which formula will correctly calculate the direct labour efficiency variance in cell B18?

O   = (C9*C4)–B13
O   = B13–(C9*C4)
O   = (C9*C4)–(150,000*8)
O   = (150,000–(C9*6))*8   **(2 marks)**

Task 2

Castilda Co uses a standard cost operating statement to reconcile budgeted contribution with actual contribution. A standard cost operating statement for Month 1 is given below with some information missing.

Complete the reconciliation for the standard cost operating statement for Month 1 shown below.

Standard cost operating statement Month 1

	$	$	
Budgeted contribution		700,000	
▼		☐	☐ ▼
Standard contribution on actual sales		☐	
Sales price variance		☐	☐ ▼
		711,680	

Cost variances			
Total direct materials variance	12,800 Adv		
Direct labour rate variance	21,000 Adv		
Direct labour efficiency variance	48,000 Fav		
Total variable production overhead variance	10,000 Fav		
		24,200 Fav	Fav
Actual contribution		**735,880**	

Picklist
Fixed overhead volume variance
Total sales variance
Sales volume variance
Adv
Fav

(6 marks)

Task 3

Castilda's management accountant thinks that the direct labour rate and efficiency variances for Month 1 could be interrelated.

Which TWO of the following could explain their interrelationship?

☐ Lower grade labour performed tasks less efficiently

☐ A productivity bonus was paid to direct labour

☐ Higher grade labour performed tasks more efficiently

☐ Actual production was less than budgeted

(2 marks)

38 Nicholson Co sells mobile telephones. It supplies its customers with telephones and wireless telephone connections. Customers pay an annual fee plus a monthly charge based on calls made.

The company has recently employed a consultant to install a balanced scorecard system of performance measurement and to benchmark the results against those of Nicholson Co's competitors. Unfortunately the consultant was called away before the work was finished. You have been asked to complete the work. The following data is available.

Nicholson Co	
Operating data for the year ended 30 November 20X0	
Sales revenue	$480 million
Sales attributable to new products	$8 million
Average capital employed	$192 million
Profit before interest and tax	$48 million
Average number of customers	1,960,000
Average number of telephones returned for repair each day	10,000
Number of bill queries	12,000
Number of customer complaints	21,600
Number of customers lost	117,600
Average number of telephones unrepaired at the end of each day	804

Task 1

Calculate the following ratios and other statistics for Nicholson Co for the year ended 30 November 20X0.

Return on capital employed   [   ] %

Return on sales (net profit percentage)   [   ] %

Asset turnover   [   ] times

Average wait for telephone repair   [   ] days

(6 marks)

Task 2

Calculate the following statistics for Nicholson Co. (Give your answers to two decimal places.)

Percentage of customers lost per annum   [   ] %

Percentage of sales attributable to new products   [   ] %

(2 marks)

Task 3

Complete the following explanation of a balanced scorecard.

A balanced scorecard measures performance from four perspectives: customer satisfaction, growth, financial success and [▼]

Picklist

process flexibility
process efficiency
non-financial success

The scorecard is balanced in that it requires managers to:

[▼]

Picklist

offset bad performance in one area with good performance in another
deliver performance in all four areas
achieve on an equal number of KPIs in each perspective

(2 marks)

(Total = 100 marks)

Answers to Mock Exam 1

DO NOT TURN THIS PAGE UNTIL YOU HAVE
COMPLETED THE MOCK EXAM

Section A

1 The correct answer is: Functional benchmarking

2 The correct answer is: Setting a cost by subtracting a desired profit margin from a competitive market price

3 The correct answers are: Process F Abnormal loss Process G Abnormal gain

   F: normal loss = 65,000 × 8% = 5,200. Actual loss (65,000 − 58900) = 6,100

   G: normal loss = 37,500 × 5% = 1,875. Actual loss (37,500 − 35,700) = 1,800

   Therefore F shows an abnormal loss and G shows an abnormal gain

4 The correct answer is: $27,000

   OAR = Budgeted overhead/budgeted production = $63,000/14,000 = $4.50 per unit

   Inventory has risen by 2,000 units so absorption costing will report a higher profit than marginal costing. 2,000 × $4.50 = $9,000

Absorption costing profit	$36,000
	$9,000
Marginal costing profit	$27,000

5 The correct answer is: Differences in workforce motivation

6 The correct answer is: Random sampling

7 The correct answer is: 147,000 kg

Production (units)	= Closing inventory + sales − opening inventory
	= 3,000 + 19,000 − 4,000
	= 18,000
Raw material purchases	= Closing inventory + production − opening inventory
	= 53,000 kg + (18,000 × 8 kg) − 50,000 kg
	= 147,000 kg

8 The correct answer is: Graph D

9 The correct answers are: It helps coordinate the activities of different departments and It establishes a system of control

10 The correct answer is: 2 only

   Participative budgeting increases the motivation of junior managers

11 The correct answer is: 30%

Return on investment	= Profit/capital employed
Profit	= $36,000 + ($200,000 × 12%)
	= $60,000
ROI	= $60,000/$200,000
	= 30%

12 The correct answers are: An increase in material prices and An increase in raw material usage per unit

13 The correct answer is: $130,000

   (Budgeted sales volume − actual sales volume) × standard profit per unit = $10,000 (A)

   Standard profit on actual sales = (actual sales units × standard profit per unit) = $120,000

   Fixed budget profit = $120,000 + $10,000 = $130,000

14   The correct answers are: 1 and 2

Return on investment and market share

15   The correct answers are: 0 and -0.94

The correlation coefficient should be between -1 and 1

16   The correct answer is: Sales volume variance

17   The correct answer is: $13,680

Use the high-low method to determine the fixed and variable elements

100	$15,120
60	$11,280
40	$3,840

$3,840/40 = $96 per %

Fixed element: $15,120 – (100 × 96) = $5,520

For 85% capacity, production cost would be 5,520 + (85 × $96) = $13,680

18   The correct answer is: 12.5%

$$\text{IRR} = A + \left[\frac{a}{a-b} \times (B - A) \right]$$

$$= 10 + \left[\frac{50}{50-30} \times 1 \right]$$

$$= 12.5\%$$

19   The correct answer is: $128,500

	P	Q	X	Y
Total overhead	95,000	82,000	46,000	30,000
Reallocate Y	9,000	18,000	3,000	(30,000)
			49,000	
Reallocate X	24,500	24,500	(49,000)	
	128,500			

20   The correct answer is: EOQ: Lower   Annual holding cost: Lower

A decrease in the ordering cost would reduce the EOQ (as smaller quantities could now be ordered) and also the holding cost (as lower inventories would be kept)

21   The correct answer is: $19,910

	$
Opening WIP	1,710
Completion of 300 units (300 × 40% × 10)	1,200
1,700 units @ $10	17,000
Total value 2,000 units	19,910

22   The correct answers are: True and True.

One of the main uses of Big Data analytics is to help understand customers. Being able to process Big Data means that business processes can be analysed in real time.

23   The correct answer is: 25%

Coefficient of variation = (Standard deviation/mean) × 100 = (3/12) × 100 = 25%

24   The correct answer is: Piece rate

25   The correct answers are:

Absorption costing profit/(loss)   *Marginal costing profit/(loss)*
Month 1	Month 2	Month 1	Month 2
$	$	$	$
200	3,200	(400)	4,400

Closing inventory at the end of Month 1 = opening inventory + production – sales

26   The correct answer is: 1 and 2 only

27   The correct answer is: 75%

Cost per unit of finished output (480,000/10,000) $48

Cost per unit of work-in-progress (144,000/4,000) $36

Therefore the WIP is 75% completed

28   The correct answer is: Quantified short term targets the organisation seeks to achieve

29   The correct answer is: $180

Production in one standard hour = 20 units

Pay for 200 units = 200/20 × 18 = $180

This is above the guaranteed rate.

30   The correct answer is: Under absorbed by $3,875

Overhead absorbed (30,000 × $3.5)	105,000
Actual overhead	108,875
Under-absorbed	3,875

31   The correct answers are: No strict rules govern the way in which the information is presented. It may be presented in monetary or non-monetary terms

32   The correct answer is: 61 degrees

$$\frac{51,000}{300,000} \times 360° = 61°$$

33   The correct answer is: 2.28%

Z-score = (80 – 56)/12 = 2

From the normal distribution table, 2 = 0.4772

To find the probability of scoring more than 80: 0.5 – 0.4772 = 0.0228

34   The correct answer is: 1,461

$$EOQ = \sqrt{\frac{2CoD}{Ch}} = \sqrt{\frac{2 \times 20 \times (4 \times 20,000)}{25 \times 6\%}} = \sqrt{\frac{3,200,000}{1.5}} = 1,460.59$$

35   The correct answer is: $39,200

$40,000 + $900 – $1,000 + $700 – $500 – $900 = $39,200

$38,500 is arrived at by not including overheads.

$40,800 is arrived at by deducting adverse variances and adding favourable variances.

$41,500 is arrived at by deducting adverse variances and adding favourable variances and not including overheads.

Section B

36 **Task 1**

(i)	Computerised tracking system investment of $2,100,000	Relevant
(ii)	Depreciation of $420,000 in each of the five years	Irrelevant
(iii)	Staff training costs of $425,000	Relevant
(iv)	New staff total salary of $120,000 per year	Relevant
(v)	Staff training costs of $75,000	Irrelevant
(vi)	Interest cost of $150,000 per year	Irrelevant

Relevant costs are future incremental cash flows. Non-relevant costs include sunk costs, committed costs and notional (imputed) costs.

(i) Relevant. This is a future incremental cash outflow.

(ii) Irrelevant. This is not a cash flow.

(iii) Relevant. This is a future incremental cash outflow.

(iv) Relevant. This is a future incremental cash outflow.

(v) Irrelevant. This cost has already been incurred and is therefore a sunk cost.

(vi) Irrelevant. The interest is only relevant if it represents an identified lost opportunity to use the finance for some alternative purpose.

Task 2

Incremental sales in Year 1 (W1)	$800,000
Savings in vehicle running costs in Year 1 (W2)	$110,000
Present value of the maintenance costs over the life of the contract (W3)	Answer range:
	$284,000 - $285,000

Workings

1 If the tracking system did not go ahead then the sales in Year 1 would be $10 million + $200,000 = $10,200,000.

If the tracking system did go ahead then the sales in Year 1 would be $11,000,000. The incremental sales are the difference between what the sales would have been without the tracking system and what they would be with the tracking system.

$11,000,000 – $10,200,000 = $800,000.

2

	Year 1
	$'000
Sales	11,000
Vehicle running savings (1%)	110

3 The maintenance cost is an annuity, ie, it is the same amount every year for the five years. We can therefore use the cumulative discount factor for 5 years at 10%.

NPV = $75,000 × 3.791 = $284,325.

It is also possible to calculate the present value of each year and add them up. There will be a small rounding difference.

	Year 1	Year 2	Year 3	Year 4	Year 5
	$	$	$	$	$
Maintenance cost	75,000	75,000	75,000	75,000	75,000
Discount factor	0.909	0.826	0.751	0.683	0.621
Present value	68,175	61,950	56,325	51,225	46,575
NPV	284,250				

Task 3

The correct answer is: The project is worthwhile because the IRR is greater than the cost of capital.

'The project is worthwhile because the IRR is a positive value' is incorrect because the IRR needs to exceed the cost of capital to make the project worthwhile.

'The project is not worthwhile because the IRR is less than the ROCE' is incorrect because the IRR needs to exceed the cost of capital to make the project worthwhile.

'The project is not worthwhile because the payback is less than five years' is incorrect because the cut-off period for deciding on the payback period is arbitrary and we don't know what Cab Co considers to be acceptable.

37   Task 1

= (C9*C4) – (150,000*8)

Task 2

Standard cost operating statement Month 1

	$	$	
Budgeted contribution		700,000	
		16,800	Fav
Sales volume variance (W1)			
Standard contribution on actual sales		**716,800**	
Sales price variance (W2)		**5,120**	Adv
		711,680	
Cost variances			
Total direct materials variance	12,800 Adv		
Direct labour rate variance	21,000 Adv		
Direct labour efficiency variance	48,000 Fav		
Total variable production overhead variance	10,000 Fav		
		24,200	Fav
Actual contribution		**735,880**	

Workings

1

Budgeted sales volume	25,000 units
Actual sales volume	25,600 units
Sales volume variance in units	600 units (F)
× standard contribution per unit	× $28
Sales volume variance	$16,800 (F)

2

	$
Sales revenue from 25,600 units should have been (× $120)	3,072,000
but was (× $15.30)	3,066,880
Selling price variance	5,120 (A)

313

Task 3

The correct answers are:

- A productivity bonus was paid to direct labour

- Higher grade labour performed tasks more efficiently

When two variances are interdependent (interrelated) **one** will usually be **adverse** and the other **one favourable**.

If employees in a workforce are **paid higher rates** for **experience and skill**, using a highly skilled team should incur an **adverse rate variance** at the same time as a **favourable efficiency variance**.

38

Task 1

Return on capital employed (W1)	25%
Return on sales (net profit percentage) (W2)	10%
Asset turnover (W3)	2.5 times
Average wait for telephone repair (W4)	Answer range: 29-30 days

Task 2

Percentage of customers lost per year (W5)	6.00%
Percentage of sales attributable to new products (W6)	Answer range: 1.66-1.67%

Task 3

Complete the following explanation of a balanced scorecard.
A balanced scorecard measures performance from four perspectives: customer satisfaction, growth, financial success and **process efficiency**

The scorecard is balanced in that it requires managers to:
deliver performance in all four areas

Workings

1   Return on capital employed $= \dfrac{\text{Profit}}{\text{Capital employed}} = \dfrac{\$48\,\text{million}}{\$192\,\text{million}} \times 100\% = 25\%$

2   Net profit percentage $= \dfrac{\text{Net profit}}{\text{Sales}} \times 100\% = \dfrac{\$48\,\text{million}}{\$480\,\text{million}} \times 100\% = 10\%$

3   Asset turnover $= \dfrac{\text{Sales}}{\text{Capital employed}} \times 100\% = \dfrac{\$480\,\text{million}}{\$192\,\text{million}} = 2.5$

4   Average wait for telephone repair =

$\dfrac{\text{Average number of telephones unrepaired at end of day}}{\text{Number of telephones returned for repair}} \times 365\ \text{days}$

$= \dfrac{804}{10{,}000} \times 365 = 29.3\ \text{days}$

5   Percentage of customers lost per year $= \dfrac{\text{Number of customers lost}}{\text{Total number of customers}} \times 100\%$

$= \dfrac{117{,}600}{1{,}960{,}000} \times 100\% = 6\%$

6   Percentage of sales attributable to new products =

$$\frac{\text{Sales attributable to new products}}{\text{Total sales}} \times 100\%$$

$$= \frac{\$8m}{\$480m} \times 100\% = 1.67\%$$

Mock Exam 2

Foundations in Accountancy/ACCA

FMA/MA

Management Accounting

Mock Examination 2

Questions	
Time allowed	2 hours
This examination is divided into two sections:	
Section A – 35 questions, each worth 2 marks	
Section B – 3 questions, each worth 10 marks	
All questions within each section are compulsory	

DO NOT OPEN THIS EXAMINATION UNTIL YOU ARE READY TO START UNDER EXAMINATION CONDITIONS

Section A – ALL 35 questions are compulsory and MUST be attempted

1   Three years ago the price index appropriate to Material Z had a value of 140. It now has a value of 180. The material costs $3,500 per kg today.

What was its cost per kg three years ago?

○ $1,167
○ $2,722
○ $4,500
○ $6,222   **(2 marks)**

2   Which of the following statements are true?

(i)   Quota sampling is a non-probability sampling method
(ii)   Stratified random sampling involves dividing the population into categories

○   Statement (i) is true and statement (ii) is false
○   Statement (i) is false and statement (ii) is true
○   Both statements are true
○   Both statements are false   **(2 marks)**

3   A manufacturing company has four types of cost (identified as T1, T2, T3 and T4)

The total cost for each type at two different production levels is:

Cost type	Total cost for 125 units	Total cost for 180 units
	$	$
T1	1,000	1,260
T2	1,750	2,520
T3	2,475	2,826
T4	3,225	4,644

Which TWO cost types would be classified as being semi-variable?

☐   T1

☐   T2

☐   T3

☐   T4   **(2 marks)**

4   D Co has presented information on a particular cost in the form of a line graph.

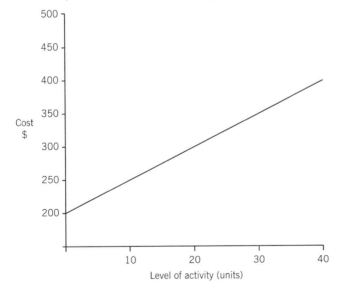

Based on the graph, which TWO of the following statements are correct?

☐ Statement 1   At a level of activity of 30 units the total cost is $350

☐ Statement 2   The fixed element of the cost is $200

☐ Statement 3   The cost appears to be non-linear

☐ Statement 4   The variable element of the cost is $10 per unit   **(2 marks)**

5   The performance of a publicly funded hospital is monitored using measures based upon the 'three Es'.
     The most important performance measure is considered to be the achievement of hospital targets for the
     successful treatment of patients.

     Which of the three Es best describes this above measure?

     ○   Economy
     ○   Externality
     ○   Effectiveness
     ○   Efficiency   **(2 marks)**

6   Are the following statements true or false?

     (i)   Life cycle costing assesses a product's profitability over its entire life
     (ii)   The aim of life cycle costing is to understand product profitability more fully

     ○   Statement (i) is true and statement (ii) is true
     ○   Statement (i) is false and statement (ii) is true
     ○   Both statements are true
     ○   Both statements are false   **(2 marks)**

7   Which of the following tasks would usually be carried out first in the budgetary planning process?

     ○   Identify the principal budget factor
     ○   Establish the level of sales demand
     ○   Calculate the predetermined overhead absorption rate
     ○   Establish the organisation's long term objectives   **(2 marks)**

8   Which of the following statements are correct?

     (i)   Strategic information is mainly used by senior management in an organisation
     (ii)   Productivity measurements are examples of tactical information
     (iii)   Operational information is required frequently by its main users

     ○   (i) and (ii) only
     ○   (i) and (iii) only
     ○   (i) only
     ○   (i), (ii) and (iii)   **(2 marks)**

9   A company manufactures two products P1 and P2 in a factory divided into two cost centres, X and Y. The following budgeted data are available:

	Cost centre	
	X	Y
Allocated and apportioned fixed overhead costs	$88,000	$96,000
Direct labour hours per unit:		
Product P1	3.0	1.0
Product P2	2.5	2.0

Budgeted output is 8,000 units of each product. Fixed overhead costs are absorbed on a direct labour hour basis.

What is the budgeted fixed overhead cost per unit for Product P2?

○ $10
○ $11
○ $12
○ $13   **(2 marks)**

10   A manufacturing company uses a machine hour rate to absorb production overheads, which were budgeted to be $130,500 for 9,000 machine hours. Actual overhead incurred were $128,480 and 8,800 machine hours were recorded.

What was the total under absorption of production overheads (to the nearest whole number)?

$[   ]   **(2 marks)**

11   Which TWO of the following are disadvantages of flexible budgets?

☐   They are not very useful for decision-making

☐   They are more time consuming to prepare than fixed budgets

☐   They fail to provide an appropriate yardstick for cost control purposes

☐   They are based on a set of assumptions which may be over simplistic   **(2 marks)**

12   A company operates a job costing system. Job number 605 requires $300 of direct materials and $400 of direct labour. Direct labour is paid at the rate of $8 per hour. Production overheads are absorbed at a rate of $26 per direct labour hour and non-production overheads are absorbed at a rate of 120% of prime cost.

What is the total cost of job number 605?

○ $2,000
○ $2,400
○ $2,840
○ $4,400   **(2 marks)**

13   Which TWO of the following are advantages of a participative approach to budgeting?

☐   Improved acceptance of the budget

☐   Budgetary slack is reduced

☐   Improved motivation

☐   Relatively fast budget preparation   **(2 marks)**

14 Which of the following variances would be shown in an operating statement prepared under a standard marginal costing system?

   (i)   Variable overhead expenditure variance
   (ii)   Variable overhead efficiency variance
   (iii)   Fixed overhead expenditure variance
   (iv)   Fixed overhead volume variance

○   (i), (ii) and (iv)
○   (i), (iii) and (iv)
○   (i), (ii) and (iii)
○   (ii), (iii) and (iv)   **(2 marks)**

15 A company's budgeted sales for last month were 10,000 units with a standard selling price of $20 per unit and a contribution to sales ratio of 40%. Last month actual sales of 10,500 units with total revenue of $204,750 were achieved.

What were the sales price and sales volume contribution variances?

Sales price variance ($)	Sales volume contribution variance ($)
○ 5,250 Adverse	4,000 Favourable
○ 5,250 Adverse	4,000 Adverse
○ 5,000 Adverse	4,000 Favourable
○ 5,000 Adverse	4,000 Adverse **(2 marks)**

16 A company operates a standard absorption costing system. The standard fixed production overhead rate is $15 per hour.

The following data relate to last month: Actual hours worked   5,500
Budgeted hours   5,000
Standard hours for actual production   4,800

What was the fixed production overhead capacity variance?

○ $7,500 Adverse
○ $7,500 Favourable
○ $10,500 Adverse
○ $10,500 Favourable   **(2 marks)**

17 Value analysis can achieve which TWO of the following?

☐   Eliminate costs

☐   Reduce costs

☐   Increase quantity sold

☐   Increase sales price

                                                  (2 marks)

18 How does setting objectives relate to the mission statement of an organisation?

○   The mission gives managers a focus for setting objectives
○   The mission states what the objectives are
○   The mission has nothing to do with setting objectives
○   The mission and the objectives are identical   **(2 marks)**

19   Which of the following statements best describe critical success factors?

    (i)   The financial ratios used by analysts to evaluate the organisation
    (ii)   The personal objectives of the strategic management team
    (iii)   Derived from the mission statement and objectives of the organisation
    (iv)   The key areas that a business needs to succeed in, to ensure it achieves overall aims

    O   (i), (ii), (iii) and (iv)
    O   (ii) and (iv) only
    O   (i) and (iii) only
    O   (iii) and (iv) only   **(2 marks)**

20   Which of the following best describes tactical information?

    O   Mainly qualitative with some numerical analysis
    O   Sourced largely from external and informal sources
    O   Mainly quantitative, internal and generated frequently
    O   Based on operational information with some interpretation applied   **(2 marks)**

21   A company has two production departments and two service departments with the following fixed overheads:

Production		Service	
A	B	C	D
$'000	$'000	$'000	$'000
1,000	1,200	1,200	1,600

Service department C divides its time between the other departments in the ratio 3:2:1 (for A, B, and D respectively). Department D spends 40% of its time servicing Department A and 60% servicing Department B. If all service departments' overheads are allocated to production departments, the total fixed overhead cost of Department A is:

    O $2,400,000
    O $2,200,000
    O $1,320,000
    O $2,320,000   **(2 marks)**

22   Which TWO of the following will lead to an abnormal loss arising?

    ☐ Total losses are less than expected

    ☐ Total losses are greater than expected

    ☐ Total output is less than expected

    ☐ Total output is greater than expected   **(2 marks)**

23   An investment will produce an annual return of $1,500 in perpetuity with the first receipt starting in 3 years' time.

    What is the present value of this perpetuity discounted at 6%?

    O $21,000
    O $22,250
    O $25,000
    O $25,250   **(2 marks)**

24   Organisations often have to make a trade-off between short-term and long-term objectives. Which of the following statements are correct?

	True	False
Making short-term targets realistic can encourage a long-term view	O	O
Linking managers' rewards to share price may encourage a long-term view	O	O

                                                                   (2 marks)

25   A company uses 9,000 units of a component per year. The component has a purchase price of $40 per unit and the cost of placing an order is $160. The annual holding cost of one component is equal to 8% of its purchase price.

What is the Economic Order Quantity (to the nearest unit) of the component?

☐☐☐☐ units

(2 marks)

26   Consider the following statements:

(i)   Job costing is only applicable to service organisations.

(ii)   Batch costing can be used when a number of identical products are manufactured together to go into finished inventory.

Is each statement TRUE or FALSE?

	Statement (i)	Statement (ii)
O	False	False
O	False	True
O	True	True
O	True	False

(2 marks)

27   An organisation absorbs overheads on a machine hour basis. The planned level of activity for last month was 30,000 machine hours with a total overhead cost of $247,500. Actual results showed that 28,000 machine hours were recorded with a total overhead cost of $238,000.

What was the total under absorption of overhead last month?

$☐☐☐☐

(2 marks)

28   The following information relates to a manufacturing company for next period:

	units		$
Production	14,000	Fixed production costs	63,000
Sales	12,000	Fixed selling costs	12,000

Using absorption costing for the profit for next period has been calculated as $36,000.

What would the profit for next period be using marginal costing?

$☐☐☐☐

(2 marks)

29   Information relating to two processes (F and G) was as follows:

Process	Normal loss as % of input	Input litres	Output litres
F	8	65,000	58,900
G	5	37,500	35,700

For each process, was there an abnormal loss or an abnormal gain?

	Abnormal gain	Abnormal loss
Process F	O	O
Process G	O	O

(2 marks)

30   Last month 27,000 direct labour hours were worked at an actual cost of $236,385 and the standard direct labour hours of production were 29,880. The standard direct labour cost per hour was $8.50.

What was the labour efficiency variance?

O $17,595 Adverse
O $17,595 Favourable
O $24,480 Adverse
O $24,480 Favourable

(2 marks)

31 The pharmacy in a busy hospital uses pre-determined rates for absorbing total overheads, based on the budgeted number of prescriptions to be handled. A rate of $7 per prescription has been calculated, and the following overhead expenditures have been estimated at two activity levels.

Total overheads	Number of prescriptions
$	
97,000	13,000
109,000	16,000

During a particular period fixed overheads were $45,000.

Based on the data above, what was the budgeted level of activity in prescriptions to be handled during the period in question?

[_____] prescriptions   **(2 marks)**

32 Which one of the following would be classified as indirect labour?

O   Assembly workers on a car production line
O   Bricklayers in a house building company
O   Forklift truck drivers in the stores of an engineering company
O   Tutors in a private education business   **(2 marks)**

33 The correlation coefficient (r) for measuring the connection between two variables (x and y) has been calculated as 0.6.

How much of the variation in the dependent variable (y) is explained by the variation in the independent variable (x)?

[_____] %   **(2 marks)**

34 In a process where there are no work–in–progress inventories, two joint products (J and K) are created. Information (in units) relating to last month is as follows:

Product	Sales	Opening inventory of finished goods	Closing inventory of finished goods
J	6,000	100	300
K	4,000	400	200

Joint production costs last month were $110,000 and these were apportioned to joint products based on the number of units produced.

What were the joint production costs apportioned to product J for last month?

O $63,800
O $64,000
O $66,000
O $68,200   **(2 marks)**

35 Budgeted results and actual results for September are shown below.

	Fixed budget 12,000 units	Actual 11,200 units
	$	$
Sales	600,000	571,200
Direct costs	(144,000)	(145,600)
Fixed costs	(70,000)	(69,500)
Profit/(loss)	386,000	356,100

What is the profit for the flexed budget?

O $360,267
O $355,600
O $356,100
O $425,600   **(2 marks)**

Section B – ALL THREE questions are compulsory and MUST be attempted

36   Graffs Co has produced the graph below showing the standard fixed overhead cost per unit, the total budgeted fixed overhead cost and the actual fixed overhead cost for the month of June. The actual number of units produced in June was 7,500 units.

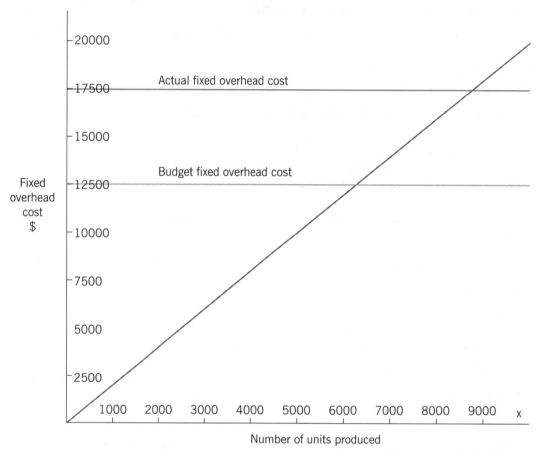

Number of units produced

Task 1

Calculate the following figures.

The over- or under-absorbed overhead for June	$ ____	Over-/Under-
The fixed overhead expenditure variance for June	$ ____	Adverse/Favourable
The fixed overhead volume variance for June	$ ____	Adverse/Favourable

(6 marks)

Task 2

Which TWO of the following factors should be considered before investigating an adverse material usage variance?

☐   Worldwide increase in cost of raw material

☐   Tolerance limits

☐   Interrelationship with adverse labour rate variance

☐   Cost involved in the investigation

(2 marks)

Task 3

Graffs Co is considering using standard marginal costing as the basis for variance reporting in the future. **Which variances for fixed production overhead would be shown in a marginal costing operating statement?**

	Yes	No
Fixed production overhead expenditure variance	O	O
Fixed production overhead capacity variance	O	O
Fixed production overhead efficiency variance	O	O

(2 marks)

37   HF Co is considering two different (mutually exclusive) investment options, investment A and investment B.

Task 1

A net present value (NPV) table has been partially completed for investment A. Complete the present values to two decimal places for each cash flow, using a discount rate of 10%.

Year	Cash flow $'000	Present value $'000
0	(350)	
1	50	
2	110	
3	130	
4	150	
5	100	

(3 marks)

What is the net present value of investment A to the nearest whole thousand dollars?

$ _____   **(2 marks)**

Task 2

Investment B requires an initial investment of $250,000, and has a net present value of $40,000 using a cost of capital of 10%. At a cost of capital of 15%, the net present value is $(1,000).

Calculate the Internal Rate of Return (IRR) of investment B to the nearest whole number.

_____ %   **(3 marks)**

Task 3

The IRRs and NPVs for investments A and B have been compared.

Are the following statements true or false?

	True	False
Investments with a positive NPV are worthwhile.	O	O
On the basis of NPV, he investment with the higher NPV should be chosen.	O	O
Investments with IRR above zero are always worthwhile.	O	O

(2 marks)

38 The management accountant of Vin Co has collected the following information for the year ending 31 December 20X8.

Vin Co operating data for the year ended 31 December 20X8

Capital employed	$4,000,000
Operating profit	$600,000
Sales revenue	$3,600,000
Number of buses in operation	40 buses
Total number of passenger seats available	1,920 seats
Total number of passenger kilometres travelled	39,000,000 passenger kilometres
Total bus kilometres travelled	3,250,000 kilometres
Total fuel consumed	764,705 litres

Required

Task 1

Calculate the following ratios and other statistics for Vin Co for the year ended 31 December 20X8.

Return on capital employed (to the nearest whole number) ☐ %

Return on sales (to the nearest whole number) ☐ %

Average maximum capacity per bus (to the nearest whole number) ☐ seats per bus

Average bus occupancy as a percentage of maximum capacity

(to the nearest whole number) ☐ %

Average bus km travelled per litre of fuel (to two decimal places) ☐ km/litre

(6 marks)

Task 2

Which TWO of the following are reasons for using non-financial performance measures?

☐ To discourage short-termism

☐ To prevent scrutiny of financial performance

☐ To provide leading indicators for financial performance

☐ To appear socially responsible

(2 marks)

Task 3

Select the correct type of benchmarking for each scenario from the drop down list.

Comparing the fuel consumption of vehicles with those of a road haulage company.

Select... ▼
Internal
Functional
Competitive
Strategic

Comparing bus kilometres travelled with those of a rival bus company.

Select... ▼
Internal
Functional
Competitive
Strategic

(2 marks)

(Total = 100 marks)

Answers to
Mock Exam 2

Section A

1 The correct answer is: $2,722

$$\$3,500 \times \frac{140}{180} = \$2,722$$

2 The correct answer is: Both statements are true.

3 The correct answers are: T1 and T3

Cost type	Total cost for 125 units	Cost per unit @ 125 units	Total cost for 180 units	Cost per unit @ 180 units
	$	$	$	$
T1	1,000	8.00	1,260	7.00
T2	1,750	14.00	2,520	14.00
T3	2,475	19.80	2,826	13.75
T4	3,225	25.80	4,644	25.80

Cost types T1 and T3 have different costs per unit at different activity levels and are therefore most likely to be classified as semi-variable costs.

Cost types T2 and T4 have the same cost per unit at different levels of activity and are therefore wholly variable costs.

4 The correct answers are: Statements 1 and 2.

The variable element of the cost is calculated using any number of units.

Using 10 units, total cost less fixed element = $250 – $200 = $50

$50 / 10 = $5 per unit.

Therefore statement 4 is incorrect. Statement 3 is incorrect because a straight line on a graph shows that the cost is linear.

5 The correct answer is: Effectiveness

6 The correct answer is: Both statements are true.

Life cycle costing tracks and accumulated costs and revenues attributable to each product over the entire product life cycle. This means that more accurate feedback information is available on the organisation's success or failure in developing new products.

7 The correct answer is: Establish the organisation's long term objectives

The annual budget is set **within the framework of the long-term plan.** It acts as the first step towards the **achievement of the organisation's long-term objectives.** Therefore the long term objectives must be established before any of the other budget tasks can be undertaken and the correct answer is 'Establish the organisation's long term objectives'.

8 The correct answers are: (i), (ii) and (iii)

Statements (i), (ii) and (iii) are all correct.

9 The correct answer is: $13

Cost centre

	X	Y
	$	$
Overheads	88,000	96,000
Budgeted direct labour hours		
Product P1	24,000 hours	8,000 hours
Product P2	20,000 hours	16,000 hours
	44,000 hours	24,000 hours

Budgeted overhead absorption rate

$$\text{Cost centre X} = \frac{\$88,000}{44,000\,\text{hours}} = \$2 \text{ per direct labour hour}$$

$$\text{Cost centre Y} = \frac{\$96,000}{24,000\,\text{hours}} = \$4 \text{ per direct labour hour}$$

Budgeted fixed overhead cost per unit – Product P2

Cost centre x = 2.5 hours $2 per direct labour hour
          = $5
Cost centre y = 2 hours @ $4 per direct labour hour
          = $8
∴ fixed overhead per unit of Product P2 = $(5+8)
                        = $13

10   The correct answer is: $880

	$
Overhead absorbed (8,800 machine hours × $14.50*)	127,600
Actual overhead	128,480
Under-absorbed overhead	880

$$\text{* Budgeted overhead absorption rate} = \frac{\$130,500}{9,000\,\text{machine hours}} = \$14.50 \text{ per machine hour}$$

11   The correct answers are: They are more time consuming to prepare than fixed budgets and They are based on a set of assumptions which may be over simplistic

Managers may not have time available to prepare flexible budgets to cover all possible scenarios. Therefore they will often make simplifying assumptions. They are useful for decision making as they are flexed to the actual level of activity, and therefore allow actual costs to be compared against the standard costs for that actual activity.

12   The correct answer is: $2,840

Total cost – job number 605

	$
Direct materials	300
Direct labour	400
Prime cost	700
Production overheads ($26 × $400/$8)	1,300
	2,000
Non-production overheads (120% × $700)	840
Total cost – job number 605	2,840

13   The correct answers are: Improved acceptance of the budget and Improved motivation.

It usually takes longer to produce a participative budget than to produce an imposed budget. In the process of participative budgeting, managers may deliberately overestimate costs, introducing budgetary slack, so that they will not be blamed for possible future poor results.

14   The correct answers are: (i), (ii) and (iii).

The fixed overhead volume variance represents the over- or under-absorption of overheads caused by a change in production volume. This means that the fixed overhead volume variance cannot arise in a standard marginal costing system, only in an absorption costing system.

15   The correct answers are: Sales price variance $5,250 Adverse. Sales volume contribution variance $4,000 Favourable.

	$
Sales revenue from 10,500 units should have been × $20)	210,000
but was	204,750
Sales price variance	5,250 (A)

$$\frac{\text{contribution per unit}}{\$20} = 0.4$$

∴ contribution per unit   = 0.4 × $20

              = $8

Budgeted sales	10,000 units
Actual sales	10,500 units
Sales volume variance	500 units (F)
× standard contribution per unit	× $8
Sales volume contribution variance	$4,000 (F)

16   The correct answer is: $7,500 Favourable

Budgeted hours of work	5,000 hours
Actual hours of work	5,500 hours
Fixed production overhead capacity variance	500 hours (F)
× standard fixed production overhead rate	× $15
Fixed production overhead capacity variance (in $)	7,500 (F)

17   The correct answers are: Eliminate costs and Reduce costs

Value analysis focuses on costs, not sales volumes or prices.

18   The correct answer is: The mission gives managers a focus for setting objectives

The mission statement gives the purpose and strategy of the organisation. The business will then use this as a focus for setting appropriate objectives.

19   The correct answer is: (iii) and (iv) only

By monitoring the critical success factors, management ensure that they are on track to succeed in their mission and objectives. The personal objectives of the strategic management team should mirror the critical success factors of the organisation, but are likely to contain personal objectives such as individual development targets. The CSFs may contain some of the financial ratios used by analysts to evaluate the organisation but there will be other qualitative factors as well. The CSFs should drive the information requirements of the organisation – not the other way round.

20   The correct answer is: Based on operational information with some interpretation applied

Tactical information is medium term and drawn largely from internal/operational sources. It is the job of middle management to analyse it further in order to use it for decision making. Quantitative information that is generated frequently is normally found at the operational level and qualitative information from a range of sources will be found more at the strategic level.

21   The correct answer is: $2,320,000

	A	B	C	D
	$'000	$'000	$'000	$'000
Fixed overheads	1,000	1,200	1,200	1,600
C (3:2:1)	600	400	(1,200)	200
				1,800
D (40:60)	720	1,080		(1,800)
	2,320			

22   The correct answers are:

If more losses have been incurred than expected, the loss is abnormally high.
If output is less than expected, losses must be higher than expected.

23   The correct answer is: $22,250

Value of income one year before first receipt is due:

$1,500/0.06 = $25,000

Discounting back to today using a discount factor of 6% over 2 years:

PV   = $25,000 × 0.890

       = $22,250

24   The correct answer is: Both are true.

If budget targets are unrealistically tough, a manager will be forced to make trade-offs between the short and long term. Linking managers' rewards to share price may encourage goal congruence.

25   The correct answer is: 949 units

$$EOQ = \sqrt{2 \times C_o \times D / C_h}$$

$C_o = \$160$
$D = 9,000$ units
$C_h = 8\% \times \$40 = \$3.20$

$$EOQ = \sqrt{2 \times 160 \times 9,000 / 3.2}$$

$= 949$ units

26   The correct answer is: Statement (i) is false and statement (ii) is true.

Job costing can also be used in manufacturing organisations.

27   The correct answer is: $7,000

Overhead absorption rate = $247,500/30,000 = $8.25
Absorbed overheads = 28,000 × $8.25 = $231,000
Actual cost = $238,000
Under absorption = 238,000 – 231,000 = $7,000

28   The correct answer is: $27,000

The fixed overhead absorbed into the inventory valuation is the difference in the marginal costing profit.

Inventory = 14,000 – 12,000 = 2,000 units

Value of fixed production costs absorbed into inventory

= 2,000 × 63,000/14,000

= $9,000

Marginal costing profit = 36,000 – 9,000 = $27,000

29   The correct answer is: Process F Abnormal loss. Process G Abnormal gain.

Process F: Expected output = 92% × 65,000 = 59,800 litres

                  Actual output = 58,900 litres

                  There is an abnormal loss

Process G: Expected output = 95% × 37,500 = 35,625 litres

                  Actual output = 35,700 litres

                  There is an abnormal gain

30   The correct answer is: $24,480 Favourable

Labour efficiency variance

	$	
5,500 units should have taken (× 3 hours per unit)	29,880	hrs
but did take	27,000	hrs
Labour efficiency variance (in hours)	2,880	hrs (F)
x standard rate per unit	× $8.50	
	$24,480	(F)

31   The correct answer is: 15,000

Variable overhead + fixed overhead = total overhead

∴ Fixed overhead per prescription = $7 – $4 = $3

Total fixed overheads   = $45,000

∴ Budgeted activity level $= \dfrac{\$45,000}{\$3} = 15,000$ prescriptions

32   The correct answer is: Forklift truck drivers in the stores of an engineering company

      The drivers are not working directly on engineering projects

33   The correct answer is: 36%

      The variation is given by the coefficent of determination, r^2

      $r^2 = 0.6 \times 0.6 = 0.36 = 36\%$

34   The correct answer is: $68,200

      Production in units:

      J: 6,000 – 100 + 300 =   6,200
      K: 4,000 – 400 + 200 =   3,800
                                       _____
                                       10,000

      Joint costs apportioned to J:
      6,200/10,000 x $110,000 = $68,200

35   The correct answer is: $355,600
      Budgeted sales per unit = $600,000/12,000 = $50 per unit
      Budgeted direct costs per unit = $144,000/12,000 = $12 per unit
      Budgeted fixed costs are $70,000

      Flexed budget for 11,200 units

                                          $
      Sales (11,200 × $50)   560,000
      Direct costs (11,200 × $12)   (134,400)
      Fixed costs   (70,000)
                                      _____
      Profit   355,600

Section B

36

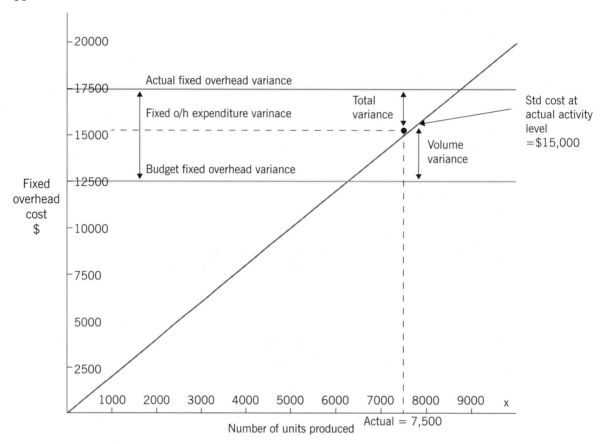

Fixed overhead cost $

Number of units produced — Actual = 7,500

Task 1

The over- or under-absorbed overhead for June (W1)	$2,500	Under-
The fixed overhead expenditure variance for June (W2)	$5,000	Adverse
The fixed overhead volume variance for June (W3)	$2,500	Favourable

Workings

1   Actual fixed overhead cost – fixed overhead absorbed = $17,500 – $15,000 = $2,500 Under absorbed

2   Fixed overhead expenditure variance = $12,500 – $17,500 = $5,000 Adverse

3   Fixed overhead volume variance = $15,000 – $12,500 = $2,500 Favourable

Task 2

The correct answers are: Tolerance limits and Cost involved in the investigation.

Tolerance limits relate to materiality. Variances should only be investigated if they are significant and worthy of investigation.

Similarly, a variance should only be investigated if the benefits outweigh the costs and therefore the costs involved in the investigation need to be considered.

A worldwide increase in the cost of raw material should not affect the material usage and therefore does not need to be considered. An adverse labour rate variance will not be related to an adverse material usage variance and therefore does not need to be considered.

Task 3

The correct answers are:

Fixed production overhead expenditure variance	Yes
Fixed production overhead capacity variance	No
Fixed production overhead efficiency variance	No

In a marginal costing system the only fixed overhead variance is an expenditure variance

37 Task 1

Calculation of net present value at a discount rate of 10%.

Year	Cash flow $'000	Discount factor 10%	Present value $'000
0	(350)	1.000	(350.00)
1	50	0.909	45.45
2	110	0.826	90.86
3	130	0.751	97.63
4	150	0.683	102.45
5	100	0.621	62.10
			48.49

The NPV is $49,000 (to the nearest $'000)

Task 2

The correct answer is: 15%

$$\text{IRR} = 10 + \left[\frac{40}{40+1} \times (15-10)\right]\% = 14.9\% \ (15\% \text{ to the nearest whole number})$$

Task 3

Investments with a positive NPV are worthwhile.	TRUE
On the basis of NPV, the investment with the higher NPV should be chosen.	TRUE
Investments with IRR above zero are worthwhile.	FALSE

Statement 1 is true. A positive NPV means that the **present value** of the cash **inflows** from a project is **greater** than the **present value of the cash outflows**.

Statement 2 is true. On the **basis of NPV** alone, the project with the **higher NPV should be chosen**.

Statement 3 is false. If a project earns a higher rate of return than the cost of capital, it will be worthwhile undertaking.

38 Task 1

Return on capital employed (W1)	15%
Return on sales (W2)	17%
Average maximum capacity per bus (W3)	48 seats per bus
Average bus occupancy as a percentage of maximum capacity (W4)	25%
Average bus km travelled per litre of fuel (W5)	4.25 km/litre

Workings

1   *Return on capital employed*
    (Operating profit ÷ Capital employed × 100)
    $600,000 ÷ $4,000,000 × 100 =   15%

2   *Return on sales (net profit percentage)*
    Operating profit ÷ Sales revenue × 100
    $600,000 ÷ $3,600,000 × 100   17%

3   *Average maximum bus capacity*
    Total number of passenger seats available ÷ number of buses
    1,920 seats ÷ 40 buses   48 seats per bus

4   *Average bus occupancy*
    Total number of passenger km travelled ÷
    (Total km travelled × Average maximum bus capacity)
    39,000,000 km ÷ (3,250,000 × 48 seats) × 100%   25% of maximum capacity

5   *Average km travelled per litre of fuel*
    Total km travelled ÷ Total fuel consumed
    3,250,000 kilometres ÷ 764,705 litres   4.25 km/litre

Task 2

The correct answers are: To discourage short-termism and To provide leading indicators for financial performance.

A key reason why non-financial performance measures are used is that they are considered to be a leading indicator of financial performance. For example, if customer satisfaction is low, this could imply a future fall in profits due to decreased sales demand. The non-financial measure of poor customer satisfaction has given an indication that the financial measure of future sales (and therefore profit) may change.

Task 3

Comparing the fuel consumption of vehicles with those of a road haulage company = Functional benchmarking.

Comparing bus kilometres travelled with those of a rival bus company = Competitive benchmarking

REVIEW FORM

Name: _____   **Address**: _____

_____

Date:_____   _____

How have you used this Practice & Revision Kit?
(Tick one box only)

☐ On its own (book only)

☐ On a BPP in-centre course_____

☐ On a BPP online course

☐ On a course with another college

☐ Other _____

Why did you decide to purchase this Practice & Revision Kit? *(Tick one box only)*

☐ Have used complementary Interactive Text

☐ Have used BPP Texts in the past

☐ Recommendation by friend/colleague

☐ Recommendation by a lecturer at college

☐ Saw advertising

☐ Other _____

During the past six months do you recall seeing/receiving any of the following?
(Tick as many boxes as are relevant)

☐ Our advertisement in *ACCA Student Accountant*

☐ Our advertisement in *Teach Accounting*

☐ Other advertisement __

☐ Our brochure with a letter through the post

☐ ACCA E-Gain email

☐ BPP email

☐ Our website www.bpp.com

Which (if any) aspects of our advertising do you find useful?
(Tick as many boxes as are relevant)

☐ Prices and publication dates of new editions

☐ Information on Practice & Revision Kit content

☐ Facility to order books

☐ None of the above

Have you used the companion Interactive Text for this subject?   ☐ Yes   ☐ No

Your ratings, comments and suggestions would be appreciated on the following areas

	Very useful	*Useful*	*Not useful*
Introductory section (How to use this Practice & Revision Kit)	☐	☐	☐
'Do You Know' checklists	☐	☐	☐
'Did You Know' checklists	☐	☐	☐
Possible pitfalls	☐	☐	☐
Questions	☐	☐	☐
Answers	☐	☐	☐
Mock exams	☐	☐	☐
Structure & presentation	☐	☐	☐
Icons	☐	☐	☐

	Excellent	*Good*	*Adequate*	*Poor*
Overall opinion of this Kit	☐	☐	☐	☐

Do you intend to continue using BPP products?   ☐ Yes   ☐ No

Please note any further comments and suggestions/errors on the reverse of this page.
The author of this edition can be emailed at: learningmedia@bpp.com

REVIEW FORM (continued)

Please note any further comments and suggestions/errors below